Sweetheart,

For all those
fabulous meals to

[barcode] D0984770

THE JOY OF JAPANESE COOKING

THE JOY OF JAPANESE COOKING

Kuwako Takahashi

SHUFUNOTOMO CO., LTD.

Seventh printing, 1997

© Copyright in Japan 1986 by Kuwako Takahashi
Illustrations by Office Two One
Sumi Paintings by Kuwako Takahashi
Photographs by Dean Stone and Hugo Steccati
            Takehiko Takei

Published by SHUFUNOTOMO CO., LTD.
2-9, Kanda Surugadai, Chiyoda-ku Tokyo, 101 Japan

ISBN:4-07-975150-8
Printed in Japan

This book is dedicated to my husband Yasundo Takahashi—for his encouragement, criticism, and for having been such a patient and willing "guinea pig".

CONTENTS

★ indicates photo pages in color.

FOREWORD

Kuwako Takahashi, the author, affectionately nicknamed Ponchan, is one of those rare individuals who, when transplanted to a foreign country, can settle in and enjoy the challenges of new ways of living. And what makes her more unusual is that when called upon, she takes great pleasure in sharing her extensive knowledge of the customs and culture of her native land.

Ponchan came from Tokyo in 1958 with her thirteen year old daughter and her professor husband to Berkeley and quickly adjusted to a very different milieu. The American way of entertaining at home, as opposed to the Japanese practice of inviting guests out to restaurants, was a delightful experience. Her dinner parties were not only beautiful presentations of traditional Japanese foods, but her house was a showcase for her talents as a top ranking teacher of the Sogetsu School of Japanese flower arrangement. Soon her involvement with ikebana developed into a primary interest and she became the founder of three highly successful Bay Area ikebana associations. As first president of the San Francisco Bay Area Chapter of Ikebana International she continues to be its guiding spirit. The second group she formed, a study group actually for students and teachers of Sogetsu, keeps expanding. The last organization to benefit from her expertise as first president was the Ikebana Teachers Federation.

As the Takahashis' social circles widened to include friends throughout the Bay Area, so did Ponchan's reputation as a gourmet hostess become well known. A local Japanese TV station invited her to do some programs on Japanese home cooking, adapting the materials available in the California markets. The research necessary for these appearances was the beginning of long years of experimentation which have resulted in this book.

The innovative format of the book owes much to her experience as an organizer. Each recipe was worked and reworked and repeatedly tested. Superfluous details were eliminated, yet those knowledgeable insights which guide the reader over unfamiliar territory, remain. Her trained artist's eye insures that the first prerequisite of Japanese cuisine, its esthetic appearance, is more than satisfied.

For more than a quarter of a century I have had the privilege of friendship with this very special lady and my admiration continues to grow as new facets of her many talents keep unfolding. Kuwako Takahashi has set forth for you exciting adventures in Japanese home style cooking. As an added reward you will find you have produced meals that are not only tasty and nutritious, but on the whole are less expensive than current Western alternatives.

Fay Kramer

Fay Kramer, President Emeritus
Ikebana International

San Francisco

PREFACE

Recently Japanese cooking has been recognized in Western countries as a very elegant and healthful way of preparing food. Many who are interested in cooking Japanese dishes at home have been frustrated by not being able to get certain ingredients or utensils, but now basic ingredients like soy sauce, *miso* and *tofu* are widely available in the United States. In general, Western kitchens are very well furnished and some Western equipment works wonders in preparing Japanese dishes. In a few minutes a food processor does work that takes half an hour using the traditional ceramic mortar. An ordinary oven can cook rice without watching, bake "*Atsuyaki Tamago*" (a thick omelet) and roast a quantity of sesame seeds evenly.

Japanese people are known for their knack of absorbing new things and coming out with something unique of their own. Now they use more Western vegetables such as bell pepper, celery, green asparagus, okra, etc., and certainly more meat than in the past. In the United States, especially on the West Coast, vegetables such as Chinese cabbage, *daikon*, Japanese eggplant and cucumbers, fresh *shiitake* and *enokidake* mushrooms are appearing regularly in the markets. This abundance makes our cooking choices more flexible and opens a wider scope of possibilities. In this book I have made it a point to list alternative choices for the materials listed.

In the following recipes you will learn how to create dishes from the original, basic ingredients—from "scratch," so to speak,—whenever possible. For example, the sweet, pickled ginger and fluffy shrimp that are used in making *sushi* are sold in packages, but if you make them yourself, they are more economical and taste better. Besides, you gain the confidence that you can make them anywhere out of the raw materials!

I have included in this book some traditional items such as Sesame *Tofu* made with *kuzu* (arrowroot). These may not be of interest to all Westerners, but Japanese people living abroad will no doubt make use of them.

One of the characteristics of Japanese cooking is its keen appreciation and consciousness of the seasons. Japan is a country with four definite seasons. Not only do cooking ingredients reflect seasonal changes, but great care is taken to reflect the seasons in the presentation of foods. Careful choice of dishes and garnishes heightens the feeling of season and occasion, not only making the meal enjoyable to the palate, but a celebration of life!

Kuwako Takahashi

ACKNOWLEDGEMENTS

In writing this book I was helped by many friends. My grateful thanks to Fay Kramer for her advice and introduction, Joan Finnie for going through the draft, Sally Sutherland for helping me with my English and for editing the copy, Pearl Kimura for proofreading, and Hugo Steccati for visualizing my ideas in his artistic photographs. I am greatly indebted to Miss Toshi Takamura of Shufunotomo Company for conceiving the idea of this book, Mr. Kazuhiko Nagai and Mrs. Michiko Kinoshita, also of Shufunotomo, for their patience and encouragement, and Mr. Takehiko Takei for his beautiful photographs taken in Tokyo.

PART-1

Japanese Ingredients
Seasonings in Japanese Cooking
Utensils and Equipment
Tableware
Measurements and Equivalents
Basic Techniques

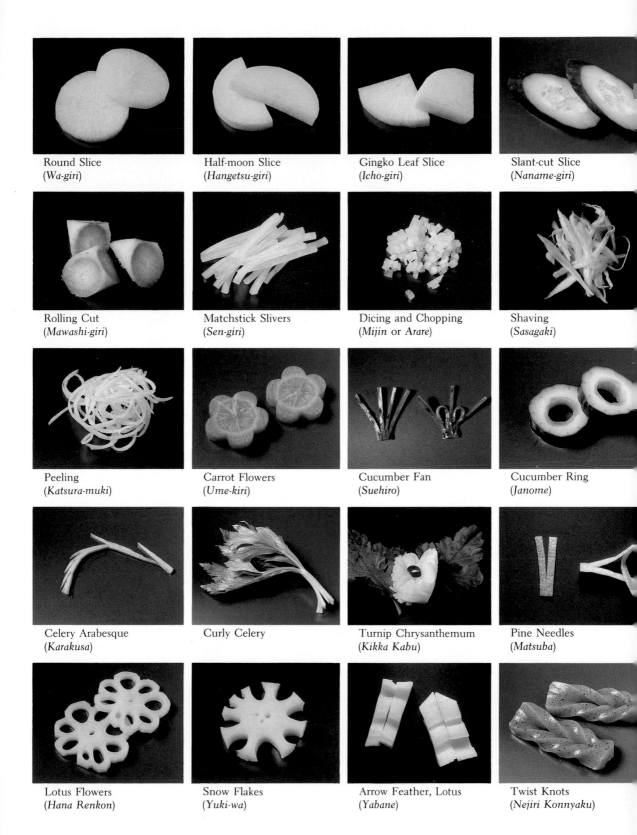

Round Slice
(*Wa-giri*)

Half-moon Slice
(*Hangetsu-giri*)

Gingko Leaf Slice
(*Icho-giri*)

Slant-cut Slice
(*Naname-giri*)

Rolling Cut
(*Mawashi-giri*)

Matchstick Slivers
(*Sen-giri*)

Dicing and Chopping
(*Mijin* or *Arare*)

Shaving
(*Sasagaki*)

Peeling
(*Katsura-muki*)

Carrot Flowers
(*Ume-kiri*)

Cucumber Fan
(*Suehiro*)

Cucumber Ring
(*Janome*)

Celery Arabesque
(*Karakusa*)

Curly Celery

Turnip Chrysanthemum
(*Kikka Kabu*)

Pine Needles
(*Matsuba*)

Lotus Flowers
(*Hana Renkon*)

Snow Flakes
(*Yuki-wa*)

Arrow Feather, Lotus
(*Yabane*)

Twist Knots
(*Nejiri Konnyaku*)

Cutting Techniques on pages 48–51.

13

1. Trefoil (*Mitsuba*), p. 30
2. *Enoki* Mushrooms (*Enokidake*), p. 25
3. *Daikon* Sprouts (*Kaiware*), p. 27
4. Perilla Seedpods (*Hojiso*), p. 29
5. Citrus Fruit, Aromatic (*Yuzu*), p. 21
6. Oyster Mushrooms (*Shimeji*), p. 25
7. Black Forest or *Shiitake* Mushrooms (*Shiitake*), p. 25
8. Chrysanthemum Greens (*Shungiku*), p. 21
9. Japanese Horsradish (*Wasabi*), p. 23
10. *Myōga* (Bud of ginger family plant), p. 29
11. Prickly Ash (*Sansho*), p. 30

1. Agar-Agar (*Kanten*), p. 17
2. Buckwheat Noodles (*Soba*), p. 25
3. Wheat Noodles (*Udon*), p. 25
4. Pounded Rice Cake (*Mochi*), p. 28
5. Dried *Daikon* (*Kiriboshi Daikon*), p. 27
6. Dried *Shiitake* Mushrooms (*Hoshi Shiitake*), p. 19
7. Dried Red Beans (*Azuki*), p. 19
8. Dried *Nori* Seaweeds Sheets (*Nori*), 30
9. Dried Gourd Rind (*Kampyō*), p. 23
10. Bean Threads (*Harusame*), p. 20
11. Wheat Gluten Cake (*Fu*), p. 32
12. Rice, Grain, p. 28

14

1. Kelp (*Kombu* or *Kobu*), p. 24
2. *Wakame* Seaweed (*Wakame*), p. 24
3. Bonito Flakes (*Kezuri Bushi*), p. 20
4. Japanese Cayenne Red Pepper (*Taka-no-tsume*)
5. Black Sesame Seeds (*Kuro Goma*), p. 31
6. Dried Black Mushrooms (*Kikurage*), p. 25
7. Gingko Nuts (*Gin-nan*), p. 23
8. Grained *Dashi* (Instant *Dashi*), p. 43
9. Seven-Taste Pepper (*Hichimi Tōgarasi*), p. 26
10. White Sesame Seeds (*Shiro Goma*), p. 31

1. Deep-Fried Soybean Puffs (*Age* or *Aburage*), p. 18
2. Fried *Tofu* Cutlet (*Atsu Age* or *Nama-Age*), p. 18
3. *Tofu* Patties (*Ganmodoki*), p. 19
4. Soymilk Film, Dried (*Yuba*), p. 13
5. Bean Curd Cake (*Tofu*), p. 17
6. Freeze-Dried *Tofu* (*Kōya Dofu*), p. 18

1. *Kamaboko*, Fish Cake, p. 22
2. Jellied Loaf from Devil's Tongue Plant (*Konnyaku*), p. 23
3. *Konnyaku* Noodles (*Shirataki*), p. 26
4. Crab Sticks
5. *Chikuwa*, Fish Cake, p. 22
6. *Hanpen*, Fish Cake, p. 22
7. Fish Cake with Swirl Design (*Naruto*), p. 22

1. Pickled *Daikon* (*Takuan Zuke*), p. 27
2. Fermented Bean Paste, Red (*Aka Miso*), p. 37
3. Fermented Bean Paste, Wheat (*Mugi Miso*), p. 37
4. Fermented Bean Paste, White (*Shiro Miso*), p. 37
5. Plum, Salt-Pickled (*Umeboshi*), p. 26

Japanese Ingredients

Agar-Agar (*Kanten*) *page 14
Freeze-dried seaweed gelatin. Wash and soak in water for one hour. Squeeze out the water and tear into pieces. Boil in measured water until it melts. The standard amount of water is 2 cups for one stick of *kanten*. Unlike other gelatins which need ice water to jell, *kanten* will jell in cold tap water.

Bamboo Shoots (*Takenoko*)
Fresh bamboo shoots in spring have an unforgettable aroma, (see page 132). Unfortunately, canned bamboo shoots do not have this aroma, but they do have the crunchy texture and are easy to use since they are already boiled and are ready to use.

Bean Curd Cake (*Tofu*) *page 15
Tofu is now manufactured in many places in the United States and is sold at most markets. It comes in polyethylene boxes weighing 15–21 ounces (450 g – 630 g).

Storing and Draining *Tofu*:
1. Keep *tofu* refrigerated at all times. It spoils easily. But do not freeze it since freezing will change the texture completely.
2. Usually a date is printed on the plastic cover and the *tofu* should be consumed before that date. Of course, the fresher the *tofu* the better.
3. Except when *tofu* is used in soup or poached, it must be drained well. Otherwise water seeps out onto the serving dish. Wrap *tofu* with a paper towel, place on a dish and refrigerate for one to two hours, changing the towel once. Or slice it and arrange on paper towels spread on a board. Change the paper towels when wet.

Varieties of *Tofu*
There are various types, but these are the basic categories:

1. **Regular *Tofu* (*Momen Dofu*).**
   This is the all-purpose *tofu*, good for eating raw, poaching, sautéeing, grilling, deep-frying, or mashing and reshaping. Soymilk is made into curd with a coagulant (natural *nigari*, calcium sulfate, or lactone), separated from the whey, plac-

★ Indicates photo in color

ed in a cotton cloth-lined mold, and pressed lightly. The Japanese word for "cotton" is *"momen,"* hence *"momen dofu."* When the *tofu* has set, it is immersed in water, cut under water, packed into containers and sealed with plastic film. This *tofu* has body with some porousness. It should be eaten within a week. After purchase, open the cover and change water daily.

2. **Soft *Tofu* (*Kinugoshi Dofu*)** (In Chinese: *Shui Doufu*)
   The Japanese name means silk-strained, and the Chinese name means water *tofu*. Both refer to the smooth, silken texture of the soft *tofu*. The soft *tofu* made here is formed right in the polyethylene containers and sterilized. It lasts much longer than regular *tofu*—up to three weeks. The date before which it should be consumed is printed on the package. Do not open the package until needed. But once opened, change the water every day and finish it in a few days. Pull the edges of the container to release the *tofu* before turning it out.

3. **Ever-Fresh Silken *Tofu*.**
   This is packaged soft *tofu* which lasts six months without refrigeration. It is smaller (10½ oz. or 300 g.); slightly firmer than regular soft *tofu*. It can be sautéed, broiled, fried or eaten raw. The paper package is easily cut and the *tofu* cake slides out in perfect shape. One request we could make of the manufacturer: print the date of manufacture on the package!

4. **Instant *Tofu*.**
   A package containing soymilk powder and coagulant with directions for making homemade soft *tofu* is sold at Japanese stores.

5. **Firm *Tofu*.**
   Firm *tofu* is a Chinese variety. Firmer and denser than regular *tofu*, the need for pressing is eliminated before preparing Mashed *Tofu* (page 130), *Tofu* Patties (page 130), or *Tofu* Burger (page 130).

Tofu products

Deep-fried Soybean Puffs (*Agé* or *Aburage*)   *page 15*
Crinkly, golden puffs which are sold in bags. They may be frozen. See page 127.

Fried *Tofu* Cutlet (*Atsu Age* or *Nama Age*)   *page 15*
A slice of *tofu* about ¾" (2 cm) thick, fried skin-deep. Inside it retains the *tofu* texture. See page 127.

Freeze-dried *Tofu* (*Kōya Dofu*)   *page 15*
A lightweight, sponge-like, dried *tofu* which keeps indefinite-

ly. It expands about three times its original size when softened. It is very nutritious. See page 128.

Grilled *Tofu* (*Yaki Dofu*)
Used in *sukiyaki* in Japan, this lightly browned *tofu* is firmer
and has a slightly nutty flavor. You can pat-dry the pressed
or firm *tofu* and broil it. At this time, it is not sold on the West
Coast.

Tofu Patties (*Gan Modoki*)   *page 15
Tofu mash is mixed with vegetables and seeds and then deep-
fried to make golden patties (page 130). They are very nutritious and can be frozen.

Beans

Fava Beans (*Sora Mame*)
In California from May to fall, fresh fava beans in shells are
sold at Japanese, Mexican and Chinese groceries.
   These are giant-sized beans. Choose shells with firm beans
inside. After shelling and boiling in salt water, fava beans are
enjoyed as snacks or appetizers (see page 197).

Red Beans, Dried (*Azuki*)
These tiny, dark red beans are used to make Red Rice (*Sekihan*)
for auspicious occasions. They can also be boiled and sweetened to make a sweet bean paste which is the base for many
Japanese sweets.

Soybeans, Dried (*Daizu*)
These are cooked like other dried beans after soaking in water
for 10 to 12 hours. Puréed, diluted and strained, these make
soymilk which in turn becomes *tofu* when mixed with
coagulants.

Soybeans, Fresh (*Eda Mame*)
Soybean products such as *miso*, soy sauce, and *tofu* are all well
known, but their mother—the fresh soybean—is still little
known. They are easy to grow. Sow dry soy beans in the spring
and by summer you will notice the beans growing in their
green, hairy pods. At Japanese markets frozen soybean pods
are sold in bags. From summer to fall, boiled soybeans are a
favorite appetizer or snack (see page 197).

Bean Pastes

Bean Paste, Fermented (*Miso*)   *page 16
Another soybean product which is indispensable to Japanese
cooking. It is used to season soups, poached foods and "*nabemono*," as well as sauces. There are many varieties—see page
37 under Seasonings.

Sweet Bean paste (*Azuki An*)

See page 266 for preparation instructions. This is also sold in cans. "*Koshi an*" or "*neri an*" is a smooth paste, while "*tsubushi an*" is a paste with partially crushed beans.

Bean Threads (*Harusame*) *page 14

"*Harusame*" means spring rain. These transparent vermicelli or cellophane noodles are sold in packages at Oriental food stores and are quite similar to Chinese bean threads, except *harusame* are made from potatoes while Chinese beans threads are made from green beans. Both can be used identically—in salads, soups and *nabemono*. To prepare, soak in lukewarm water for 10 minutes to soften, then parboil until transparent. Drain and rinse with water. Be careful when cooking *harusame* (the Japanese variety) not to leave them in hot liquid too long or they will disintegrate. Add these to soups or "*nabemono*" at the last minute. For unusual fritters, "*Harusame Age*," coat prawns or fish in flour, then dip into slightly beaten egg white, and roll in bean threads which have been cut into ½–1" (1.2–2.5 cm) lengths. Deep-fry in clean oil. In frying, the threads will puff up for crisp, white fritters.

Bonito

Dried Bonito (*Katsuo Bushi*)

This dried fish looks and feels like a slab of dark, brown wood and can be kept indefinitely in a cool, dry place. The time-honored method of making stock (*dashi*) with freshly shaved bonito flakes and "*kombu*" (kelp) cannot be surpassed for flavor. "*Katsuo dashi*" (bonito stock) is the basis of Japanese cooking.

Bonito Flakes (*Kezuri Bushi*) *page 15

This is sold in various sized vacuum packs. In addition to being used to make *dashi*, it is also used as a topping or garnish.

Burdock (*Gobō*)

Burdock is a curious, dark brown, root vegetable used only in Japan. It resembles French salcify, but is longer and woodier throughout. It is ½–1" (1.2–2.5 cm) in diameter and is 1–2 feet (30~60 cm) long. It dries out quickly, so use it as soon as possible and keep it tightly wrapped in plastic in the refrigerator. Do not peel the skin—just scrub it with a vegetable brush. Cuttings should be dropped into water to prevent discoloring. It should be blanched before cooking. The flavor is earthy and bland, but it adds authenticity to many Japanese dishes.

Cabbage, Chinese (*Hakusai*)

Now available nearly all year long in many markets on the West Coast, this is a wonderful vegetable because it is good raw, stir-fried, boiled or pickled. Since it does not have a cabbage odor when boiled, it is ideal for "*nabemono.*"

Chestnuts (*Kuri*)
Chestnuts are the only nuts that should not be dried out—the fresher the better. However, the chestnuts we buy in markets are dry whether they come from California or Italy. No matter how you plan to use them, make a cut on the shell and soak them in water for at least one day. If you change the water every fourth or fifth day, they will keep several weeks in the refrigerator, or they can be frozen.

To shell these nuts, use a blunt-edged knife. To peel skins, place the shelled nuts in a pot, cover with water, bring to a boil and boil for 1 minute. Drain and place in cold water. Peel the skin off with a small knife and drop into water to prevent discoloration. Drained chestnuts may be frozen.

Chestnuts in Syrup (*Kuri Amani*)
Available in a can or jar, these are very handy to use as an additional garnish or in "*kinton*" (sweet potato mash) on page 147. They can also be used in a Japanese sweet, Steamed Chestnut Bean Paste Square, found on page 268.

Citrus Fruit, Aromatic (*Yuzu*)   **page 14*
Slivers of *yuzu* rind—green from summer to fall or golden from late fall to winter—add so much aroma to soups and other food. The juice is used for "*chirizu*" (page 90), for *sashimi*, or some "*nabemono.*" A substitute is green or ripe, yellow lemon.

Chrysanthemum Greens (*Shungiku*)   **page 14*
This is a green, aromatic vegetable, used like spinach.

Coloring, Natural Green (*Aoyose*)
A green "essense" which is used to color dressing or rice dumplings. To make about 1 tablespoon, place 2 cups of spinach leaves with stems removed and ¼ cup water in a food processor or blender. Process for a few minutes. Strain the green liquid through double cheesecloth into a pot, using about ¾ cup more water to wash the container out. Bring the liquid in the pot to a boil, then lower the heat. In about one minute, some green "essense" will come to the surface, leaving the liquid completely clear. Remove the pot from the heat. After spreading a piece of finely woven cloth or paper towel over a colander, pour out the contents of the pot. What remains on the cloth or paper towel is the natural green coloring essense. Wrapped in plastic, it can be frozen.

Cucumber, Japanese (*Kyūri*)
This is much smaller and thinner than American cucumbers, has fewer seeds and a thinner skin. The English cucumber is closest to the Japanese.

Eggplant, Japanese (*Nasu*)

This is also much smaller than its American counterpart, with fewer seeds. Buy shiny, unblemished ones that are firm. When you use these sliced, soak in water to cover for 15 minutes to prevent discoloring and bitterness. When cooked whole, it is not necessary to soak them first. Chinese and Italian eggplants, when available, are also good.

Fish Cake

Kamaboko   *page 16

This solid-textured fish cake is formed in semi-circular shapes on boards. They come in white, surface-tinted (red for festive color), or lightly browned. They can be served as is, or blanched in boiling water just to warm through. Served with soy sauce and *wasabi*; grilled, then brushed with soy sauce, deep-fried, or poached in a seasoned liquid. They keep well in the refrigerator for one week. Since it can be cut into many shapes, it is very useful as a soup garnish.

Chikuwa   *page 16

Chikuwa is a cylinder-shaped fish cake that can be eaten right out of the package with soy sauce, poached, grilled or fried.

Hanpen   *page 16

Hanpen is a soft fish cake. White and fluffy, this spongy-textured cake comes in squares or rounds. As with other fish cakes, it may be eaten as is with soy sauce and grilled, deep-fried or poached. It will swell up when boiled. It keeps up to one week in the refrigerator—or it may be frozen.

Naruto (Fish cake with swirl design)   *page 16

This is a white, cylinder-shaped fish cake. When sliced, each slice has a decorative red swirl which make it a nice garnish in soup or *nabemono*.

Ginger (*Shōga*)

Fresh ginger roots are now sold at most supermarkets. If you cannot find them, go to an Oriental food market or store. Smaller roots are better than big ones, which are too fibrous. Keep ginger roots in a plastic bag in the refrigerator. As needed, cut off a portion, peel and soak in water 5–10 minutes before grating or slicing. This will prevent discoloration.

Red Pickled Ginger (*Beni Shōga*)

Originally ginger was pickled with a red brine from the salt plum pickle with red "*shiso*" leaves (beefsteak plant). Now the color is from food dye. It has a tart, salty taste and is indispensable in making Mixed *Sushi* (page 245), *Nori* Rolls (page 249), or *Inari Zushi* (page 248).

Sweet Pickled Ginger (*Gari*)
This is an essential accompaniment to *nigiri* and other *sushi*.
See page 241 for the recipe.

Young Ginger (*Shin Shōga*)
You can grow young ginger root if you have a hot summer
climate. In the spring, plant ginger roots in sandy soil. Water
them well. By the end of summer, dig up the clump. There
will be young shoots with roots which are the young ginger.
This has a fresh, mild taste. Cut off the stem, leaving about
2″ (5 cm) of the stem. Scrap off the skin and make a slit in
the root if it is too big. Deep-fried in *tempura* batter (page 98),
these are excellent served after seafood *tempura*. Or parboil
young ginger for 1–2 minutes in boiling water and marinate
it in sweetened vinegar for Sweet Pickled Young Ginger (*Hajikami*). This keeps for a week or so in the refrigerator and is
excellent as a garnish for fish or meat. *Hajikami* is also available
in jars.

Gingko Nuts (*Gin-nan*) *page 15*
Sold already cooked in cans or jars, these are tender nuts with
an interesting taste. They are often used in steamed dishes such
as Custard Soup (page 113) or Steamed Turnips (page 151). Also,
they may be threaded on pine needles and used as garnish on
an appetizer tray.

Gourd Rind, Dried (*Kampyō*) *page 14*
Off-white, cream-colored strips of dried gourd rind is folded, tied,
and sold in packages. As it ages, the color becomes yellowish tan,
so buy light colored, white *kampyō*. Before cooking, wash with
water, sprinkle with salt and rub, rinse again with water. Boil
in boiling water for a few minutes and drain. Simmered in seasoned *dashi*, it is essential in Mixed *Sushi* (page 245) or *Nori* Roll
(page 249).

Horseradish, Japanese (*Wasabi*) *page 14*
Grated *wasabi* is vital as a spice for *sashimi* and some *sushi*. Fresh
wasabi roots are now sold at some Japanese markets. Peel the
skin as needed and grate with a fine grater. Wrapped in plastic
wrap, it will keep several weeks in the refrigerator. Fresh *wasabi*
has a wonderful aroma.

Powdered *Wasabi*
This comes in small cans. Mix with water to make a thick
paste.

***Wasabi* paste**
Sold in tubes, this paste is squeezed out to use. Once opened, this must be kept in the refrigerator.

Jellied Loaf from Devil's Tongue Plant (*Konnyaku*) *page 16*
A gray-colored, translucent loaf is made from the starch of tubers

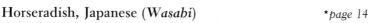

of the devil's tongue plant. The Japanese like its resilient, slippery texture. It has no calories but is a good source of fiber. It is sold in cans or bags. Always parboil it about 5 minutes before cooking to remove its limestone odor. It will keep 1 to 2 weeks if you change the water every few days. It is also made in noodle shapes (see Noodles page 25).

Kelp (*Kombu* or *Kobu*) *page 15
Japan is unique in utilizing seaweed—sea vegetables—for eating and for making stock. *Kombu* is dried kelp and looks almost black-colored. There are many kinds and grades, but they can be divided into two categories. One is kelp for making stock, "*dashi kombu*"; the other is "*nikombu*" kelp for eating. *Dashi kombu* is wide—4 to 12″ (10—3 cm)—and several feet long. Wide, thick and dark-colored with a greenish tinge means it is good quality. The essence of the flavor dissolves easily in water, so do not wash it—just wipe. It will enhance the flavor of dried bonito stock. And it is also used alone as *kombu* stock (page 43).

Leek, Japanese (*Negi*)
This has white stems up to 1″ (2.5 cm) thick and is about 1 foot (30 cm) long. It may be found in Japanese markets on the West Coast. It is succulent and tender, and marvelous in *sukiyaki* or for "*yakitori*" (page 105).

Lotus root (*Renkon*)
Renkon is the root of the water plant with beautiful flowers. It has a crunchy texture and earthy sweetness, enjoyed both in Japanese and Chinese cooking. Because of its holes, the slices are decorative. (See page 51).

Fresh Lotus Root
Summer to winter, these roots are available in Chinese or Japanese stores. Buy lighter-colored, unblemished roots. As soon as peeled or sliced, drop into vinegared water (1 tablespoon vinegar to 1 cup water), and parboil in vinegared water to prevent darkening of the creamy color.

Canned Lotus Root
These are water-boiled. The color is light gray, so cook in soy sauce-seasoned cooking liquid, as in directions for Braised Chicken with Vegetables on page 107.

Mushrooms

Black Mushrooms, dried (*Kikurage*) *page 15
Also called "cloud ear" or "wood ear," these are used in Chinese and Japanese cooking for their crunchy texture and black color. Shrunken and leathery when dry, these mushrooms expand about four times when soaked in warm water for 10–15 minutes. The hard parts of the stem must be removed and discarded, and the soaked mushrooms are usually

cut into fine julienne (matchstick pieces). They are sold in Chinese and Japanese food markets.

Black Forest or *Shiitake* Mushrooms (*Shiitake*)   *page 14

Both dried and fresh *shiitake* are quite commonly found now. "Shii" is the golden oak tree (Pasania Cuspedata), and "*take*" means mushroom so in English the name should be *Shii* Mushroom. Dried *shiitake* should be soaked in lukewarm water for 15 to 30 minutes until tender. If soaked too long the flavor will be lost in the water. Save and use the soaking water for poaching. Fresh *shiitake* are fresh from the farm if they have brown caps with white undersides.

Enoki Mushrooms (*Enokidake*)   *page 14

One of the cultivated mushrooms now sold widely, they look like bean sprouts with tiny caps and thin stems that grow in tight bunches. All yellowish-brown parts should be cut off and discarded. Rinse with water in a colander. To prepare them to be eaten uncooked in salads, blanch them lightly by pouring boiling water and then rinsing immediately with cold water again to retain crispness.

    "*Enoki*" means Chinese nettle tree. "*Enokidake*" is the mushroom that grows on a Chinese nettle tree.

Oyster or Abalone Mushrooms (*Shimeji*)   *page 14

The stems of this small mushroom with its flat, gray cap grow in a cluster. The cultivated mushrooms are sold quite widely, and they are good in soups, *nabemono*, salad and in rice.

Pine Mushrooms (*Matsutake*)

"*Matsu*" means pine, "*take*" means mushrooms. *Matsutake* are so called because they grow under red pine trees in the fall. They are very fragrant and flavorful. In Japan the mushroom-growing mountain areas are rapidly diminishing, sending prices sky high! Japanese-Americans have found them in Washington, Oregon, the Great Lakes States and in Colorado. On the West Coast, they are sold at Japanese markets in October for about $15 and up per pound. They are also exported to Japan because they are cheaper. American mushrooms are whiter than Japanese, and not as fragrant.

Noodles

Wheat Noodles   *page 14

Varieties of wheat noodes are "*udon*" (thick noodles), "*kishimen*" (flat noodles), "*hiyamugi*" (thin noodles—always served cold with dipping sauce), and "*sōmen*" (vermicelli).

Buckwheat Noodles (*Soba*)   *page 14

Light brown noodles made with buckwheat flour are also popular.

Cooking Noodles

Boil a large quantity of water in a big pot over high heat. When it boils rapidly, separate the noodles and drop all the noodles into the boiling water. Stir with chopsticks. When the water begins to boil over, add a cup of cold water. Repeat this twice. Lower the heat slightly and keep boiling until the noodles are cooked (not al dente), about 8–10 minutes, depending on the thickness of the noodles. Turn off the heat and leave covered for a few minutes. Drain in a basket or colander, then rinse with water. Use the Standard Cooking Liquid (page 36) as the soup to pour over, and the *Tempura* Dipping Sauce (page 35) as the sauce for the drained noodles.

Cellophane Vermicelli (*Harusame*)
See Bean Threads (page 20).

Konnyaku Noodles (*Shirataki*)   *page 16
These are made of the starch of tubers called devil's plant. "*Shirataki*" means white waterfall in Japanese. They are also called yam noodles or *sukiyaki* noodles because they are also used in *sukiyaki*. Parboil 5 minutes to remove the limestone odor before cooking.

Peas, Snow (*Saya Endo*)
These are sold at most markets. Choose the smaller pods for tenderness—the larger pods tend to be tougher. Pull off the stringy fiber from both seams before using.

Pepper, Seven-Taste (*Shichimi Tōgarashi*)   *page 15
This is a ready-mixed spice used for noodles or in *miso* soup. It is a mixture of powdered red pepper, *sansho* berries, hemp seeds, poppy seeds, rakeseeds, and dried orange peel. It comes packaged in small shakers.

Persimmon (*Kaki*)
The most commonly available persimmon in markets in the USA is the "*hachiya*" variety with a tall, pointed shape and a beautiful bright orange color. Unless these are very tender, they will be bitter. However, my friend Pearl Kimura has a wonderful method to make firm *hachiya* persimmons sweet. Remove the stem but leave the calyx. Make a small hole and fill it with 1–2 teaspoons vodka or gin. Place them upright in a tight container and let stand 4–5 days in a cool, dark place. The persimmons may then be eaten. The alcohol is completely evaporated and no alcohol flavor remains. Another variety, sold mostly in Japanese markets, is the "*fuyu*" persimmon. These are rather flat shaped, but are sweet when orange-colored and still firm. These are marvelous in salad (see page 216 for "*Kaki Namasu*") or Persimmon Cup (page 265) as well as for dessert.

Plum, Salt-pickled (*Umeboshi*)   *page 16
Green, Japanese plums are salt-pickled, sun-dried, and pickled

again with red *shiso* leaves (beefsteak plant, page 29). These plums are often used in rice balls, or puréed to add to sauces or dressing. They keep indefinitely.

Pumpkin (*Kabocha*)

The most common Japanese pumpkin is the "*kiku kabocha*," with a fluted shape that resembles a chrysanthemum flower. Another variety, the "*kuri kabocha*" or "chestnut pumpkin" is so called because of its taste and meaty texture. It is also called "hatchet pumpkin" because of its extremely hard skin. It is delicious when poached. To choose a tasty one, try to mark the skin with your fingernail. One with skin hard to mark is a good one. It resembles a buttercup squash which is also excellent.

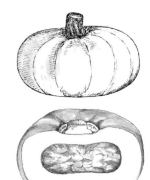

Radish, Giant White or Icicle (*Daikon*)

This giant radish with a diameter of 2–3″ (5–8 cm) and 1–1½ feet (30–45 cm) long is one of the most common vegetables in Japan. Available year round, but best in late fall or winter. On the West Coast it is now sold widely. Choose a radish with a smooth, unblemished skin, and one that is heavy, since it will more likely be succulent. The Chinese *daikon* called "*luopo*" is squatter and darker-skinned, but it is also very good.

Daikon is served raw in a salad, grated for garnish or spice, or it may be simmered.

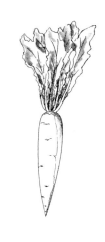

Dried *Daikon* (*Kiriboshi Daikon*)

Shredded or sliced *daikon* is sun-dried until it becomes shriveled. It has a concentrated, natural sweetness that emerges nicely in a pickle (Sweet-Sour Pickle, page 259), or in Braised, Dried *Daikon* on page 137 or as soup garnish.

Pickled *Daikon* (*Takuan Zuke*) *page 16

A yellow-colored, salty pickle which is one of the most common pickles, served with rice at the end of the meal. It is also used as the filling of thin *Nori* Roll, page 249.

Daikon Sprouts (*Kaiware*) *page 14

Young *daikon* sprouts about 2–3″ (5–8 cm) long with only two leaves are very popular in Japan. These appear in many dishes such as salad, *sashimi* garnish, soups and *sushi*. These can easily be home grown. Just select a small container with sides about 2–3″ (5–8 cm) high (such as a *tofu* or cottage cheese container).

Make a shallow bed of soil in a 18 oz. foam plastic cup used for hot or cold water. Seed the soil heavily with *daikon* seeds. Keep moist and you can harvest them in about 10–15 days. A good growing place is a kitchen window sill. Radish seeds grow faster than *daikon* seeds, and they produce a delicate pink sprout. To harvest, the best way is to cut the stems with kitchen scissors above the roots.

Rice (See "Cooking Rice" under Basic Techniques)

Glutinous Rice (*Mochi Gome*)
This rice is stickier and absorbs more water than regular rice. It is not sweet, even though in English it is sometimes called "sweet" rice!

Steamed Glutinous Rice (*Kowameshi*)
After washing the rice, soak in water for 2 hours. Drain in a colander. Spread on a rack of a steamer covered with a well-wrung towel and steam over high heat about 40 minutes, sprinkling with water two or three times in the last 20 minutes.

Red Bean Rice (*Sekihan*)
The rice is soaked in the cooking liquid of red beans (*azuki*) and steamed with the red beans. This is a traditional rice for auspicious occasions.

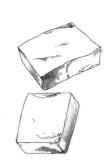

Pounded Rice Cake (*Mochi*)   *page 14
The Japanese associate "*mochi*," the product of pounding steamed glutinous rice with a heavy pestle in a mortar, with the preparation of New Year festivities. Sticky, soft, fresh *mochi* may be eaten right away with grated *daikon* and soy sauce or sweet bean paste, but usually it is shaped into rounds for offerings or rolled out and dried for one or two days to harden and then cut into squares. For eating, either grill it until puffy and browned (bake in a 400°F./210°C. oven), or boil it in water or soup until tender. Soup with *mochi* is called "*zōni*." This is the single most important New Year food, with many variations depending on the region and family traditions.

Rice Vinegar (*Komezu*)
Manufactured from fermented rice, this mild, mellow vinegar is best used for *sushi* and salad. One can substitute white wine vinegar for it if unavailable.

Rice Wine (*Sake*)
Just like wine in French cooking, *sake*, besides being a good drink to serve with a Japanese dinner, is invaluable in cooking. It improves flavor, tenderizes meat and removes some odors. *Sake* is now manufactured in the USA, using the excellent rice grown here. It has an alcohol content of 16–19%. As a substitute for *sake*, use dry vermonth or sherry. For instructions on serving *sake*, see page 277.

Rice Wine Lees (*Sakekasu*)
"Lee" is what remains when rice wine (*sake*) is filtered out during the production process. From winter to spring, when *sake* is manufactured, *sakekasu* is sold in thick paste form or as pressed sheets. It retains some alcohol and a subtle sweetness and is used as a pickling bed or is added to soup. An old-fashioned snack for wintertime, *sakekasu* sheet is grilled and dipped into

soy-sugar syrup.

Rice Wine Lees Pickles (*Narazuke*)
These are luscious, deep amber-colored pickles, usually made of cucumber melon or cucumber, and they are nurtured in a bed of *sake* lees for months. Sold in packages, you should wash the pickle and slice for serving.

Roe, Fish Eggs

Codfish Roe, Salted (*Tarako*)
This is an elongated, kidney-shaped membrane which contains miniscule pink eggs under the thin skin. They are grilled and sliced for serving. Uncooked roe (eggs) may also be removed from the skin and used to coat and mix with fish or vegetables to make *aemono*.

Flying Fish Roe, Salted (*Tobiko*)
These are tiny orange-red eggs sold in plastic cups. They make good *sushi* toppings.

Salmon Roe, Salted—Red Caviar (*Ikura*)
This jewel-like red caviar is very useful as *sushi* topping or as an appetizer.

Roe, Sea Urchin (*Wuni*)
Raw, sea urchin roe (*nama wuni*) is sold at Japanese markets. It is eaten like *sashimi*, with soy sauce mixed with *wasabi* and lemon juice. *Wuni* is a good garnish for *Nigiri Zushi*. Bottled, salted roe (*shio wuni*) and seasoned sea urchin roe (*neri wuni*) may be served in small quantities as is, diluted to be mixed with other things or as a glaze. See page 194.

Seasonings and Garnishes

Myōga *page 14
A bud of a plant related to the ginger family. Harvested in summer, shredded *myōga* makes a nice aromatic garnish for *sashimi*, salads or soups.

Perilla (*Sisho*) *page 14, 57
An annual plant which is a little like basil and easy to grow from seed. The leaves have a pleasant aroma. They make a nice garnish for *sashimi*, grilled fish or meat, or mixed with rice, salads and pickles. Young *shiso* seed pods, (flowers just turning to pods), left on the stalk make a nice garnish for *sashimi*. Stripped off the stalk into soy sauce, they impart an interesting bite and aroma in *sashimi* dipping sauce. Both the leaves and seedpods on stalks are good in *tempura* (see page 97). Red *shiso* is called beefsteak plant because of its shape and color. It is used for pickling salted plums. Red *shiso* sprouts are popular as *sashimi* garnish.

Prickly Ash (Sansho) (Botanical: Zenthoxylum Piperitum)
This is a shrub with thorns. Its leaves, flowers and berries are used as an aromatic garnish. The leaf is called *"kinome"*; the flower is *"hana zansho"*; the green berries *"ao zansho,"* and the popped seedpods are called *"wari zansho."* All make attractive garnishes for soup, grilled or poached foods.

Sansho powder (*kona zansho*) is a powder ground from the dried seed pods. It is used as a spice for grilled items like barbecued eel, or mixed in salads or soups. It is sold in a shaker.
*page 14

Trefoil (Mitsuba) *page 14
These delicate, three-leafed, fragrant greens with long white stems are very good in soup, *nabemono*, or in salad. Sometimes it is available in Japanese markets, but it is not yet commonly sold. It is a perennial plant easily started from seeds.

Seaweeds

Dried Bits (Hijiki)
Sold in packages, these small bits of dried seaweed resemble coarse black tea. When soaked in water for 10 to 15 minutes, they expand more than three times.

Dried Sheets or Squares (Nori) *page 14
The standard, packaged size is 8″ by 7″ (20 × 18 cm). Dark, almost black colored, thick sheets indicate good quality. Ten sheets are folded in half and packed in a cellophane bag. The outside of the folded sheet is the "right side." *Nori* sheets are used to wrap rice balls or *sushi* (see *Nori* Rolls on page 249 and Thin *Nori* Rolls on page 250). *Nori* is best toasted to make it crisp and fragrant. However do not toast the sheets when they are used as wrappers for rice balls or *sushi* that will be kept for hours, since the crispness and aroma diminishes quickly and the untoasted sheets hold better.

To toast *nori*: Place oven rack in middle of oven. Place one layer of *nori* on rack. Set oven at 300° F. (150° C.) and toast *nori* for 2–3 minutes. When the *nori* is crisp and the color has turned slightly green, it is done.

Toasted Nori (Yakinori)
Ten sheets of pretoasted, standard-sized *nori* are sold in bags. Several bags may be sealed in a square, tin can. These toasted *nori* are always packed flat.

Small Sized Nori
Nori is cut 2″ by 2½ ″ (5 × 7 cm) and toasted (*yakinori*) or seasoned (*ajitsuke nori*). These are sold in small packs or round cans. The Japanese like to dip this *nori* in soy sauce, put some hot rice on it and eat. The small white bag in the pack or can

is a chemical which keeps the contents dry. Do not use it in cooking—just discard it.

Dried Strips (*Wakame*) *page 15

These are dark, green-brown, nearly black strips. When soaked in water for 5 or 10 minutes, they spread out to enormous size! The veins should be cut out before using. *Wakame* is often used in soup or salad.

Green Seaweed (*Ao Nori*)

Crumbled green seaweed comes in small jars. Sprinkle it over food as a garnish.

Sesame Seeds (*Goma*) *page 15

There are both black and white sesame seeds. Toasted sesame seeds can be used as a topping on many kinds of food. Toast them in a dry frying pan or a small roaster (page 39), shaking constantly until a few seeds pop. To release even more flavor, they may be roughly chopped.

Soups, Instant *page 15

Many kinds of instant soups are now available in both Japanese and American supermarkets. Some are sold in packages containing three or four small envelopes—each making one serving. To prepare, place the contents in a soup bowl and pour in boiling water. There are both clear soups and *miso* soups. All have some garnishes, but the addition of some greens improves the taste.

There are also several types of instant *"dashi"* to make stock: concentrated liquids, granular types to be dissolved and a type packaged like a small tea bag to boil (see page 43).

Soymilk Film, Dried (*Yuba*) *page 15

The film that is formed at the surface of boiling soymilk is called *"yuba."* It is dried and sold in small swirls or rolled or folded sheets. It is beige-colored and brittle. Before using it in soups or poached foods, soften it in lukewarm water. Deep-fried, *yuba* makes crisp appetizers.

Soy Sauce (*Shōyu*)

This is a refined liquid strained from a long-brewed mixture of fermented soy beans, wheat and brine. Its flavor has a subtle natural sweetness, as well as a salty taste. There are several kinds of soy sauce—see page 33 under "Seasonings."

Sweet Rice Wine for Cooking (*Mirin*)

This sweet cooking wine is used extensively in Japan as a sweetener. It improves the flavor of fish or meat. *Mirin* sold in Japan and Europe and *mirin* sold in the USA are not the same, however. Because of tax regulations, *mirin* sold in the USA is sweeter with less alcohol, whether produced here or imported from Japan. (See page 34 under "Seasonings"). Recipes in this book are based on the use of American *mirin*.

Taro, Japanese (*Satoimo*)
Harvested in summertime and stored for winter, this is one of the staple vegetables in Japan. Since it is very slimy after peeling, sprinkle on some salt and let it stand for about 5 minutes. Then rinse before cooking. See page 150.

Vinegar, Rice (*Komezu*)
See "Rice Vinegar."

Wheat Gluten Cake (*Fu*)

Raw Wheat Gluten Dough (*Nama Fu*)
Well-kneaded wheat flour dough is rinsed and washed, leaving a rubbery mass of dough which is formed into various shapes with some coloring or additional flavors. Dainty flowers or decorated handballs make a festive soup garnish. Rectangular slices are poached, fried, and also used in soup. These should be frozen to keep.

Baked Wheat Gluten Cake (*Yaki Fu*)   *page 14
These look like lightweight sponges and come in various shapes. They are sold in packages and will keep indefinitely. To soften, soak in water and then squeeze the water out before cooking. They are used in soups, *nabemono*, or poached with other materials.

Pine Mushroom Gluten Cake (*Matsutake Fu*)
This is baked *fu* in the shape of a mushroom slice and scented with pine mushroom aroma. It is marvelous in *sukiyaki* (page 230). Soften in water and squeeze out excess water.

Seasonings in Japanese Cooking

All recipes in this book have been carefully tested. However, occasionally you may wish to make a slight adjustment in the seasonings listed because of the seasonal variations in ingredients or their state of freshness. Always taste before adding the entire amount of seasoning. When poaching, it is best to save some of the seasoning for a last minute addition, since simmering may have concentrated the flavor. One of the goals in Japanese cooking is to serve good materials as naturally as possible.

SOY SAUCE

Soy sauce is the most common Japanese seasoning—the one ingredient we cannot do without! Fortunately it is now manufactured in the USA and is available at most markets.

Soy sauce is the liquid which is refined and strained from a long-brewed mixture of fermented soybeans, wheat and brine. It has a sweetness and flavor as well as a salty taste.

There are several kinds of soy sauce.

Regular Soy Sauce (*Koikuchi Shōyu*)
This is an all-purpose soy sauce commonly referred to as "*shōyu*" (soy sauce). "*Koikuchi*" means "dark."

Light Soy Sauce (*Usukuchi Shōyu*)
A lighter-colored soy sauce which is widely used in the Kansai area of Japan (Kyoto and Osaka). It is preferred by professional chefs because of its lighter color. Use slightly less of this type than regular soy sauce because it is saltier than *koikuchi shōyu*.

Tamari **Soy Sauce**
A darker and thicker soy sauce made of fermented soybeans and brine. It is popular in the Nagoya area. It is not saltier than regular soy sauce but has a richer flavor, thicker taste, and some people prefer *tamari* as the dipping sauce for *sashimi*. It is also useful for making barbecue sauce.

Available in the USA are "*Sashimi Tamari*" which is a mixture of *tamari* and soy sauce.

Note: In the USA the name "*tamari*" is mistakenly used for natural soy sauce which is not *tamari*.

White Soy Sauce (*Shiro Shōyu*)
A very light-colored soy sauce—the color of medium sherry. It is made mostly from wheat and brine and has an excellent mellow flavor. It is not yet commonly used outside the Nagoya area.

Milder Soy Sauce
This is manufactured for those who must restrict their salt intake. The salt content is reduced to nearly half. Salt can also be reduced by diluting regular soy sauce with *dashi* or *sake*.

The Japanese Ministry of Science and Technology, Natural Research Commission, provided the following analysis of soy sauce.

Per 100 grams of:	Protein	Carbohydrates	Salt
Regular soy sauce	7.5 g	7.1 g	14.8%
Light soy sauce	5.7 g	6.5 g	16.29%
Tamari soy sauce	10.0 g	9.0 g	14.8%
White soy sauce	2.5 g	17.4 g	14.8%
Milder soy sauce	——	——	7.6%

MIRIN (Sweet Cooking Rice Wine)

The use of *mirin* is another characteristic of Japanese cooking. It is used in place of sugar in cooking to improve the flavor of materials, to make a more refined, mellow sweetness and to add a sheen to sauces. It is now manufactured in the USA.

It is important to be aware that all *mirin* sold in the USA—whether manufactured here or imported for sale here—is sweeter than *mirin* sold in Japan, Europe, and everywhere except the USA. So if you are using a recipe written for cooks in Japan, the results will be sweeter than the original recipe intended! However, all recipes in this book are based on the use of *mirin* which is purchased in the USA.

An analysis of *mirin* shows:

Per 100 grams	Sugar	Alcohol Content
Sake	5.0 g	15.4–16.0 %
Mirin sold in Japan & Europe	46.0 g	14.0%
Mirin sold in USA	62.0 g	8.0 %

If it is necessary to make a substitute for *mirin*, use *sake* or sherry with 30% sugar added. For example, for 1 tablespoon *mirin*, substitute 1 tablespoon *sake* or sherry mixed with 1 teaspoon sugar.

COMBINATIONS OF SOY SAUCE AND *MIRIN*

In Japan, equal parts of *mirin* and soy sauce provide a delicious balance of seasonings used in many ways. The following recipes have been adjusted for use of *mirin* sold in the USA, with its higher sugar content than that sold in Japan.

TERIYAKI MARINADES FOR FISH, CHICKEN, AND MEAT

	Standard Marinade	Less Sweet Marinade	Sweeter Marinade
Soy sauce	1 cup	1 cup	1 cup
Mirin	¾ cup*	½ cup	1¼ cups
Sake	¼ cup	½ cup	0

*Two possible substitutes for *mirin* in the Standard Marinade are either 1 cup *sake* plus ⅓ cup sugar, or 1 cup sherry plus ¼ cup sugar.

GLAZE FOR *TERIYAKI*
Boil down the marinade to ⅔ the original amount. You may add 1–2 tablespoons dark corn syrup to 1 cup marinade before boiling.

DIPPING SAUCES

For *Tempura* or Noodles:

⅓ cup	1 part	soy sauce
4 tablespoons	⅔ part	*mirin*
2 tablespoons	⅓ part	*sake*
1 cup	3 parts	*dashi*

Bring all to a boil, then cool. Makes 1⅔ cups sauce.

A Milder *Tempura* Dipping Sauce:

⅓ cup	1 part	soy sauce
4 tablespoons	⅔ part	*mirin*
2 tablespoons	⅓ part	*sake*
1⅓ cups	4 parts	*dashi*

Bring all to a boil, then cool. Makes 2 cups sauce.

COOKING LIQUIDS

Standard Cooking Liquid:

Used in cooking vegetables or as the broth for noodles or "yosenabe," a casserole assortment. This liquid is called "happo dashi" (eight-direction dashi) because it is so useful and the seasoning is diluted eight times.

1/3 cup	1 part	soy sauce	Bring all to
4 tablespoons	2/3 part	mirin	boil. Makes
2 tablespoons	1/3 part	sake	3 1/3 cups.
2 2/3 cups	8 parts	dashi	

Light-Colored Cooking Liquid

1 cup dashi
1–2 tablespoons mirin (or 1–2 teaspoons sugar)
1 teaspoon soy sauce
1/3 teaspoon salt

Colorless Cooking Liquid

Good for keeping the green color of vegetables.
1 cup dashi
1 tablespoon mirin (or 1 teaspoon sugar)
1/2–2/3 teaspoon salt

CONCENTRATED BASE

If you cook Japanese food frequently, it is helpful to have on hand a Concentrated Base to which you simply add water whenever necessary.

1 cup soy sauce
3/4 cup mirin (3/4 cup sake or sherry plus 1/4 cup sugar)
1/4 cup sake
10 g bonito flakes* or 1 1/2 teaspoons instant dashi granules or liquid dashi concentrate

*Sold in packages with four 5 gram, cellophane bags.

Bring all to a boil and simmer 1 minute. Strain and keep in a bottle. This will keep indefinitely in the refrigerator.

Note: A little sugar may be added to the base, depending on use. The strained bonito flakes can be stir-cooked over low heat until dry and used as topping for rice.

USING THE CONCENTRATED BASE

For Dipping Sauce
Dilute 1 part concentrated base with 1½–2 parts water.

For a Standard Cooking Liquid and Broth
Dilute 1 part concentrated base with 4 parts water

MISO—FERMENTED SOYBEAN PASTE

Historically, soybean paste has been not only a seasoning for the Japanese, but a staple source of protein. There are many varieties, but they can be divided into three categories:

Kome-Miso

Soybean paste fermented with *"kome kōji"*—rice cultured with the aspergillus mold. Eighty percent of the *miso* currently consumed in Japan, and most of the *miso* produced in the USA, belongs in this category. Some varieties are:

> *Kyō Miso*: sweet, white
> Mellow White, Hawaiian Style: mild and sweet
> *Inaka Miso*: yellow and salty
> *Aka Miso*: red, salty

Mugi Miso

This is fermented with barley *kōji*. A reddish-brown *miso* favored in the Kyushu area.

Mame Miso

Fermented with soybean *kōji*. Chocolate brown in color, *mame miso* has the highest protein content. It is popular in the Nagoya area. *"Hatchō miso"* made in Okazaki is the king of the whole *miso* family. This has a sharp, concentrated flavor, but it becomes slightly bitter if boiled too long. This *miso*, usually mixed with one-third *aka miso*, is commonly called *"aka dashi"* (red soup), and is served in restaurants all over Japan.

Mixing of Miso:

In making soups or dressing, one kind of *miso* may be used, but you can enjoy more variety by combining various kinds of *miso*.

Utensils and Equipment

Since the theme of this book is to do Japanese cooking in typical kitchens in Western countries, we like to use kitchen utensils and equipment that are common in America.

KNIVES
It is very important to have several sharp knives. While they do not have to be of Japanese origin, these are the most useful types and styles:

1. One with a thin blade for cutting vegetrables.
2. A long, narrow knife for cutting fish, chicken and meat.
3. A Chinese cleaver for rough cutting.
4. A small knife or boning knife for delicate cutting.

POTS
If you cook rice often, it is handy to have an electric rice cooker. Be sure to buy a large model, since you can only cook up to $\frac{2}{3}$ the capacity of any rice cooker. Or you can use heavy iron or aluminum pots with heavy lids. See Basic Technique—Cooking Rice (page 43).

FOOD PROCESSOR
In a matter of seconds or minutes, the food processor does grinding and puréeing that formerly took 15 to 30 minutes to do by hand with a *suribachi* (mortar and pestle). Making ground fish or chicken for "*shinjo*," a quennelle-like cake, mixing eggs with fish purée for "*Atsuyaki Tamago*" (thick baked egg omelet), grinding sesame seeds for sesame *tofu*, and grinding boiled red beans for sweet bean paste are all so easy!

SQUARE ELECTRIC SKILLET WITH NON-STICK SURFACE
This skillet can be used to make "*Dashi-maki Tamago*," a layered, rolled omelet, and is also handy for *sukiyaki* and other *nabemono*.

SQUARE NON-STICK CAKE PAN (9″ × 9″ or 23 × 23 cm)
This pan will bake "*Atsuyaki Tamago*" (thick baked egg) in the oven beautifully.

CASSEROLES

A corning ware casserole can be used to cook directly on the stove top, and is very convenient for cooking rice with its see-through glass top. A Japanese *"donabe"* (earthenware pot) is useful as casserole, but the unglazed bottom should be completely dry before cooking on top of the stove.

GRATER

Japanese markets have several types of small graters which are handy for grating *daikon* or ginger. Although a food processor can grate *daikon* with the addition of a little water, it tends to make the texture too fine. The *"daikon oroshi"* we prefer has more body and includes crushed fibers.

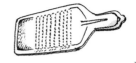

COOKING CHOPSTICKS

These are quite long, but once you get used to them, they are so convenient you will find you cannot do without them!

BAMBOO MAT (*Makisu*)

For rolling *sushi* or for shaping a rolled-up omelet. If you cannot find this, you might use a scrap of bamboo matchstick blind. The regular size is 10″ × 10″ (25 × 25 cm). A larger one, for rolling egg roll, is 14″ × 14″ (35 × 35 cm).

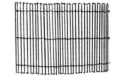

DROP-LID (*Otoshi-buta*)

Japanese cooks use wooden lids that come in various sizes. But you can use any lid that is flat and slightly smaller that the diameter of the pot you cook in. At kitchen hardware shops you can buy a lid with holes, and this is very useful. When using a wooden lid, wash it well before use so it will not be stained or absorb any odor.

Also, you may make a paper drop-lid by cutting parchment paper to fit inside the pot and cutting a small hole in the center for steam to escape. This paper-lid is helpful when poaching foods which tend to crumble.

STAINLESS STEEL SKEWERS

Thin, round skewers with pointed ends are nice to have because they pierce through foods easily and do not make big holes in the food.

WOODEN OR BAMBOO RICE PADDLE

Have these if possible because they are gentler to cooked rice than a metal spoon.

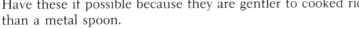

SMALL ROASTING PAN

This is similar to an old-fashioned American corn popper used over a flame, but much smaller, about 4″ (10 cm) diameter with a handle. This is handy for roasting sesame seeds or tea.

Tableware

MINIMUM TABLEWARE

SOUP BOWL, RICE BOWL AND CHOPSTICKS

Lacquer soup bowls are expensive, but there are quite good looking plastic bowls coated with lacquer which are not so expensive. Lacquered bowls retain heat longer, and they have a softer feel when you drink from them.

Chopsticks may be wood stained, lacquered, or made of bone. To Western people it may sound strange, but for formal dinners, the chopsticks are unstained cedar, not silver or gold. An unstained virgin wood tray or chopsticks that are used only once or twice are real luxuries to the Japanese mind. This respect for unstained wood comes from the *Shinto* ceremonies where all the sacred utensils are made of unstained wood. Unstained cedar chopsticks must be soaked in a shallow pan filled with water and wiped dry.

ADDITIONS TO BASIC TABLEWARE

TINY DISHES FOR *SASHIMI* DIPPING SAUCE
SMALL AND MEDIUM BOWLS
SMALL AND MEDIUM DISHES

A Japanese dinner uses many small dishes and bowls. Fortunately, it is more fashionable to use different, but coordinated, patterns and colors of dishes rather than a uniform set. For larger dishes and plates, you can use Western dishes. Here it is nice to use fresh leaves or paper to add a Japanese feeling. One charm of elegant Japanese dinners is the exquisite choice of tableware, suitable for each occasion. But in an average household there is no room for an endless collection of tableware. My advice is to start with plain simple dishes which set off any food, and you can change the feeling with the addition of leaves or paper, and do improvise! Custard soup served in glass bowls is more interesting than in orthodox bowls for *"Chawan Mushi."*

WOODEN TRAYS AND BASKETS

These can be very useful. If you find a piece of nicely grained wood, cut it into any desirable rectangular shape, glue two pieces of chopstick-sized sticks on the back, and you have a nice tray for serving appetizers. (See the cover photograph of this book.)

Spraying the trays with unglossy varnish is a good idea.

Some baskets can double as vegetable drainers in the kitchen and also as nice serving baskets on the table.

CHOPSTICK HOLDERS
These give the feeling of the season or occasion to the table setting. You can also use well-washed pebbles or shells for a patio dinner, or a twig of flowering tree for a Spring dinner.

Measurements and Equivalents

Measurements for all recipes in this book are given in American cups and spoons.

American Spoons & Cups	Volume Measurements Abbreviation	Metric	Weight Measurements American	Metric
1 teaspoon	1 t.	5 cc	$\frac{1}{6}$ oz.	5 g
1 tablespoon	1 T.	15 cc	$\frac{1}{2}$ oz.	15 g
2 tablespoons	2 T.	28 cc	1 oz.	28 g
1 cup (16 tablespoons)	1 c. (16 T.)	230 cc	8 oz.	230 g
2 cups (1 pint)	2 c. (1 pt.)	450 cc	1 lb. (16 oz.)	450 g
4 cups (1 quart)	4 c. (1 qt.)	900 cc	2 lbs.	900 g
$6\frac{2}{3}$ tablespoons	$6\frac{2}{3}$ T.	100 cc (1 decilitre)	$3\frac{1}{2}$ oz.	100 g
1 cup + 1 tablespoon	1 c. + 1 T.	250 cc ($\frac{1}{4}$ litre)	$8\frac{1}{2}$ oz.	250 g
$4\frac{1}{3}$ cups	$4\frac{1}{3}$ c.	1000 cc (1 litre)	2.2 lbs.	1000 g (1 kg)

Note: For Japanese readers, the standard Japanese cup equals 200 cc.

Basic Techniques

MAKING SOUP STOCK (*DASHI*)

A unique feature of Japanese cuisine is that the basic soup stock is not made from animal products, but from dried fish. You might think it would be very fishy, but *"katsuo bushi"* (dried bonito fillet) is as hard as wood and it has no smell at all! It is shaved on a wooden box with a plane iron. The outer, dark brown shavings are used for *miso* soup or *nimono* (poached foods). The inner, red-colored part produces delicate, curly, pink shavings that make *dashi* for clear soup. It is always used with dried giant kelp called *"dashi kombu"* because the two combine to augment the flavor.

Dashi made from bonito flakes and dried kelp has a clean and refreshing taste and is completely free from fat. Used as a base for many Japanese dishes, it sets off and brings out the natural flavor of foods and there is no need to add oil or fat to make it taste richer.

FIRST SOUP STOCK (*Ichiban Dashi*)

This first soup stock (*ichiban dashi*) is the best stock for clear soup.

To make 4 cups:
4½ cups water
5″ (12.5 cm) square of dried kelp (dashi kombu)
1–2 cups bonito flakes (10–20 g)*

* One brand of bonito flakes comes packaged in bags of 19 g (0.67 oz.) and one bag will do. When using a smaller quantity of bonito flakes, supplement by adding MSG.

1. Wipe the kelp with a towel. Place it in a pot and cover with cold water. Let it stand 30–60 minutes to draw flavor from the kelp.
2. Cook over medium heat. When bubbles start to come up from the bottom, remove the kelp. If left longer, it will become slimy and leave an odor. Reserve the kelp.
3. Bring the water to a boil, add ¼ cup cold water to lower the temperature and add the *katsuo* flakes all at once.
4. When it comes to a boil again, take the pot from the heat.
5. Wait 30 seconds, then strain through double thickness of cheese cloth. Do not wait for the flakes to settle because commercially packed flakes do not settle down, and if left too long the broth will develop a slightly bitter taste. Reserve the strained *katsuo* flakes and kelp for use in making "Second Soup Stock."

SECOND SOUP STOCK (*Niban Dashi*)

This is used as a cooking liquid.
You may add some fresh bonito flakes to make it tastier.

1. Cook fish flakes in the water.
2. Just before it comes to a boil, remove the kelp. Then continue boiling for 5 minutes more.
3. Strain through double thickness of cheese cloth.

3 cups water
Kelp and fish flakes
already used once for
making First Soup
Stock.

VEGETARIAN *DASHI* WITH KELP (*Kombu Dashi*)

1. Wipe the kelp clean with a paper towel.
2. Soak it in the measured water for 3 hours (1 hour in summer).
3. Heat the pot slowly. When bubbles start to form at the bottom of the pot, remove the kelp.

To make 4 cups:
4¼ cups water
6×8″ (12×25 cm) piece dashi
kombu

INSTANT *DASHI* PRODUCTS

There are many instant *dashi* products that are widely used in Japan. They are very convenient to use and very good for cooking liquid and sauces. There are three types:

"*Hondashi*" grains to dissolve:
  Use ¼ teaspoon per cup of boiling water.

"*Katsuo dashi*" liquid concentrate:
  Use ⅓ teaspoon per 1 cup of water.

"*Dashi-no-moto*" teabag type:
  Use 1 package per 3 cups boiling water. Let stand for 5 minutes, adding a sliver of lemon rind.

Note that all three types of instant *dashi* contain a little salt. Taste before adding any seasonings!

COOKING RICE

Rice is an essential, basic part of any Japanese meal and cooking it perfectly is of the utmost importance. Because rice is usually served plain, any defect in its texture and resiliency is very obvious. Follow these directions for cooking perfect rice— Japanese style.

Buy short-grain, Japanese style rice for authenticity. Some producers of Japanese rice say it is not necessary to wash it. However, for the best results, it should be washed and polished. Well-washed rice looks glossy when cooked and it will also keep longer. There are four steps in cooking perfect rice: washing, soaking, cooking and steaming.

WASHING

1. Measure the rice into a bowl or cooking pot.
2. Pour in enough water to cover it. Stir the rice with your hand, and quickly discard all the water. Repeat this three times. The first washing water is white and smells of rice bran. Since the rice will absorb much water during the first minute of washing, it will retain this rice bran odor unless you change the water quickly.
3. By handfuls, roll the rice between your palms. Then pour in more water, stir and pour out. Repeat this 2 or 3 times.
4. Rinse the rice in water a few times.
5. Finally, drain the rice in a colander.

MEASURING WATER TO COOK RICE

You will need 10% to 20% more water than the rice measured before washing. For example, for 2 cups of dry rice, measure 2¼ cups to 2½ cups of water for cooking. The larger the amount of water, the softer the rice will be, so choose the amount of water to match your preference for firm or soft rice. Also, the amount of water needed to cook *"shin-mai"* (newly harvested rice which comes to market in October) should only be equal to the measured amount of dry rice.

SOAKING

Rice should be soaked before cooking to allow time for the water to penetrate to the core of the rice. Place the washed rice in a cooker, pour on the measured amount of cold water, and soak it for 30 minutes during the summer, or 50 minutes during the winter. During this time the rice will absorb the water fully. If you are in a hurry, use lukewarm water and soak it for 15 minutes minimum. It is possible to soak rice longer, like overnight, but keep in a cool place.

Another way to moisturize rice is to let the drained rice stand in a colander (30 minutes in summer or 50 minutes in winter). Moisture will penetrate to the core of the rice during this time. If you must leave it longer before cooking, cover it with a well-wrung damp towel to prevent its drying out.

COOKING

Types and Sizes of Cooking Pots
Choose a pot at least four times the capacity of the dry rice since it will expand 2½ times during cooking.

Rice may be cooked in an automatic rice cooker, on the top of the stove or in the oven. A heavy, deep pot with a heavy lid is best for cooking rice. When using an automatic rice cooker, cook no more than ⅔ of the cooker's capacity. If you cook the full capacity, the rice will be heavy and gummy. However, even in a large 10-cup cooker, you can successfully cook as little as one cup of rice. It is wiser to buy a cooker somewhat larger than you think you need!

Automatic Rice Cookers

It is not an exaggeration to say that the liberation of Japanese women began with the invention of the electric, automatic rice cooker! Cookers come in various sizes and the latest ones even keep the cooked rice piping hot for several hours. To use one:

1. Measure the rice into the cooker. Then wash and soak it as explained above.
2. Push the start button about half an hour before you plan to eat. The actual cooking time is 10–15 minutes, depending on the quantity.
3. Steaming will take an additional 10–15 minutes. After the light goes off, the rice will continue to cook at the high temperature, so do not remove the lid during this period.
4. When the steaming is finished, remove the cover and fluff up the rice with a wooden paddle. The rice is now ready to serve. Cover the rice with a dry cloth to absorb any moisture that drips down from the lid. Or you may transfer the rice to a wooden container.

Cooking over Direct Heat

Use a heavy, deep pot for this method. A glass top is convenient. Rice water tends to boil over and splatter. Start with boiling water—it is quicker and does not splatter.

1. Wash and drain the rice in a colander. Let it stand 30 to 50 minutes to moisturize.
2. Measure water into the pot and bring it to a boil.
3. Add the rice all at once. Stir to make the temperature even.
4. Cover the pot and cook over high heat for a couple of minutes.
5. Lower the heat to medium and cook until steam starts to come out.
6. Reduce the heat to very low. Cook about 10 minutes until the water is completely absorbed. Do not remove the lid because that will lower the temperature. However, if you are not sure whether or not all the water has been absorbed, slide the lid off just a little, peek in and close the lid immediately.
7. Turn the heat off. Let the rice steam for 10 to 15 minutes.
8. Fluff up the rice with a wooden paddle and place a dry towel between the lid and pot to absorb condensed moisture.

Cooking in the Oven

Any deep, covered ovenproof casserole may be used.
1. Wash and soak the rice in the casserole or pot.
2. Place the pot on the middle shelf of the oven.
3. Turn on the oven and bake at 350°F. (175°C.). For 1 to 2 cups of rice, bake for 25 minutes. For 3 or more cups, bake for 30 minutes, until the water is absorbed.
4. Turn the oven off and let the rice steam in the oven for 10 to 15 minutes.

Note: Use small, individual casseroles to prepare cooked rice for *"kama meshi"*—a popular rice dish with various garnishes which is served in miniature cauldrons.

KEEPING COOKED RICE

Unless the weather is very hot, cooked rice will keep about 1 or 2 days. If you plan to eat it within one day, do not refrigerate rice. Low temperatures make the starch in cooked rice very crisp, hard and brittle. A boxed lunch with rice or *sushi* should be kept in a cool place, but not refrigerated.

If you must refrigerate cooked rice, steam it before serving. In the refrigerator, cooked rice will keep about one week.

PREPARING FISH

Freshness is the most important factor in cooking fish. Buy only very fresh fish. The eyes should be clear, not reddish. The body should be firm and shining.

Preparation:
As soon as you get home, clean the fish before putting it into the refrigerator.

1. Rinse and scale the fish. Scrape it with a knife, scraping from the tail toward the head.
2. Insert the tip of a knife under the gill cover and cut off the gills.
3. Split the belly from the head to the vent. Remove the gills and entrails.
4. Rinse well under running water and scrub inside well with a wire brush.
5. Wipe the fish dry with paper towels. Now the fish is ready to be cooked whole, or to be cut later.
6. Wrap and store in the refrigerator. Or freeze it if you are not cooking it within a day or two.

Cutting Fish into Two Pieces (*Nimai Oroshi*)
1. Cut the head off the cleaned fish.
2. Cut from the tail, sliding a knife along the upper side of the backbone.
3. Turn the tail to your right. Holding the fish with your left hand, push a knife through to the belly side and up toward the nape, keeping the knife flat on the bone. You now have two fillets. The boneless part of the fillet can be made into *sashimi*. The fillet with bone can be cut into pieces and broiled or boiled.

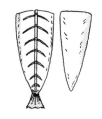

Cutting Fish into Three Pieces (*Sanmai Oroshi*)
Place the fillet with bone, bone side down, on a cutting board. Insert a knife just above the bone and slide it along the backbone. Now you have two fillets and the bone. The bones can be used to make fish stock. If the bones are not too large and hard, cut into pieces and fry until crisp. Sprinkle with salt and serve as an appetizer. This is called *"hone senbei"* (bone cracker).

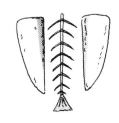

Trimming Fillets
1. Place the fillet skin side down on a cutting board and slice off the belly bones.
2. Separate the skin from the flesh at the tail end. Holding the skin with one hand, move the knife, scraping the skin.
3. Remove small bones with tweezers.

Cutting Fish into Five Pieces (*Gomai Oroshi*)
In Japan we say "five" pieces—counting the bone. Larger fish fillets can be cut further into pieces. There is a slightly darker line in the center of a fillet. Cut lengthwise, following this line. Cut off any bones.

BONING CHICKEN

Chicken is a very versatile meat widely used in Japanese cooking, but most recipes require boneless chicken. So you have to learn to bone them, either a whole chicken or parts like breasts or legs. Save the bones in your freezer until you have enough to make soup stock.

Separating a Whole Chicken into Parts
Use a knife only at crucial points, like cutting the skin and the joints. The rest is done by pulling it with your hands.

1. Separate the legs:
   Hold a leg out and cut the skin close to the body. Pull the leg straight out until the joint is visible. Dislodge the joint by pulling hard. Cut the leg off.

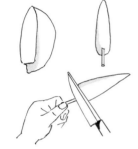

2. Separate the wings:
    Cut the skin near the joint close to the body. Pull the wing out and disjoint it. Cut it off.
3. Separate the breast from the back:
    Hold the breast with the pointed end up. Cut through the points where the rib cage meets the backbone. Bend the back backwards until it separates from the breast.

Boning a Leg
1. Make an incision following the bones.
2. Open up the cut, exposing the bones. Pull out and remove the white tendons.
3. Disjoint and remove the bones.

Boning a Breast
1. Place the breast skin side up on a cutting board. Cut close to the ridge of the breast bone. Continue cutting down along the rib cage, scraping the flesh off the bones. Now you have half a breast with the skin on.
2. Place it skin side down. On top there is a narrow strip of meat which adheres to the center of the breast bone. Separate it and remove the white tendon by holding it with your left hand and scraping the flesh off with a knife. Now this is a chicken tenderloin, called "*sasami*" (bamboo leaf meat) because of its shape.

CUTTING VEGETABLES

SLICING TECHNIQUES

For all five methods, cut across the grain of the vegetable.

Round slice

Half-moon slice

Gingko leaf slice

Slant-cut slice

Rolling cut

Round slice
Half-moon slice
Gingko leaf slice
Slant-cut slice
Rolling cut
 For the rolling cut, cut once on the slant. Then roll the vegetable a little, and cut it again, on the slant, from the opposite side. Continue in this fashion.

CUTTING FINE JULIENNE (Matchstick slivers)

Slice the vegetable, following the grain. Then stack the slices, partially overlapping, on a cutting board. Slice into very fine strips. A food processor may be used for thick julienne.

DICING AND CHOPPING

SHAVING

Shave the vegetable, much as if sharpening a pencil with a knife. Thick vegetables should be cut lengthwise, and then shaved.

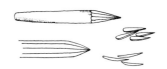

PEELING

The classic peeling technique called "*katsura muki*" is done with a thin, sharp knife. First peel a 3″ (8 cm) piece of vegetable, like *daikon*. Then roll the vegetable with one hand while using the knife to peel a long, continuous strip of vegetable—much like unrolling a roll of paper. To make "white hair" *daikon* garnish for *sashimi*, soften in salted water, roll the *daikon* sheet tightly and slice very thin.

"*Katsura muki*" takes practice, but using a potato peeler, anyone can make white hair *daikon* garnishes. First peel off long, thin sheets of peeled *daikon* from a piece about 6″ (15 cm) long. Soak in salted water to soften. Stack these, and fold to make a roll, rolling from the narrow end. Slice thin across the roll.

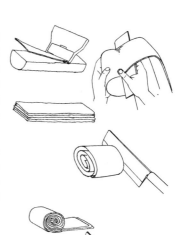

DECORATIVE CUTTING

Carrot Flowers

Trim a section of carrot into a pentagon shape. Then round the corners to a plum flower shape. Then slice across carrot to make flowers. Or use a special Japanese vegetable cutter.

Cucumber Fan

Slice a cucumber lengthwise into pieces 1½–2″ (4–5 cm). Leaving ¼″ (6 mm) at one end uncut, make incisions as shown.

A fan
A floweret

Soak in salted water and fold over the central petals.

Fan

Floweret

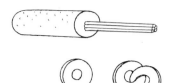

Cucumber Rings ("*Janome*"—a ring)

Cut off both ends of the cucumber. Remove the seeds by poking a chopstick through the center. Then slice into rings.

Celery and *Daikon* Arabesque

Use celery stems near the top of the stalk or *daikon* stems close to the root.

Place the stem, flat side down, on a cutting board. Make long, slanting cuts, taking care not to cut all the way through the stem.

Slice thinly, lengthwise.

Soak these pieces in water. They will curl up, making arabesque patterns. These are good as *sashimi* and soup garnish.

Curly Celery

Use the top parts of celery stalks. Cut them into pieces about 3–4″ (8–10 cm) long. Split the stem end into 4 or 5 sections. Then slit about 1″ (3 cm), and soak in water. Good for *sashimi* garnish.

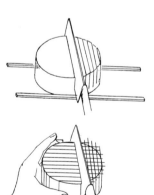

Daikon or Turnip Chrysanthemum

Slice *daikon* or turnip into pieces 1¼″ (3 cm) thick. Peel off the skin. Place thin chopsticks in front and in back of the *daikon* or turnip, and cut as thin as possible—1/16″ (2 mm) or less. The chopsticks will prevent your cutting all the way through, keeping the base intact.

Turn the vegetable a quarter turn. Cut at right angles to the previous cuts, holding tightly with your left hand. Cut into quarters to make four mums.

Soak in salted water to make them pliable. Squeeze out the water. Marinate in sweetened vinegar (¼ cup each of vinegar and *dashi* plus 2 tablespoons sugar) for one hour or more. This keeps in the refrigerator for one week.

To make the flower stamen, add a circlet of red pepper, chopped lemon rind or sieved hard-boiled egg yolk in the center.

This makes a nice garnish with *teriyaki* or any broiled fish, or it can be served as an hors d'oeuvre.

Lemon Rind Garnish

These are like pine needles, to add to soup.

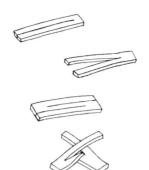

Lotus Root Flowers or Snow Flakes

Cut as shown at for right flowers:

For snow flakes, cut out the sides where the holes are—as shown:

Always soak lotus root in vinegared water (1 tablespoon vinegar in 1 cup water). Otherwise it will become grey-colored.

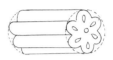

Lotus Root Arrow Feather

1. Slant cut diagonally ¾" (1.6 cm) thick
2. Cut the slice into 2 or 4 strips.
3. Turn the stick sideways to show the holes running across.
4. Put two together like an arrow feather.

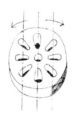

Twisted Knots

These decorative knots are often made with *konnyaku* (devil's tongue jelly), for poaching. Make these before cooking.

Cut a square of *konnyaku* into pieces 3"×1"×½" (8× 2½×1½ cm)

Make a slit on the center of each piece, leaving ½" (1.2 cm) un-cut at the ends. Open the slit and push one end of the piece through the slit.

Pull the end down through the slit and out the other side.

BROILING

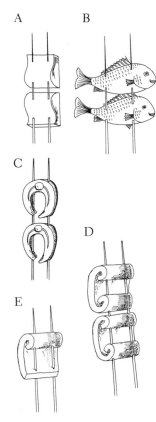

"*Yakimono*" means things that are grilled, broiled, barbecued, baked, and sautéed. The traditional and the best way to barbecue is over a charcoal fire, but in Western kitchens, oven broiling is easy and simple.

SKEWERING

Skewering makes handling easier and also shapes fish into desirable forms. Thin, rounded metal skewers are easy to insert. Bamboo skewers are good only for bite-sized foods (like "*yakitori*") that do not require long broiling.

A festive special occasion is often celebrated by serving a fish with head and tail for an individual serving, or a large fish to be divided. A whole fish is always served with its head pointing left on the plate. To keep the right side of the fish unmarred for presentation, skewer along the back side of the fish.

Techniques of Skewering
Except C & G, all the following ways of skewering are illustrated with the back side showing.

To skewer fish for "*odori-gushi*" (dancing fish) or "*nobori-gushi*" (fish going upstream), skewer as illustrated— adding a bamboo skewer sideways to connect the two fish and prevent rolling.

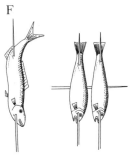

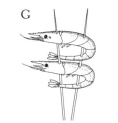

BROILING

Over charcoal, broil with the skin side down first. During broiling, twist the skewers around between your fingers to make it easier to remove them after cooking is done. For fish, broil 6" (15 cm) or more above red-hot charcoal.

For broiling in the oven, use a baking pan with slightly higher edges on which to hang the skewers. Broil with the skin side up first, about 4–6" (10–15 cm) below the broiler.

To remove the strong odor from the oven after cooking fish, sprinkle 2–3 tablespoons of tea (I use "*bancha*," which is the cheapest) on an old baking sheet. Place on the lower rack in the oven. Turn the oven on to 350°F. (180°C.) and bake until the tea starts to smoke. Turn off the heat and let the oven cool without opening the door. The tea smoke removes the fish odor.

POACHING

"Nimono," food poached in seasoned liquid, has been a very common way of preparing food in Japan. It is simple to do, very satisfying and is healthful and nutritious.

Generally speaking, there are two schools in seasoning *"nimono."* Sophisticated, restaurant-type *"nimono"* is very lightly seasoned, emphasizing the natural flavors of the ingredients. Each dish is to be enjoyed by itself or with *sake*, rather than to be eaten with rice. Hearty, home-type *"nimono"* is more strongly seasoned, and is eaten with plain rice.

Use of the *"Otoshi Buta"* (Dropped-Lid) in Poaching

This lid is a little smaller than the pot and drops inside to rest on the food being cooked. It helps circulation of the cooking liquid inside, keeps the top of the food from drying out and ensures even cooking throughout.

Poaching Fish

After the poaching liquid has come to a boil, add the fish. Finish cooking over medium-high heat, because fish cooks quickly. Use a wide, shallow pot, placing the fish in a single layer.

Parboiling Vegetables

Some vegetables need parboiling to remove odor (as with *daikon* radish), sliminess (as with *taro—satoimo*), or its dark juice (as with *gobo—*burdock)

Root Vegetables

Start cooking in cold liquid. Bring it to a boil, and then lower the heat and simmer until vegetables are tender. Watch for evaporation. If the liquid level gets too low before the food is tender, add more water or *dashi*.

Do not add all the seasonings at the beginning, because boiling down makes them stronger tasting. Before finishing cooking, taste and add more if needed to correct the seasoning.

Green Vegetables

Green asparagus, snow peas, spinach, string beans, etc. are often added for their green color to set off other food. Either of the following cooking liquids may be used to parboil green vegetables.

Cooking Liquid

Use Light-Colored Cooking Liquid (page 36), or Colorless Cooking Liquid (page 36).

1. Parboil the vegetables first in boiling salted water. Drain and rinse with cold water.

2. Bring the cooking liquid to a boil. Add the vegetables. Cook for 3–5 minutes. Turn off the heat and let them marinate in the liquid. (If a stronger flavor is desired, take the vegetables out of the liquid. Boil the liquid down and let it cool. Then mix it with the vegetables.)

STEAMING

Steaming is similar to boiling since both methods cook things with moist heat. But steaming has some merits over boiling. Steamed foods are less soggy and retain more of their natural flavor, as in the case of a steamed potato versus a boiled potato. In steaming, heat can penetrate without any danger of drying out and burning. Dietetically speaking, it is also an ideal way of cooking because it does not add extra calories, yet it retains all the natural flavor of the materials.

Steamers
A Chinese wood frame steamer with a woven bamboo top is ideal because steam passes through the top without dripping down into the food. However, water evaporates very quickly from the wok during steaming, and it must be replenished as needed.

A metal steamer is deep and holds plenty of water, but the steam cannot escape through the top and drips down into the food. To prevent this, place a dry cloth between the lid and the top of the steamer.

To improvise a steamer:
Use the deepest pot you have. Remove both ends of a can about 3″ (7 cm) high. Place the can in the center of the pot and fill the pot with water halfway up the can. Place a rack or a heatproof dish on the can.

Steaming
Bring the water to a full boil. Then place things to be steamed into the steamer. Always steam on high heat with full steam. The only exception is for egg custard, which will get bubbly when steamed on high heat. For Custard Soup, the hot bath method on page 113 works better ("Steaming a Custard Soup without a steamer").

Always watch the water level carefully while steaming, since water evaporates very quickly! Replenish as needed.

PART-II
Seafood
Chicken
Eggs
Beef
Pork
Tofu(Bean Curd)
Vegetables, Dried and
Manufactured Foods

Garnishes for *Sashimi* (*Tsuma*), page 88.
Top to bottom: *Bofu*, perilla leaves, and chrysanthemum. Shredded green onions, perilla, cucumber, *myōga*, cabbage, carrot, *daikon* and celery.

Sashimi, pages 85–92.   Halibut, tuna and yellow tail

Slicing—Above top: Straight cut.   Middle: Flat cut.   Bottom: Slant Cut., page 87.

Above: *Sashimi* Variations, page 91.
Top: Skin Broiled Bonito *Sashimi* (*Tosa Zukuri*).   Middle: *Sashimi* with Lemon (Lemon *Zukuri*).   59
Bottom: Chopped *Sashimi* (*Tataki*)

▽ Prawn *Teriyaki* in Shells, page 94.
(Vinegared Lotus Root, page 142.)

▽ Salmon *Teriyaki*, page 94.
(*Sake*-Soaked Apricots)

△ Salt Broiled Mountain Trout, page 92.
(Celery Vinegar Sauce)

Marinated & Broiled Yellow Tail, page 94
(Lady Apple Slices)

▽ Salt-Baked Casserole, page 96.
Dipping Sauce for the Salt-Baked Casserole
(Lemon Soy Sauce with Grated *Daikon*), page 97.

△ Salt Broiled Sea Bream, page 92.
(Lemon Slices and Pickled Young Ginger)

▽ *Sake*-Poached Sole, page 95.
(Green Onions)

△ Poached Mackerel with Vinegar, page 96.
(Grated Ginger)

△ *Tempura*, pages 97–101.
(Dipping Sauce) (Grated *Daikon* and Ginger

▽ *Sake* Steamed Sea Bass, page 102.
  (Red Grated *Daikon* and Chives)

△ Soy Marinated & Fried Sea Bass, page 101.
  (Red Grated *Daikon*)

Above: *Yakitori,* page 105.

Right Top: Salt Broiled Chicken, page 105.
Middle: Braised Chicken with Vegetables, page 107.
Bottom: Chicken *Teriyaki,* page 105.

64

Top: Poached Chicken and Potatoes, page 107.
Bottom: Soy Marinated Fried Chicken, page 106. (Fried Red & Green Sweet Peppers)

Steamed Chicken with a Moon, page 109.

Top and middle: Custard Soup, page 113.
Bottom: Chilled Custard Soup, page 114.

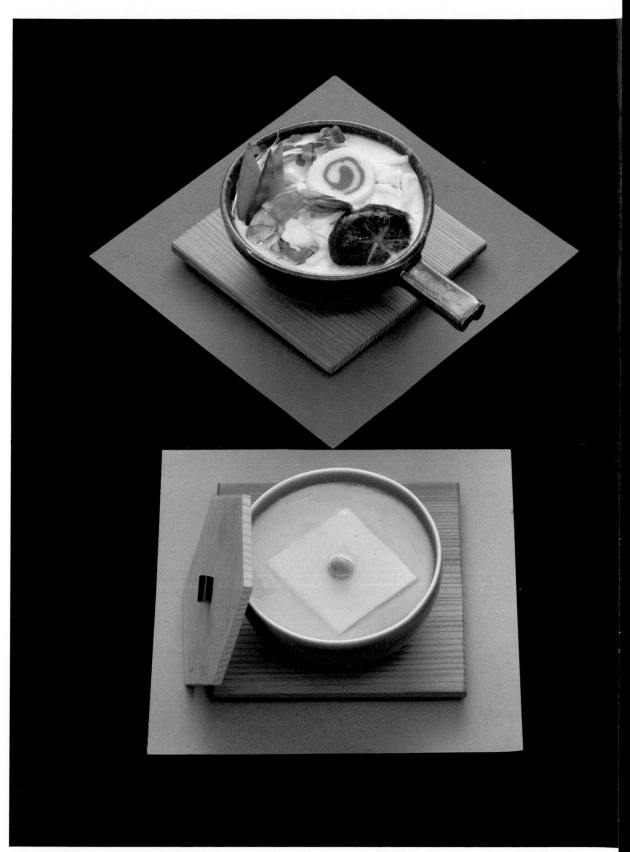

Top: Custard Soup with Noodles, page 114.
Bottom: Custard Soup with *Tofu*, page 114.

∇ Beef *Teriyaki*, page 116.

∇ Beef *Teriyaki*, page 116.
  (Chrysanthemum Turnips, page 152)

△ Broiled Beef with *Miso*, page 117.   △ Broiled Rolled Beef with Pickles, page 117
  (Green Asparagus)   (Sweet Pickled Ginger)

70

▽ Poached Beef and Potatoes, page 118.

△ *Miso* Flavored Meat Loaf, page 118.
(Cherry Tomatoes with Sweet Cucumber Pickles)

71

Top: Cold Boiled Pork, page 119. (Cucumber Fan and Tomato Slices) Bottom: Pan-Fried Pork with Ginger

72 Sauce, page 119. (Boiled String Beans and *Sake*-Soaked Apricots)

Top: Breaded Pork Cutlet, page 120. (Shredded Cabbage and Tomato Slices)   Bottom left: Breaded Pork on
Skewers, page 121.   Bottom right: Bite-Sized Breaded Pork, page 120.   73

Chilled *Tofu*, page 123. (Served with grated ginger, soy sauce, chopped green onions and bonito flakes)

Top: Poached *Tofu*, page 124.   Bottom: Pan-Fried *Tofu*, page 124.

Top left: Deep-Fried *Tofu*, page 124.   Top right: *Tofu* with Ground Chicken Sauce, page 125.   Bottom: Grilled
Tofu on Skewers with *Miso* Glaze, page 125.

Top: Dried *Tofu* with *Miso* Sauce, page 129.   Bottom: Fried & Simmered Dried *Tofu*, page 129.

78   Top: Baked *Tofu* Loaf, page 131.   Middle: Simmered *Tofu* Patties, page 130.
      Bottom: *Tofu* Burger, page 130.

Simmered Dried *Tofu* with Fishcake and *Shiitake* Mushrooms, page 128.

1: Avocado *Sashimi*, page 132.
2: Simmered Bamboo Shoots and Celery, page 133.
3: Simmered Bamboo Shoots with Bonito Flakes, page 133.
4: Stir-Fried Celery, page 136.
5: Cabbage Roll Japanese Style, page 135.
6: Braised Dried *Daikon*, page 137

7: Poached Baked Eggplant, page 138.
8: Tortoise Shell Eggplant, page 139.
9: Stir-Fried Eggplant with *Miso* Glaze, page 139.
10: Deep-Fried Eggplant, page 140.
11: Soy Glazed Grilled Asparagus, page 140.
12: Grilled Green Onions with *Miso* Glaze, page 141.

13: Braised *Konnyaku*, page 141.
14: Vinegared Lotus Root, page 142.
15: Left: Abalone Mushrooms with Sesame Sauce, page 143.
    Rigth: Poached Mushroom, page 143.
16: Grilled *Shiitake*, page 144.
17: Simmered Pumpkin, page 144.
18: Sesame *Tofu*, page 145.

19: Avocado *Tofu,* page 146.
20: Marinated Spinach, page 146.
21: Spinach with Mustard Sauce, page 147.
22: String Beans with Peanut Dressing, page 146.
23: Split Pea Sweet Purée, page 147.
   Chestnut *Kinton,* page 148.
   Apricot *Kinton,* page 149.
24: Deep-Fried and Simmered Sweet Potato, page 149.

25: Steamed Taros in Their Jackets, page 150.
26: Boiled Turnips with *Miso* Sauce, page 151.
27: Chrysanthemum Turnips, page 152.
28: Vegetable *Tempura*, page 153.

Seafood

SASHIMI ★ *page 58*

"*Sashimi*"—sliced, raw seafood—is an indispensable course in formal Japanese dinners. It usually follows appetizers (*zensai*) or soup served as the first course of the main dishes, but it can be served at the very beginning to enjoy with *sake*, or as the main dish for a simple dinner.

Sashimi itself is unseasoned and uncooked, so the sensation of eating *sashimi* depends largely on its texture which should be smooth and velvety. This is only possible with a sharp knife and excellent cutting skill! That is why Japanese chefs are judged by their knifemanship more than anything else. They jealously guard their sets of knives, keeping them well polished, and take them anywhere they go on business.

SUITABLE SEAFOOD FOR *SASHIMI*

The most popular fish for *sashimi* are tuna, albacore, sea bass, etc., but almost any seafood can be *sashimi* if it is absolutely fresh. The names of fish vary a great deal locally, so there are some duplications in the following list. I am sure there are many more possibilities. The only fish not recommended for *sashimi* are fresh-water fish because of the danger of parasites. Good seafood for *sashimi* include:

Abalone	Horse	Sand Dabs	Spanish
Albacore	Mackerel	Sardines	Mackerel
Barracuda	Jack Mackerel	Scallops	Squid
Black Jack	Lobster	Sea Bass	Striped Sea
Blue Runner	Mackerel	Sea Bream	Bass
Bonito	Perch	Shrimp	Sole
Crevalle	Plaice	Sillago	Tile Fish
Cuttlefish	Pompano	Skip Jack	Tuna
Flounder	Porgy	Tuna	Turbot
Garfish	Rock Fish	Smelt	Whitebait
Halibut	Salmon	Snapper	Yellowfin
			Tuna
			Yellow Tail

★ Indicates photo in color

UTENSILS

You will need a sharp knife such as the Japanese "*sashimi bō-cho*" (*sashimi* knife), or a 10" (25 cm) slicer, and a good-sized cutting board. It is best if you sharpen your knife the night before use for *sashimi* so it will not taste of metal. A wooden cutting board should be washed and wiped before each use to prevent staining.

PRELIMINARY CUTTING

To begin, the fish needs to be cut into long, bar-shaped pieces which will be sliced diagonally for *sashimi*.

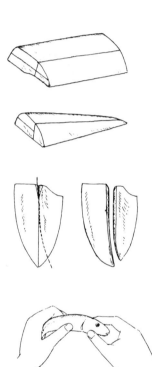

Large Fish
With a large fish like a tuna, buy only a portion of it. Cut into bar-shaped pieces, 2–2½" (5–6 cm) wide by 1" (2.5 cm) thick.

Medium Fish
Buy a whole fish or part of a fillet.
    Scrape off the belly bones by slicing them off. Remove the skin.
    Cut in half lengthwise, following the center line where the backbone was. Towards the tail end, cut into the belly side to make the width even. If there are bones and dark meat on the center line, cut in half following this line, and trim them off. Note that the belly side is thin, so it may be slant-cut or thread-cut.

Small Fish
Small fish like sardines and whitebait are very good as *sashimi* if they are almost alive. Since it is more time consuming to open many small fish, you can do it mostly with your hands. With a very small fish, an entire fillet will be a slice of *sashimi*.
    Hold the fish head with the thumb and index finger. With your other hand, twist and pull the head and the body toward the backside. Pull the head off.
    Under running water, clean inside the fish with your finger. Press your thumb close to the backbone and push up towards the tail, opening the body.
    With your thumb, loosen up the backbone and break it off. With a knife, cut it into two fillets. Cut off the tail and fins and remove the skin.

SLICING

★ *page 58*

The freshness of raw fish deteriorates quickly, so the less handling the better! That means you must work fast, with a sharp knife.

Four types of cuts are described here. Determine the texture and firmness of the fish you have and then decide which cutting style to use.

Flat Cut (*Hira-zukuri*)

This is a standard cut of *sashimi*. A bar-shaped fish fillet is cut across the grain about ⅜″ (1 cm) thick. Firm fleshed fish can be cut thinner for easier eating—as thin as ⅛″ (3 mm) thick.

Flat Cut

1. Place the bar-shaped fish skinned side up on the cutting board with the thicker part farthest away from you. This is done so that when you arrange the slices on a plate, they will stand higher in the back and lower in front.
2. Hold the knife by the upper part of the handle with your index finger over the ridge of the blade. Tilt the blade slightly to the left.

3. Start with the heel of the knife and draw it towards you. With a sharp knife you should be able to slice tender fleshed fish like tuna with one stroke, using the entire length of the blade. Do not press down while slicing!
4. The cut slice is now beside the tip of the knife. Move your knife to the right, carrying the slice with it.

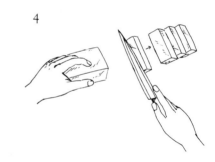

5. When you have cut several slices, slide the knife under the neat, overlapping array of slices and lift them onto a serving dish which has already been prepared with a bedding of garnish.

A good number of slices to serve are five slices in the back and four slices in front—at total of nine. But if you are serving other courses, it can be three in back and two in front. A combination of two or three kinds of seafood makes a "deluxe" *sashimi* plate.

Straight Cut (*Hikizukuri*)

This is the easiest of all *sashimi* cuts. Place the fish fillet on the cutting board, and start with the heel of the knife, as in the flat cut. But when you draw the knife, keep it straight without tilting.

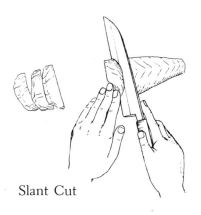

Slant Cut

Slant Cut (*Sogizukuri*)

This cut makes very thin, diagonally sliced pieces—wider slices than the flat cut and is suitable for fish with firmer flesh.

1. Start slicing from the left end of a fish fillet. Holding the end to be sliced, cut on the slant, under your fingers.
2. Carry the slice on your knife and turn it over to the left, making a pile of slices.
3. Lift the pile of slices to a dish. When slicing very thin, it is better to arrange the slices flat, like a chrysanthemum flower with a pile of grated *daikon* mixed with cayenne pepper (*momiji oroshi* or red maple grated *daikon*) and chopped chives placed in the center of the flower. Serve with Lemon Soy Sauce (*chirizu*). This cut is good for halibut or flounder.

Cube Cut

Cube Cut (*Kaku-giri*)

Cut the fish into cubes ³⁄₄–1″ (2–2.5 cm). Fish like tuna or bonito which have a tender texture may be cut into cubes.

Thread Cut (*Ito-zukuri*)

Small fish fillets or thin belly part are cut into strips. Also squid or cuttlefish is cut this way because they are chewy.

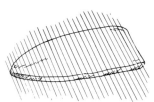

Thread Cut

1. Cut diagonally into strips measuring 2–2½″ × ¼″ × ¼″ (5–6 cm × 6 × 6 mm). If the fillet is thick, first slice it into two or three layers and then cut it diagonally.
2. With chopsticks, make a pile of strips on a dish. This cut is useful for utilizing scraps.

GARNISHES FOR *SASHIMI* (TSUMA) ★ *page 57*

"*Tsuma*" is a generic name for *sashimi* garnishes. "*Shiki zuma*" is bedding on which *sashimi* will be arranged, or a mound behind the array of *sashimi*. "*Kazari zuma*" means decorative garnishes.

These garnishes set off *sashimi*. However, their role is not only esthetic; they cleanse the palate and add vitamins which balance the high protein content of *sashimi*.

Shredded Vegetables

Shred as fine as possible one or more of the following vegetables. Crisp them in water, then drain before arranging. See page 48 for Cutting Vegetables.

Daikon, carrot, cucumber, celery, green or red cabbage, the white part of leek.

Green Perilla Leaves (*Ao Shiso*): This herb is now available on the West Coast. It is a nice addition in summertime.

Decorative Garnishes

Parsley, watercress.
Artistically Cut Vegetables (see pages 48 and 51):
Cucumber fans, *daikon* stem or celery arabesque, curly celery, radishes cut like flowers.
Young Sprouts
Daikon sprouts (*kaiware*) and *shiso* sprouts. Wash well and trim.
Baby Cucumber with Flower
If you have cucumbers in your garden, pick a tiny one still with its flower. Wash carefully.
Perilla (*Shiso*) Seedpod Stalks
A nice addition for late summer. You add the seedpods by scraping them from the stalk with your finger and add them to the dipping sauce.
Myōga
A bud of a ginger family plant. Sometimes it is available on the West Coast. Shred and soak in water, then drain. It has an interesting fragrance and taste.

Purely Decorative Garnishes
Bamboo leaves, chrysanthemum flowers and leaves, lemon flowers, maple leaves, orchid flowers, pine needles, etc.

CONDIMENTS FOR *SASHIMI*

Wasabi (Japanese Horseradish)
Wasabi is by far the most common condiment for *sashimi*. When using *wasabi* powder, mix a little less than an equal amount of water with powder and stir well to make a paste. *Wasabi* is also available as a paste in a tube. Once opened, keep the tube in the refrigerator.
Place a little mound of *wasabi* paste (about ½ teaspoon) on the *sashimi* dish. To eat, put a bit of *wasabi* paste on the *sashimi* slice, dip it into the sauce and eat. Mixing the paste in the sauce kills the fragrance.

Grated Ginger
With blue-skinned fish such as bonito, mackerel and Jack mackerel, grated ginger tastes better than *wasabi*.

Red Grated *Daikon* (Momiji Oroshi)
This is an excellent garnish for thinly sliced, firm white fish *sashimi* such as sea bream, halibut and flounder. To make it, grate peeled *daikon* and squeeze out the excess juice. Mix in cayenne pepper to suit your taste. As a dipping sauce with red grated *daikon* use lemon soy sauce "*chirizu*" (page 90). Do not use *daikon* as the garnish.

Dipping Sauces

The simplest sauce is straight soy sauce. *Tamari* soy sauce is especially good with big fish *sashimi*, since these fish contain more fat in the flesh.

For a low-salt diet, you can dilute soy sauce with *sake* or *dashi* and add a little lemon juice to perk it up.

Bonito-flavored Soy Sauce (*Tosa Jōyu*)

A delicious dipping sauce for all kinds of *sashimi*.

For ½ cup sauce:
Boil all together, then strain.
½ cup soy sauce
1 tablespoon each sake
  and mirin
½ cup shaved bonito (5 g)

Lemon Soy Sauce (*Chirizu*)

In Japan the juice of citrus fruits like *dai dai, kabosu, sudachi* and *yuzu* is called *"ponzu"* and used like vinegar. *Chirizu* is half soy sauce and half *ponzu*.

This sauce is good for *sashimi* of delicately flavored fish such as sea bream, halibut, flounder, perch, rock fish, sea bass, etc. It is also used for *"Chiri Nabe"* (page 226).

For ½ cup sauce, mix:
¼ cup soy sauce
¼ cup Meyer lemon juice or 3
  tablespoons rice vinegar
  mixed with 1 tablespoon
  fresh orange juice.
Regular lemon juice is quite
  strong, so use 2 tablespoons
  lemon juice with 2 table-
  spoons sake *or* dashi.

Vinegar Soy Sauce (*Su Jōyu*)

This is a simpler and sharper sauce than *chirizu*. Combine 6 parts soy sauce with 4 parts rice vinegar. Good for *"tataki"* (chopped *sashimi*) or steamed crab (add grated ginger).

White Miso Sauce with Vinegar (*Su Miso*)

This goes well with some shellfish and non-seafood *sashimi* like avocado slices, steamed eggplant or *konnyaku*.

5 tablespoons mellow
  white miso
3 tablespoons sugar
1½–3 tablespoons rice
  vinegar
½ teaspoon dry mustard
Combine all ingredients in a
  pot. Cook over low heat,
  stirring. Remove from heat
  and cool.

Sesame Sauce (or Peanut Sauce)

This sauce for Chicken *Sashimi* (page 104) is good for a change with some *sashimi* like halibut and non-seafood *sashimi*.

SASHIMI VARIATIONS

★ *page 59*

Sashimi with Lemon (Lemon *Zukuri*)

Tuck thin, half-slices of lemon between the slices. Cover with plastic wrap and refrigerate for half an hour. The fragrance of lemon heightens the taste of yellow tail, bonito or salmon *sashimi*.

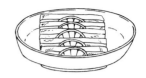

Chopped *Sashimi* (*Tataki* or "*Oki Namasu*")

When fishermen catch many small fish like horse mackerel or sardines, they chop the meat after removing the head, bones and skin, and season it with bean paste, grated ginger and chopped green onions. It is eaten with *su jōyu*. Use a sharp knife to cut it rather than pounding. Add about 5% bean paste.

Skin Broiled Bonito *Sashimi* (*Tosa Zukuri*)

Tosa is a prefecture in Shikoku Island, famous for bonito fishing. This *sashimi* of bonito, Tosa style, lets you enjoy the sleek raw fish with a slightly broiled skin. (No need to remove skin).

It is best to use larger bonito which has more fat in the flesh. Use a half fillet (split in two lengthwise), or a whole fillet if the fish is small.

For broiling, with a barbecue, burn dried straw (rice or wheat straw), grass (such as wild oats), or newspaper twisted into a tight roll. Or you may simply broil in the oven, although this method does not give the faintly smoky flavor that burned straw gives.

1. Sprinkle the fish with ½ teaspoon salt per pound. Let it stand for 10–15 minutes.
2. Skewer like a fan, as illustrated, using 4–5 skewers.
3. Broil over the burning straw or under a broiler for 2 minutes for the skin side and 1 minute for the other side until the surface changes color.
4. Slice it ⅜" (1 cm) thick, and serve with grated ginger and grated *daikon*.

Skin Broiled Bonito *Sashimi* with Spicy Sauce (*Yaki Tataki*)

Skin-broiled bonito is washed first with vinegared water and then patted ("*tataki*" means to pat) with a sauce mixed with herbs. In the Tosa area, this *sashimi* is prepared and arranged on a big platter for festive occasions.

Vinegar and water—mix 1 part of each together.

1. Marinate the skin-broiled bonito in vinegar-water for 10 minutes.
2. Drain and wipe the fish dry. Place -skin side up and slice ⅜" (1 cm) thick.
3. Mix all of the ingredients for spicy sauce and pour over the fish. Let it stand for 15 minutes.

Spicy Sauce
(for 1–2 pounds
of bonito. One pound
serves 4–5):
1 clove garlic, chopped
½" (12 mm) fresh ginger,
grated

*¼ cup chopped green onion,
chives or scallions*

*¼ cup soy sauce
2 tablespoons vinegar or lemon
juice
1–2 tablespoons* dashi
A dash of MSG

*Optional: 1 teaspoon each
chopped* shiso *leaves and
myōga*

*Condiments:
Mustard (make a paste by mix-
ing water with powdered
mustard)
Grated ginger
Red grated* daikon

4. Pat the fish with your hands several times so the fish absorbs the flavor of the sauce.
5. Arrange fish on a platter or on individual dishes. Serve with
condiments.

BROILED FISH (*Yaki Zakana*)

Before the days of city gas, charcoal was the main cooking fuel
in Japan. So broiling over red hot charcoal was the simplest and
most natural method, and it produced delicious dishes.
"Yakimono" (grilled food) was the main dish for formal dinners
at that time, and it still is.

GARNISH FOR BROILED FOODS

Broiled foods are usually served with some garnish which cleans
the palate as well as adding some color. Here are some garnishes
that are easily available.

Apple slices: Small or miniature apples make dainty slices.
Sprinkle them with lemon juice.
Apricot: Soak dried apricots in *sake* or sherry to soften.
Chrysanthemum Turnips or *Daikon*: See page 152 for the
directions. Add chrysanthemum leaves to make beautiful
garnish.
Sweet Pickled Ginger: See directions on page 241. There is also
Pickled Baby Ginger sold in a jar.
Sweet Pickled Cucumber
Lemon Slices or wedges
Vinegared Lotus Root (page 142)

SALT BROILING (*Shio Yaki*)   ★ *page 61*

If you have really fresh fish, this is a good method to bring out
the best natural flavor. Pre-salting draws out the moisture, firm-
ing up the fish. While broiling, salt quickens the coagulation of
protein around the surface of the fish, encasing and sealing the
moist flesh inside. This method adds no additional calories like
pan-frying, yet it is immensely satisfying because the fish is basted
by its own fat. Salt-broiled fish is good with many Western sauces.
Most any fish can be salt-broiled—larger fish cut into thick
slices or smaller fish broiled whole. Whole fish (*okashira tsuki*—
fish with head and tail) used to be a "must" for any festive
occasion—a big sea bream for a whole family, or a smaller fish
for individual servings.

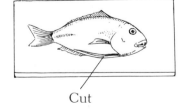

Cut

Suitable fish for salt broiling include barracuda, horse mackerel, mackerel, perch, prawns, rainbow trout, red snapper, red tile fish, salmon, sardines, sea bass, sea bream, sillago, trout, etc.

Japanese custom dictates that a whole fish be presented on the plate with the head pointing to the left. So that it will appear perfect and unmarred, make a cut in the back side of the fish to remove the entrails.

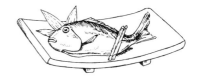

Pre-salting
Use 1–2% salt to the weight of the fish. Fish with more fat need more salt.

1. Sprinkle half of the salt onto a plate. Place the fish on the salt, then sprinkle the remaining salt over the fish.
2. Let it stand 15 minutes to 1 hour. Sliced or thinner fish takes less time for the salt to penetrate.
3. Wash and wipe dry.

Skewering
Follow the directions on page 52. Skewered fish keeps its shape better. If you are using a grill, heat it well and grease it so the fish will not stick while broiling.

Broiling
See page 52 for broiling instructions.

1. Brush the fish with vinegar or lemon juice. Sprinkle with a little salt. When broiled, vinegar makes the skin glossy and does not taste sour.
2. Broil the front side first—that is, turn the front side down facing the charcoal or facing up toward the oven broiling elements. Cook until nicely browned and half done.
3. Turn the fish and finish broiling. Do not overcook, and do not turn often. Because fish skin tears so easily, the less it is handled the better. Twist the skewers a little while broiling to prevent their sticking to the fish.
4. Remove the skewers and arrange the fish on individual plates which are lined with one or two leaves of bamboo or chrysanthemum, or add a twig of parsley. Sweet Pickled Ginger (page 241) is a nice garnish.

Serving
You may serve this simply, with lemon wedges and soy sauce, or you can make green vinegar with celery leaves.

Celery Vinegar Sauce

Grind the celery leaves in a mortar with a pestle. Add the vinegar and *dashi*. Serve this sauce in a *sake* cup for each guest, or in a small pitcher to pass around. Serve with soy sauce.

4 tablespoons chopped celery leaves
2 tablespoons rice vinegar
1 tablespoon dashi, or water with MSG

MARINATED AND BROILED FISH ★ *page 60*
(*Yūan Yaki*)

This method is similar to the well-known *teriyaki*, but more sophisticated. Most fish and chicken can be prepared this way. Suitable fish are halibut, pompano, red tile fish, salmon, trout, yellow tail, etc. Small fish are broiled whole; slightly larger fish can be filleted with their skin. Roll up both ends on skewers (see page 52). Or slice thick if you are using larger fish.

Yūan Marinade
Use the Standard Marinade or Less Sweet Marinade on page 35. Add a sliver of lemon rind.

For delicate white fish, use a little less soy sauce, and for blue fish, use *tamari* soy sauce.

1. Let the prepared fish marinate 1–3 hours, turning several times. When the fish is not extremely fresh, marinate longer—10–12 hours in the refrigerator.
2. Skewer the fish and broil, following direction on page 52.
3. Baste with the marinade once or twice while broiling.

TERIYAKI ★ *page 60*

Teriyaki means broiling with a glaze. It is good with the fattier fish, chicken or meats. Fish is first broiled until ¾ done, then basted with the glaze three times while completing the broiling. Here are three types of *teriyaki* glazes.

Broil the fish until about 80% done. Brush on the glaze and let it dry on the fish, using a lower heat or moving it further from the heat so it will not burn. Repeat several times. For an occasional change sprinkle toasted sesame or poppy seeds over before serving.

*Substitute for *mirin: Sake* or sherry with 3 tablespoons sugar.

Tokyo Style (Kanto *Area*)
½ *cup soy sauce*
½ *cup* mirin*
Combine all and simmer until reduced to half.

Kyoto-Osaka Style
(Kansai *Area*)
⅓ *cup soy sauce*
¼ *cup* mirin
⅓ *cup sake*
Combine all and simmer until reduced to half.

American Style
½ *cup soy sauce*
¾ *cup straight sherry*
2 *tablespoons sugar*
2 *tablespoons dark corn syrup*
Combine all and simmer until reduced to half.

PRAWN *TERIYAKI* IN SHELLS (*Onigara Yaki*)
★ *page 60*

Try to get prawns with the heads on. Very fresh shells are tasty when broiled. You can eat it all, and also suck the coral from the prawn. This is a treat for a special occasion.

1. Remove the black veins from the backs of the prawns with a toothpick.
2. Thread skewers through the prawns.
3. Broil both sides until almost done.
4. Brush *teriyaki* glaze on both sides and let it dry. Repeat two or three times.

PAN-FRIED *TERIYAKI*

This is an easy and delicious *teriyaki*, especially good with yellow tail and salmon.

1. Heat a skillet and add the oil. Tilt the skillet to coat it with oil.
2. Arrange fish slices in the pan. Lower the heat. Cover and cook slowly for 5–6 minutes until bottoms are nicely browned.
3. Turn the slices over and cook the other side. At this point, if you are cooking an oily fish such as yellow tail in the winter, remove skillet from the heat, pour boiling water over the fish, then pour the water off, thus rinsing away the excess fat. Return the skillet to the heat.
4. Add *mirin* and soy sauce and cook over medium heat. The sauce will become thick and can easily burn now, so watch it carefully and shake and turn the slices to coat well with the sauce.
5. Arrange the fish on dishes. Pour any sauce left over the fish. Sweet pickled ginger is a nice garnish with this dish.

4 *slices of yellow tail or salmon 1″ (2.5 cm) thick*
2 *tablespoons salad oil*
6 *tablespoons* mirin (*or 6 tablespoons* sake + 2 *tablespoons sugar*)
5–6 *tablespoons soy sauce*

POACHED FISH

★ *page 62*

SAKE-POACHED FISH (*Nizakana*)

White-fleshed fish such as halibut, perch, rockfish, sand dab, sole, etc. are delicious prepared this way. Follow directions for poaching on page 53.

Use an open, shallow pot where you can arrange the fish in one layer for easy handling. You can also use a skillet. A drop-lid is essential for this method.

For poaching, fish should be scored for quicker cooking and to let the flavors penetrate.

1. Place the fish on a cutting board tilted into a sink. Pour boiling water over the fish, just to blanch it lightly. Rinse with cold water. This blanching takes away the fishy smell and excess oil.

For 4 servings:
4 small whole fish or 4 slices
  1" (2.5 cm) thick
2 tablespoons shredded ginger

Cooking Liquid:
1¼ cup sake
¼ cup soy sauce
1–2 tablespoons sugar

Vegetable Garnish: Use one of
  the following vegatables.
½ cup celery stalks or
  daikon slices ¼" (6 mm)
  thick
1 bunch green onions,
  cut into 2" (5 cm)
  lengths

2. Lay celery or *daikon* slices on the bottom of a shallow pot, as described above. The layer of vegetables will prevent the fish from sticking to the pot. If you are using green onions, they should be added later, using the green tops for lining the bottom and discarding them after cooking.
3. Pour in the cooking liquid and bring to a boil.
4. Arrange the fish over the vegetable in one layer. Sprinkle with ginger and cover with a drop-lid.
5. Cook over fairly high heat. Fish cooks quickly and it tastes better when boiled quickly rather than simmered slowly. It takes about 10 minutes for the fish to cook and the sauce to thicken slightly.
6. With a slotted spatula, transfer the fish to serving dishes. Add vegetables at the side and pour some of the sauce over the fish.

POACHED FISH WITH VINEGAR ★ page 62
(*Suni*)

The addition of a little vinegar points up the taste of blue fish such as mackerel, Spanish mackerel, bonito, etc.

For 4 servings:
4 small whole fish or 4 slices
  1" (2.5 cm) thick
Several slices of ginger
1 tablespoon grated ginger

Cooking Liquid:
3 tablespoons vinegar
3 tablespoons mirin (or 3
  tablespoons sake with 1
  tablespoon sugar)
⅓ cup soy sauce
1 cup dashi

1. In a shallow pot, bring the cooking liquid to a boil.
2. Arrange the fish in one layer. Add the ginger slices. Cover with a drop-lid and cook over medium high heat for about 10 minutes.
3. Lift the fish onto dishes and pour the sauce over. Add a small mound of grated ginger and serve.

SALT-BAKED CASSEROLE (*Hōroku Yaki*)
★ page 61

"*Hōroku*" (or "*hōraku*" in the Kansai area) is a shallow, unglazed, earthenware pot which was used to roast nuts and beans. Using two of these as a bottom and a cover, foods are baked on a bed of coarse salt and brought to the table sizzling hot. This cooking method is especially suitable in autumn as we enjoy the bounty of the season with such delicacies as "*matsutake*" (pine mushrooms—the "king" of mushrooms—with their heavenly aroma!), or *shiitake* mushrooms, chestnuts, or gingko nuts with seafood or poultry.

   Hōroku cooking adapts well to casseroles and the oven. Heated salt absorbs fat, and the food emerges moist, delicious and not at all salty. Pine needles serve as an insulation as well as adding aroma and visual interest. Dried kelp (*kombu*) adds flavor to the food.

When using this method, avoid:
- —Using any foods which exude water or juice.
- —Using foods or materials which have an odor. Sealed baking enhances aroma as well as odors.
- —Overcrowding the materials in the *hōroku*. If they are overcrowded and touching each other, they will steam instead of bake.

Utensils:
Use ovenware casseroles, pie plates or gratin dishes—the larger the better, because you need ample space. If there is no lid, use aluminum foil to cover. Use two casseroles if one is not big enough.

Materials:
Enough rock salt to cover the bottom of a casserole ½″ (1.5 cm) deep.
Two handfuls of pine needles, washed and dried, or dried kelp (*dashi kombu*) cut to fit the bottom of the casserole.

Method:
1. Make a bed of rock salt in the bottom part of the casserole ½″ (1.5 cm) deep.
2. Place the casserole on the middle rack of the oven. Turn the oven on to 500°F. (270°C.) and heat the salt for 10 minutes.
3. Scatter most of the pine needles over the salt. Arrange the ingredients in one uncrowded layer on them, and then scatter the rest of the pine needles over. If you are using kelp, just wipe it with a dry cloth, lay it on the salt and arrange the food on it.
4. Cover with a lid or aluminum foil tucked around snugly.
5. Lower the heat to 450°F. (240°C.) and bake for 20 minutes.
6. Bring the casserole to the table still covered. Upon removing the cover, each diner reaches over to help himself, dipping the food into the sauce.

Ingredients:
For 4 servings:
8 medium unshelled prawns, deveined
Half of a chicken breast, boned and sliced diagonally into 8 pieces (or 4 pieces of white-meat fish), each about 1½ oz. (40 g).
¼ lb. (225 g) mushrooms: pine mushrooms, shiitake, or regular mushroom caps
20 snow peas
8 chestnuts shelled and peeled
4 slices white or sweet potato, sliced ⅓″ (1 cm) thick and soaked in water and pat-dried.

Lemon Soy Sauce with Grated Daikon (Mizore Zu)
This is a lemon-soy sauce mixed with grated daikon or cucumber. Makes 1½ cups. Combine and mix:
⅓ cup each lemon juice, dashi and soy sauce
¼ teaspoon sugar
A dash of MSG
½ cup grated daikon or cucumber, lightly squeezed
A dash of cayenne pepper
1 teaspoon grated lemon rind

TEMPURA

★ *page 62*

Tempura is perhaps the most internationally popular Japanese dish. And for good reason! All the natural juices and flavor are sealed in a delicate coating that crumbles in the mouth. It is very satisfying and yet not heavy. The secret of making light, crisp *tempura* is in the oil, oil temperature and the batter.

Oil

Pure vegetable oil should be used. Olive oil is too heavy and has too distinctive a flavor for *tempura*. Salad oil is highly refined and makes a very light *tempura*.

Use fresh oil. For *tempura* you should use either fresh oil or oil used only once or twice before. As oil gets older, it becomes more oxidized, thicker, and stickier—making fried things heavy. You can use older oil for other types of frying and in stir-fry. Strain used oil while it is still hot into a can to cool. Store in a tightly covered jar or bottle in a cool, dark place.

Frying temperature

For fish and shellfish, fry at 340°–355°F. (170°–180°C.)

Test by dropping a little batter into the hot oil. At these temperatures, it will drop half way down and come back up to the surface.

For vegetables, fry at 320°–340°F. (160°–170°C.)

At this temperature, the test batter drops to the bottom and then rises to the surface slowly.

Keeping oil at an even temperature

1. Use plenty of oil—at least 2″ (5 cm) deep, 3″ (8 cm) is better.
2. Do not fry too much food at one time; use less than half the oil surface. Each addition lowers the temperature of the oil, and if it takes 5 or 6 minutes to recover, *tempura* (which only takes 1–2 minutes) will not be crisp.
3. Do not overheat the oil either. Once the right temperature is reached, lower the heat to medium or medium-high to maintain the temperature. Overheating ages oil quickly and also, the oil evaporates. The quickest way to lower the temperature is to add some cold oil.

Key points for making a light batter

1. Use ice water and sifted cake flour.
2. Do not mix the flour and water until the last moment.
3. Do not stir too much. The batter should be thin and lumpy.
4. If you are not frying the materials all at once, make the batter in smaller batches.
5. Do not place the bowl of batter too close to the hot pot.

Batter "*Koromo*" Coating

For about 4 servings:
1 egg yolk
1 cup ice water
Mix together well.

1–1¼ cup sifted cake flour.
  Mix in just before frying.

Utensils

Frying pot:

Use a heavy and rather deep pot. You need 2–3″ (5–7.5 cm) depth of oil and leaving at least 1″ (2.5 cm) above the oil surface for safe and easy movement. A deeper electric skillet is convenient as it has a temperature control. A Chinese wok is handy, because the slanted bottom requires less oil but provides a broader surface, even though in a wok the temperature of the oil changes faster and more evaporation and oxidation takes place. The wok's wide upper edge helps to contain oil spatterings.

Draining tray:
  A roasting pan with a fitted rack is ideal for draining fried things.

Wire mesh ladle:
  For skimming crumbs out of the frying oil.

Handling tools:
  A pair of long wooden chopsticks or a slotted spoon for lifting fried things out of the oil, and another pair of wooden chopsticks for mixing the batter.

Serving

Like a *tempura* restaurant, serving sizzling hot *tempura* right out of the frying pot is ideal. If you use an electric skillet, perhaps you can serve this on your patio.

Serve *tempura* on dishes, baskets, or trays lined with absorbent paper folded artistically.

Dipping Sauce (see page 35)

Serve about ¼ cup sauce per person in small bowls. Grated *daikon* and a little grated ginger can be passed around.

Salt

Some people like to eat *tempura* with a little salt and lemon juice. You may serve varieties of salt with lemon wedges for the guests to choose from, such as salt mixed with freshly ground black pepper, salt with curry powder, or salt with green tea powder.

Preparation of Fish and Seafood for *Tempura*

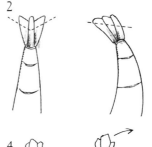

Prawns: A good size prawn for quick frying would be about 30 to 40 headless prawns to a pound.

1. Remove the shells, leaving the tail and the last segment next to the tail.
2. Cut off the tips of the tail and pointed center with scissors, and squeeze out the water.
3. Remove the black veins with a toothpick.
4. Make 3 incisions on the belly and pull towards the back to straighten. This will prevent the prawns from curling up when fried.

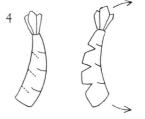

Fish: Cut small fish open from the back. Open them to lie flat and remove the backbone.

Slightly larger fish should be filleted following directions on page 47. Cut large fish into slices about double the size of *sashimi* slices ½″ (12 mm) thick.

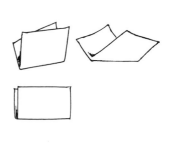

Squid and Cuttlefish: These are delicious as *tempura*, but must be prepared properly or they will splatter badly while frying.

1. Pull the inside out by holding the legs.
2. Cut off intestines from the legs. Cut off eyes.

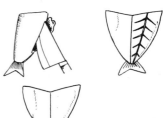

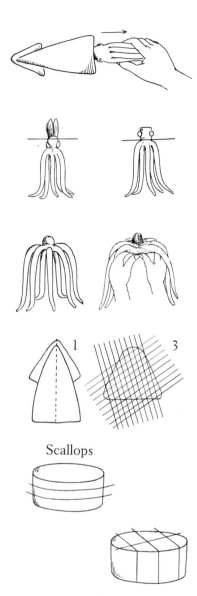

Scallops

3. Surrounding the legs are beaks. Push them out.
4. Scrape off the skin with a knife. Cut the legs into 1" (2.5 cm) lengths and use in "*kaki age*" (spoon-dropped *tempura*).

To prepare the main body:
1. Cut to open out flat.
2. Peel off the skin, both outside and inside.
3. There still remains an inner transparent skin which is difficult to peel but will splatter while frying if not removed. Score crosswise at ¼" (6 mm) intervals on both sides.
4. Cut into strips 2–3" (5–8 cm) by 1" (2.5 cm). Dredge in flour before dipping into batter. Fry at a high temperature quickly. If you fry too long, they will become tough and chewy.

Scallops: Slice in ½" (12 mm) layers, dredge in flour and dip in batter. Fry quickly like squid.

Tempura **Garnishes**
Some vegetable is usually added for color as well as a change of taste.

Some suggestions are leaves of celery, *mitsuba* (trefoil), chrysanthemum, Japanese maple, persimmon, *shiso* (perilla), spinach, etc. *Shiso* seed-pods are also good. To prepare, dip the leaves into batter only on one side and fry at a high temperature to retain crispness and green color.

Vegetables such as green asparagus, mushroom caps, okra, snow peas, string beans, and sweet green pepper are also good. Put toothpicks through the vegetables for easier handling.

An excellent garnish for seafood is young, baby ginger root with stems 2"–3" (5–7.5 cm) long. Scrape the root and slit into 2 or 3 pieces. Dip just the root into the batter and fry. Young Hawaiian ginger can be sliced thin and two or three slices may be dipped into batter and fried together.

For an unusual garnish, try softend apricots (dry apricots soaked in water), drained, dipped into batter and fried.

1½–2 lb. (700–900 g) *assorted seafood*
1 recipe tempura *batter*
¾ *cup sifted flour for dredging squid or frozen fish.*
Vegetable garnishes
Frying oil (See page 98)
1–1½ *cups dipping sauce (page 35), or seasoned salt and lemon wedges*
½ *cup grated* daikon
1 *teaspoon grated ginger*

Tempura **for Four**

To serve sizzling hot *tempura*, good timing and advance preparation are essential.

1. Defrost fish if it is frozen. Slow defrosting in the refrigerator taking 1–2 days is best.
2. Sift 2 cups cake flour into a bowl. (Set aside ¾ cup for dredging and keep the rest for batter). Mix egg yolk with ice water in a separate bowl. Keep these in the refrigerator.
3. Prepare the dipping sauce or salt.
4. Grate the *daikon* and ginger.
5. Prepare the seafood and garnish. Arrange them on a tray.
6. Set out the serving dishes. Have bowls with dipping sauce and grated *daikon* and ginger out on the table.

7. Set up a work system. With the frying pot in the center, place the raw ingredients and two bowls (one for batter and one for dredging flour) on one side. On the other side place a draining pan with a rack, a pair of long chopsticks or a slotted spoon, and a mesh ladle.

8. Heat the oil in the frying pot. Remove the flour and egg-water mix from the refrigerator and place near the two bowls.

9. When the oil is hot, mix about half the egg-water with half the flour. Test the oil temperature.

10. Hold fish or prawns by the tails, dip into batter, and slide into the oil. If the batter scatters around, it is the right consistency. Keep skimming out any scattered crumbs with the mesh ladle.

11. Prawns that are 30–40 to the pound take about 1 minute to fry. They are best when they are golden and crisp outside but still juicy and about 90% done inside. If you are not serving immediately, fry them at a slightly lower temperature a little longer to cook through so the juice will not make the coating soggy.

12. Take the fried things out and drain on the rack in one layer. Do not stack or pile one on top of the others.

13. Serve at once.

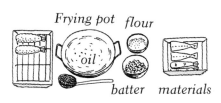

Frying pot *flour*

batter *materials*

SPOON-DROPPED *TEMPURA* (*Kaki Age*)

This is family-styled *tempura* using small shrimp, squid legs, or cut up scallops with quick cooking vegetables.

1. Heat the cooking oil.
2. Mix the batter and add ingredients.
3. Test the oil temperature—bring to 340°F. (170°C.)
4. Using a small ladle, slide a large tablespoonful of the mixture into the oil.
5. With chopsticks poke the center to spread the mound a little so the oil rises through the center. Turn a few times and fry until crisp and golden.
6. Drain on a rack. Serve with dipping sauce and grated *daikon*. Other vegetables which are suitable to fry with shellfish are mushrooms, sliced and chopped green onions, shredded string beans, and of course, if you can get *mitsuba* (trefoil), it is excellent.

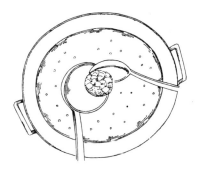

For 2–4 servings:
1 cup shelled shrimp
¹⁄₃ cup celery leaves (or green onions) coarsely chopped

Batter:
1 egg, beaten
¹⁄₂ cup ice water
³⁄₄ cup sifted cake flour

SOY MARINATED FRIED FISH (*Tatsuta Age*)

The word "*Tatsuta*" comes from the Tatsuta river which is renowned for its beautifully colored maples in the fall. In this dish the soy marinade turns the food red-brown during frying.

White-meat fish like flounder, halibut, sandab, sole, ling cod, rockfish, perch or blue fish like mackerel, bonito, and tuna are good.
★*page 63*

Whole small fish, medium fish cut into halves or thirds and scored, or a large fish fillet or steak may be used.

Marinade

Equal amounts of soy sauce and sake *(or half* sake *and half* mirin *for sweeter taste)*
Cornstarch
Frying oil
Grated daikon *mixed with cayenne pepper*

1. Marinate the fish for 30 minutes.
2. Drain it and wipe with paper towels.
3. Coat the fish with cornstarch. Shake off any excess.
4. If the fish is a boneless fillet, fry at 340°F. (170°C.) If the fish has bones, start frying at 320°F. (160°C.) and fry longer. You can also fry twice—first at a lower temperature and again at a higher temperature for one minute just before serving.
5. Serve with a small mound of grated *daikon* mixed with red pepper.

Since this fry does not need sauce, it is good for a lunch box. Also, you can prepare chicken slices the same way. *Mirin* and soy sauce are a better marinade for chicken.

STEAMED FISH

For steaming fish, see the direction for steaming on page 54.

SAKE STEAMED FISH (*Saka Mushi*) ★ *page 63*

Good fish for this dish are mackerel, perch, porgy, rockfish, rockcod, smelt, sea bream and sea bass. If using sardines, clean and steam whole. Use fillets or fish steaks cut in two. For steaming, fish must be extremely fresh!

For 4 servings:
1–1½ lb. of fish
1 teaspoon salt for each pound of fish
⅓ cup sake

Sauce:
¼ cup each vinegar and soy sauce
½ cup soup from the steamed fish

Condiments:
¼ cup grated daikon, lightly squeezed and mixed with a little cayenne pepper (red grated daikon)
2 tablespoons chopped green onion or chives

To prepare:
1. Sprinkle the fish with 1–2% salt and let stand 1 hour.
2. Arrange the fish on a tilted board and pour over boiling water. Rinse with cold water.
3. Arrange the fish on a cake pan big enough for making one layer. The pan should have raised sides to contain the liquid.
4. Pour *sake* over the fish slices. Cover the pan with aluminum foil.
5. Heat a steamer. When the water boils and steams, place the pan holding the fish into the steamer.
6. Cover and steam at high heat for 10 minutes.
7. Remove the fish to serving bowls with a slotted spatula.
8. Mix the sauce and pour over the fish.
9. Sprinkle with chopped green onion and garnish with a small mound of grated *daikon* and serve. If *daikon* is unavailable, use grated cucumber or a bit of grated ginger.

STEAMED FISH WITH *TOFU* (*Chiri Mushi*)

This is a wonderful dish to warm you up during the cold season. Use white-meat fish like cod, perch, porgy, rockfish, sea bass, scorpion fish or oysters. "*Kombu*" (kelp) with fish makes the soup, but if you do not have *kombu*, use *dashi* instead of water.

1. Salt and blanch the fish as explained in *Sake* Steamed Fish. Oysters are placed in a colander and rinsed with salted water.
2. Wipe the *kombu* clean with a paper towel.
3. Line individual bowls with the *kombu*, place the fish on the *kombu* and the *tofu* on the fish. Add mushrooms.
4. Pour 2 tablespoons *sake* into each bowl and add more water to barely cover the *tofu*. Cover bowls with aluminum foil.
5. Place the bowls in fully steaming steamer and cook about 7 minutes over high heat.
6. Add greens to each bowl and steam 3 or 4 minutes longer.
7. Serve piping hot bowls with dipping sauce and condiments.

To eat, dip the *tofu* and fish into Lemon Soy Sauce (*chirizu*), then drink the soup, adding seasonings to your liking.

For 4 servings:
About 1 pound of fish, cut in-
  to 4 pieces 2½" (6 cm)
  square
4 pieces, 2½" (6 cm)
  squares of kombu
½ cup sake
1 cake tofu, *either soft or*
  regular cut into 4 slices
4 mushrooms (any kind)
1 cup greens cut 1½" long:
  green onion, mitsuba
  (trefoil), shungiku (chrysan-
  themum family), spinach, or
  watercress
4 individual bowls
Lemon Soy Sauce
  (Chirizu) (see page 90)

Condiments:
¼ cup red grated daikon
  (squeezed, grated daikon
  mixed with cayenne pepper)
2 tablespoons chopped green
  onion

Chicken

Chicken is a wonderful food—so versatile and easily available wherever you are.

CHICKEN SASHIMI (Tori Sashimi)

"Sashimi" is primarily raw sea food, however other things, raw or lightly cooked, are also served as sashimi.

In Japan chicken sashimi is served entirely raw, or just blanched. But here is a boiled version.

For 4 servings:
2 chicken breasts, skinned and cut into 2 or 3 pieces
½ cup sake or dry white wine or water
¼ teaspoon salt
Wasabi *paste*

Dipping Sauce: Soy sauce diluted with the poached liquid.

1. Sprinkle the chicken with salt.
2. Arrange it in a sauce pan. Pour the *sake* over and cover with a drop-lid.
3. Bring to a boil and lower the heat and simmer 5 to 8 minutes. The chicken should be barely cooked through so it will be moist and tender, not dry.
4. Let cool in the juice. Chill it in the refrigerator.
5. Slant-cut it into thin slices, like *sashimi*.
6. Make a sauce by adding the poaching juices to soy sauce to your taste.
7. Arrange on the plate like *sashimi*. Sliced cucumber and tomato go well with this. Add a small mound of *wasabi* for condiment. You may serve two sauces to choose from.

A second dipping sauce for Chicken *Sashimi*:

Sesame Sauce (or Peanut Sauce)
Mix well together:
   4 tablespoons toasted ground white sesame seeds, or for Peanut Sauce, use creamy peanut butter
   2 tablespoons soy sauce
   1 tablespoon vinegar
   1½ tablespoons *dashi* or poached liquid

BROILED CHICKEN

Here, *shio yaki* and *teriyaki* are done with bones. You can also bone and flatten chicken thighs to broil in less time, or cut up cooked chicken into bite-sized pieces and serve in a more

Japanese manner.

SALT BROILED CHICKEN (*Tori no Shio Yaki*)

Like salt-broiled fish, chicken bastes itself with this method without any oil or fat added.

1. Prick the skin all over with a fork.
2. Rub with lemon slices. Sprinkle with salt and pepper.
3. Broil 6–7″ (15–18 cm) below the heat for 15 minutes. Turn over and broil 15 minutes longer. The breasts will be done.
4. With chicken legs, bake 10 minutes longer at 300°F. (150°C.).
5. Serve with soy sauce and lemon wedges. Provide knife and fork if it is not boned. ★ *page 65*

For 4 servings:
2 broiler chickens, each halved, or 4 breasts or 4 legs (about 2 lb. (900 g) altogether)
1 teaspoon salt
A dash of pepper
4 lemon slices and 4 lemon wedges

CHICKEN *TERIYAKI* ★ *page 65*

Teriyaki in Japan is primarily for fish, and it is not marinated. But with poultry and meat, which have more fat than fish, it is better to marinate first, then broil and baste with a glaze.

1. Prick the skin all over with a fork.
2. Place in a bowl and pour the uncooked *teriyaki* glaze over. Let it stand 1 to 2 hours. Drain sauce into a sauce pan.
3. Reduce the sauce by boiling until it is half the original amount.
4. Barbeque or broil the chicken. Since the marinade makes chicken brown faster, broil 7″ (17.5 cm) from the heat at 450°F. (240°C.) until nicely browned. Turn and broil the other side for 5 minutes.
5. Turn again and bake at 300°F. (150°C.) for 15 minutes, basting with the glaze two or three times.

For 4 servings:
1 broiler chicken cut up (2½–3 lb.) (1.1–1.2 kg)

Marinade and Glaze:
Use Teriyaki Glaze on page 94.
Do not reduce the liquids to a glaze immediately—first use as a marinade and then boil down to half to make the glaze. Optional additions to the marinade are grated ginger and crushed garlic.

YAKITORI (Broiled Chicken on Skewers) ★ *page 64*

"*Yakitori*" are little morsels of chicken meat or livers on bamboo skewers, barbecued over charcoal. They are very popular in Japan and a very common treat. Near train stations or in back alleys, invariably there are some little shops or stalls sending out appetizing aromas, enticing hungry people on their way home to stop for a few skewers with some *sake*.

There is a restaurant which serves *yakitori* as a whole course for dinner, using boiled quail eggs and ducks plus all the parts of chicken and varying the taste by using both "*tare*" (soy based glaze) and simple salt. The secret of good *yakitori* shops is their "*tare*" into which hundreds of grilled skewers are dipped daily, adding more flavor to the sauce. Replenished with new additions and heated daily, the sauce is handed down from generation to

generation.

Any part of a chicken can be used. Cut into small uniform pieces. One leg can be cut into 16–20 pieces—enough for 3 or 4 skewers. Wings with the tips cut off, cut in two at the joint, can be skewered with the bone in. Duck, beef and pork are also very good.

In Japan, Japanese leeks and small sweet green peppers are standbys. Thick, green onion root parts or thin leeks (split in two if they are too thick), and bell peppers can be used. Green asparagus and mushrooms are another good choice.

Equipment:
A barbecue and charcoal
2–4 bricks
Skewers: 8″ (20 cm) for dinner; 6″ (15 cm) for appetizers. Soak in water for 5 minutes.

Ingredients:
For 4 servings as a main dish:
4 chicken legs, boned, cut bite size
4–8 chicken livers
3 tablespoons each sake and soy sauce
2 bunches green onions, cut bite size
1 green pepper
8 green asparagus
8 button mushrooms

Tare (*Glaze*):
½ cup soy sauce
½ cup mirin
¼ cup sake
2 teaspoons sugar
Combine all, boil and simmer until reduced to 80% original volume.

Condiments: Kona sansho or shichimi togarashi

Optional: Browned chicken bones or parts boiled in the sauce add more flavor.

1. Start the charcoal fire in a barbecue. When the charcoal is red and covered with ash, spread the coals into a narrow, rectangular-shaped bed. Arrange two rows of bricks, about 4″ (10 cm) apart, wide enough so the ends of the skewers can rest on the bricks. (When broiling in the oven, fold a strip of aluminum foil around ends of skewers to protect from heat.)
2. Mix 2 tablespoons each of soy sauce and *sake* with chicken. Mix 1 tablespoon each of soy sauce and *sake* with the livers. Let stand 10 minutes.
3. Cut green onion (root part) into 1″ (2.5 cm) pieces.
4. Cut green pepper and asparagus into bite sizes.
5. Skewer chicken pieces with green onion and green pepper pieces. Do not mix chicken pieces with the chicken livers—make separate skewers.
6. Skewer the asparagus and mushrooms together. Brush with oil.
7. Grill both sides until lightly browned.
8. Dip the skewers into the sauce, or brush them with sauce. Dry over the fire. Repeat this two or three times.
9. Serve with a little shaker of "*kona sansho*" (powdered prickly ash berries) and "*shichimi togarashi*" (seven-taste pepper) to sprinkle on if you like.

SOY MARINATED FRIED CHICKEN
(*Tatsuta Age*)
★ *page 66*

Cut slices of chicken into bite-sized pieces and marinate in half soy sauce and half *mirin* for 30 minutes to an hour for larger cuts. Follow the directions for Fish *Tatsuta Age* on page 101. Grated *daikon* is not served with chicken.

Chicken Dishes with Vegetables

Here are some recipes which combine bland vegetables with a small amount of chicken and makes the vegetables delicious!

BRAISED CHICKEN WITH VEGETABLES
(Iridori or Chikuzen Daki*) ★ *page 65*

Chicken and several kinds of vegetables chosen from the list below are first stir-fried, then poached in a seasoned liquid. An easy dish to prepare for a crowd, it keeps well for boxed lunches.
* *Chikuzen* is the name of a region in southern Japan, Kyushu Island.

Preparation:
1. Soak *shiitake* mushrooms in lukewarm water to soften. Discard the stems. Cut mushrooms into halves or quarters, depending on size.
2. Cut *konnyaku* into bite-sized pieces with a knife or spoon to make irregular-shaped pieces. Parboil 5 minutes.
3. Peel taro root and cut each into 3 or 4 pieces. Sprinkle with salt and rinse with water to remove sliminess. If you are using potato, cut as for stew and soak in water.
4. Peel carrot and cut into chunks. (rolling cut, page 48)
5. Scrub the burdock with a hard brush and cut like carrot. Drop pieces into water to prevent them from darkening. Parboil 5 minutes.
6. Green peas, snow peas, or string beans with ends trimmed should be boiled in salted, boiling water for a few minutes until tender. Drain and rinse with cold water.

Cooking Method:
1. In large, heavy pot, heat the oil. Stir-fry *konnyaku*, taro root (or potato), carrot and burdock over medium high heat for 2–3 minutes.
2. Add the chicken pieces and continue to stir-fry for a few minutes more until the chicken changes color.
3. Pour in *dashi* to barely cover the materials. Add half the seasonings. Cover with a drop-lid and cook over medium heat about 15–20 minutes.
4. Taste the liquid and add more seasonings to your taste.
5. Continue to cook until there is just enough liquid to coat the materials. Add the green peas or beans and stir well so everything is well coated with the sauce. Serve hot or cold.

For 8–10 servings:
1 lb. chicken (450 g), cut up as for stew. Can be with or without bones. Legs and wings are good for this.
1 small can bamboo shoots (7 oz.–200 g)
2–3 carrots
1½ lb. (700 g) taro roots or potato
8 dried shiitake mushrooms
1 loaf konnyaku 9.5 oz. (270 g)

Optional:
1 burdock
1 can lotus root
½ cup green peas, snow peas, or string beans
3 tablespoons oil
About 2½ cups dashi, or water with MSG
3–4 tablespoons sugar
4–6 tablespoons soy sauce

Cut *konnyaku*
with a spoon.

POACHED CHICKEN AND POTATOES
(Jagaimo to Tori no Fukume-ni) ★ *page 66*

1. Cut the chicken at the joints. Save the wing tips to add to the water.
2. Grill or broil the chicken pieces until nicely browned.

For 4 servings:
4–6 chicken wings or 2 legs
4 cups water
2–3 tablespoons sugar
3 tablespoons soy sauce
A *dash of* MSG
2–3 medium-sized boiling
  potatoes, about 1½ lb.
  (700 g)
Optional: Needle thin lemon
  rind as topping

3. Place them in a stewing pot. Add water and the wing tips. Bring to a boil. Remove any scum. Lower the heat and cook until the chicken is tender.
4. Peel the potatoes and cut into large, egg-sized pieces. Soak in water.
5. Add the drained potatoes to the pot. Season and cover with a drop-lid.
6. Poach until the potatoes are cooked through and the liquid is boiled down to one-third original volume.
7. Arrange in small individual bowls and pour the liquid over.

POACHED *DAIKON* WITH GROUND CHICKEN (*Daikon Soboro-ni*)

On the West Coast *daikon* is now sold at many markets and is becoming popular as an ideal low calorie food. In addition to eating it raw, *daikon* is very good in soups and poached. However, when it is boiled it takes on a slight odor, so it is better to parboil it. Peel the skin, but there is no need to peel the skin if it is very fresh and unblemished.

Ground chicken tends to stick together when boiled. So here it is blanched in a seasoned liquid, then chopped, ground or put through a food processor.

For 6–8 servings:
2 lb. (900 g) daikon
⅓–½ lb. (150~230 g) chicken
  breast

Cooking Liquid:
3 cups dashi
3 tablespoons sugar
1 tablespoon soy sauce
1 teaspoon salt

1. Cut the *daikon* crosswise into slices ⅔–¾" (1.5–2 cm) thick.
2. Place in a pot, cover with water and parboil about 5 minutes.
3. Drain and rinse with water.
4. Combine the *dashi* and seasonings in a pot and bring to a boil.
5. Blanch the chicken in the liquid for 2 or 3 minutes.
6. Grind the blanched chicken meat to make it crumb-like.
7. Add the *daikon* to the broth and top with the ground chicken.
8. Bring to a boil. Remove any scum.
9. Lower the heat to medium and cover with a drop-lid. Poach until the liquid is reduced to one-third. Watch carefully at this last stage, because it is very easy to burn the bottom.
10. Serve warm with the sauce poured over.

Variations: Ground beef or pork may be used in place of chicken. They do not adhere like chicken, so just use ground meat. Also, turnips may be used in place of *daikon*. Peel and halve or quarter.

CAULIFLOWER WITH CHICKEN SAUCE
(*Hana Kyabetsu Tori-soboro An Kake*)

A poached liquid is thickened and poured over as the sauce. Vegetables may be cucumber, potato, pumpkin or taro potato.

1. Cut the cauliflower head into 8–12 pieces.
2. Place these in a pot and cover with the cooking liquid. Poach until tender. Remove and keep warm.
3. Measure 2 cups of the liquid into a smaller pot, add the seasonings for the sauce and bring to a boil. Blanch the chicken and grind or chop it. Return it to the pot.
4. Simmer for a few minutes. Taste and adjust the seasonings if necessary.
5. Thicken with cornstarch mixed with a little water.
6. Arrange the cauliflower pieces in individual bowls and pour the chicken sauce over.

Optional: Sprinkle a little bit of grated or needle-thin lemon rind on the sauce.

For 8–10 servings:
1 head cauliflower

Cooking Liquid:
3–4 cups water
2 tablespoons sugar
1 tablespoon soy sauce
2 teaspoons salt

Sauce:
1/3 pound chicken breast
2 cups cooked liquid
2 teaspoons sugar
1 1/2 teaspoons soy sauce
1 tablespoon cornstarch

STEAMED CHICKEN WITH A MOON
(*Tori no Tsukimi Mushi*)   ★ *page 67*

Here a steamed egg is poetically referred to as a moon. Moon viewing (*tsukimi*) is always associated with autumn, and so are the mushrooms. Use one or two kinds of mushrooms. Pine mushrooms are superb, but use *shiitake* (fresh or softened, dried ones), regular mushooms, or other cultivated mushrooms such as abalone or oyster mushrooms or *enoki* mushrooms.

1. Slice the chicken diagonally as thin as possible. Sprinkle with a little salt and *sake*. Let it stand 10 minutes.
2. Cut large mushrooms into smaller pieces. With *enoki* mushrooms, cut off the root.
3. Arrange the chicken slices and mushrooms in the bottom of the bowls and add the green vegetables.
4. Make an indentation in the center and break the raw eggs into the indentations. Pour 3 tablespoons of sauce into each bowl. Cover with aluminum foil.
5. Steam for 8–10 minutes.
6. Serve hot, with a spoon.

For 4 servings:
1/3–1/2 lb. (150–230 g) chicken breasts without bone or skin
4 shiitake *mushrooms*
1 bunch enoki *mushrooms*
1/2–1 cup any of the following green vegetables such as green onions, spinach leaves, boiled string beans or mitsuba (trefoil)
4 eggs

Cooking Liquid:
(Same as milder tempura dipping sauce)
1/2 cup dashi
2 tablespoons soy sauce
1 1/2 tablespoons mirin
Boil all together

4 individual bowls (cereal bowls, coffee cups, medium-sized custard cups, etc. may be used.)

Eggs

Something which seems to amaze Westerners at Japanese inns is that raw eggs are served at Japanese breakfast! Among the Japanese people, there used to be an almost religious faith in the value of eating fresh eggs raw. A box of fresh eggs was a welcome gift to the young and old, especially to someone ill.

One of the favorite Japanese dishes consists of steaming hot rice and raw eggs. An egg is broken over a bowl of hot rice, soy sauce is drizzled on, bonito flakes sprinkled on top, and the whole mixture is stirred with chopsticks. Raw eggs become halfcooked by the hot rice and seasoned with soy sauce and bonito shavings. It is simple but good.

SCRAMBLED EGGS (*Iri Tamago*)

Eggs are stir-cooked without oil. You can change the seasonings to salt and pepper and a little MSG.

For 2 to 3 servings:
4 eggs
¹/₄ teaspoon salt
2–4 teaspoons sugar
2 teaspoons soy sauce

1. Break eggs into a bowl. Add the seasonings. Stir well to break eggs and mix with the seasonings.
2. Place a heavy pot or a frying pan on medium heat. When it is warm, pour in the eggs.
3. Stir with 2 or 3 pairs of wooden chopsticks. When the eggs are cooked to a soft scramble, take the pot off the heat. The retained heat of the pan will finish the cooking.
4. Serve piled in small bowls or as a topping for rice.

BAKED EGGS (*Tamago Yaki*)

There are several varieties of *Tamago Yaki*, from thin egg crepes to omelettes, layered rolled eggs, and thick-baked eggs.

EGG CREPES (*Usu Yaki Tamago*)

This recipe makes 4 crepes 8″ (20 cm) in diameter, using a frying pan. Crepes may also be baked. See page 246, last line.

Sweet Crepes
3 eggs
¹/₄ teaspoon salt
1 tablespoon sugar

1. Break the eggs into a bowl. Add the seasonings and stir with two or three pairs of chopsticks or use a hand mixer for one or two seconds to cut the egg whites but do not beat or make bubbly.
2. Strain through a sieve.
3. Heat a frying pan until it is sizzling hot. Wipe the pan with an oil-soaked cotton or paper towel. Lower the heat to low.

4. Pour in a small ladleful of the egg mixture and tilt the pan so the egg spreads evenly over the bottom.
5. Cover and cook over a low heat about 40–50 seconds until the surface is set and the edges are dry. Insert a spatula or chopsticks under the crepe and flip it over to cook just a few seconds more.

Sweet crepes are used to wrap *sushi* rice. Non-sweet crepes are used to roll up crab meat or ham for hors d'oeuvres.

GOLDEN THREAD EGGS (*Kinshi Tamago*)

Shred egg crepes very fine. Shredded sweet crepes are used for the topping of "*Chirashi Zushi*" (loose *sushi*). Shredded non-sweet crepes make a pretty addition to salads.

ROLLED OMELETTE (*Dashi-maki Tamago*)

This is a popular dish for breakfast, lunch or supper. In Kanto (Tokyo area) it is sweeter, while in Kansai (Kyoto-Osaka area), very little sugar and more *dashi* is used.

In Japan a special rectangular omelette pan is used. However, a square or rectangular electric skillet with temperature control is very convenient to use.

1. Lightly stir eggs with seasonings.
2. Heat an electric skillet to 350°F. (180°C.).
3. Pour in about 2 tablespoons of oil and heat. Pour out the oil and wipe the pan with a cotton ball. Lower the heat to 325°F. (165°C.).
4. Pour in a ladleful (½ to ⅔ cup) of eggs. Tilt the skillet to spread the eggs evenly.
5. When the edges begin to set but the center is still runny, use a couple of wooden or plastic spatulas to roll the eggs from one end to the other.
6. Wipe the skillet with a cotton ball dipped in oil. Wipe the open space in the skillet, as well as under the omelette.
7. Pour in another ladleful of eggs. Spread evenly. Lift the first roll and let the eggs flow underneath it.
8. Again with the spatulas, roll the omelette to the opposite side.
9. Continue in this fashion, alternating the direction of rolling the omelette, until all the egg mixture is used.
10. Lift the roll onto a cutting board. Cut into slices 1″ (2.5 cm) thick and serve with a mound of grated *daikon* seasoned with a little soy sauce.

If you have a wide bamboo mat, roll up the egg in it for a few minutes for a neater shape. For serving cold, perhaps in a lunch box, keep it rolled until completely cool.

Non-sweet Crepes
3 eggs
¼ teaspoon salt
A dash of MSG

For one roll which serves 4–8 made in a 10″–11″ (25–28 cm) square skillet:

Regular Roll:
8 eggs
½ cup dashi
1 teaspoon to 4 tablespoons sugar
½ teaspoon salt
2 teaspoons soy sauce

Thin Roll:
4 eggs
¼ cup dashi
½ teaspoon to 2 tablespoons sugar
¼ teaspoon salt
1 teaspoon soy sauce

THICK BAKED EGGS (Atsu Yaki Tamago)
THICK ROLLED EGGS (Date Maki Tamago)

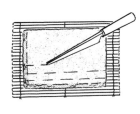

This is the ultimate of baked egg dishes, considered by most Japanese as too difficult to make at home. But equipped with a food processor and an oven, it is easy to prepare.

Utensils: A bamboo mat called "*makisu*," which is used for rolling *sushi*. In Japan, there is a special mat for "*datemaki*" made of thick bamboo sticks which makes a fluted surface for the roll. See section on utensils.
    A non-stick pan about 9″ (23 cm) square.

For a 9″ (23 cm) square pan This amount makes an egg sheet ⅔″ (1.5 cm) thick which is cut into 36 rectangles for the topping of "nigiri zushi", or a roll that provides 16 thick slices

8 eggs
½ cup (100 g) raw shrimp meat or white-meat fish (shelled and boned), or 2 hanpens*
3 tablespoons sugar
2 tablespoons mirin
¼ cup dashi
1 teaspoon soy sauce
⅙ teaspoon salt

* Hanpen is a soft, spongy, white fish cake sold frozen at Japanese grocery stores. It is easier to grind than raw fish.

1. In a food processor, process coarsely chopped shrimp or fish, or cubed *hanpens*, until smooth, scraping down the sides.
2. Add the seasonings gradually.
3. Break eggs in a bowl, then add to the mixture through the feed tube with the machine running. Do not overmix as it makes the eggs bubbly.
4. Heat the oven to 350° F. (180° C.). Grease the pan and heat it in the oven. If you have a baking sheet, line the pan with it. There is no need to heat the pan.
5. Pour the egg mixture into the heated pan all at once. Cut any large bubbles by stirring with a bamboo stick.
6. Place the pan on the middle shelf of the oven, and turn the heat down to 325° F. (170° C.). Bake for 13–14 minutes. The eggs should be cooked and the surface beginning to dry. If not, bake a few minutes longer.
7. Turn the oven to broil (550°F. or 280°C.) and bake the surface until it is golden. This only takes one minute or less.
8. Remove the pan from the oven. Run a spatula around the sides of the pan to loosen the egg sheet.

For Thick Baked Eggs (Atsuyaki)
9. Turn out on a board and invert the sheet again on a rack to cool to make the right side up.

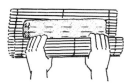

For Thick Rolled Eggs (Datemaki)
9. Place the bamboo mat on the pan, making sure the smooth side of the mat is facing up—not toward the egg sheet. Invert the pan onto the mat. Now the fluted side of the mat is against the egg sheet and will leave the fluted design on the roll.
10. Make parallel, shallow slits at 1″ (2.5 cm) intervals with a knife. This will make the rolling easier.
11. Roll the egg sheet, keeping the mat as tight as possible. Hold the roll with one or two rubber bands around the bamboo mat and leave it until the roll is completely cool.
12. Slice the roll in pieces ¾″ (2 cm) thick.

STEAMED EGG DISHES

These are like custard, even though they are not sweet. Depending upon the proportion of *dashi* to eggs, the thin custards are served as soup, while the firmer ones are served like *tofu*.

Steaming Custard Soup without a Steamer

Steaming custard soup is tricky. The high steam makes it bubbly, and steaming at low heat takes such a long time for the custard to set! Recently my friend in Japan, Tamaye Murayama, told me a wonderful method which is quicker and does not require a steamer.

1. Prepare the custard base with warm (not hot) *dashi* and eggs.
2. In a wide-mouthed pot big enough to hold all the bowls, boil about 1–2″ water (less than ⅓ the height of the bowls to be steamed.)
3. Cover bowls with foil or plastic. When the water boils, place the bowls in, lower the heat to low or medium low. Cover the pot and steam about 6–8 minutes until set.

STEAMED CUSTARDS

CUSTARD SOUP ★ *page 68*
(Chawan Mushi, meaning Steamed Bowl)

This is steamed in bowls that are a little larger than teacups, and served with a spoon. It is very popular for winter because it really warms you up.

Prepare the soft egg soup base shown at the right. This amount makes 6–8 servings depending upon the size of the bowls.

Garnishes:
6–8 thin, bite-sized pieces of chicken breast sprinkled with drops of soy sauce
6–8 shrimps, shelled and deveined, sprinkled with *sake*
12–14 snow peas
3–4 *shiitake* mushrooms, softened and cooked in *dashi* with soy sauce and *mirin*

1. Add seasonings to *dashi*, heat until dissolved.
2. Break the eggs into a large bowl. Stir eggs, trying to cut the whites.
3. Pour the warm *dashi* into the eggs and mix. Strain through a sieve.
4. Line up the bowls or cups. Distribute the garnishes. Pour in the egg soup and cover each bowl with aluminum foil or plastic.

Custard Soup
Soft:
4 eggs (1 cup)
3 cups dashi*
1 teaspoon salt
1 tablespoon soy sauce
1 teaspoon mirin *or* ⅓
    teaspoon sugar

Medium:
4 eggs (1 cup)
2 cups dashi*
⅔ teaspoon salt
1 teaspoon soy sauce
⅔ teaspoon mirin *or* ¼
    teaspoon sugar

Egg Tofu
Firm:
4 eggs (1 cup)
1 cup dashi*
¼ teaspoon salt
¼ teaspoon soy sauce
* You may replace dashi *with clear chicken stock.*

5. Follow directions for steaming custard without a steamer.
6. When the custard is set, insert a bamboo skewer and if it comes out clean and the liquid in the hole is clear, it is done.
7. Place each bowl on a saucer, cover with a lid and serve with a spoon. Lemon rind cut into needle thin slivers may be placed in the center for flavor before covering with the lid.

VARIATIONS:

CHILLED CUSTARD SOUP   ★ *page 68*
(*Hiyashi Chawan Mushi*)

Very good for summer!

For 6 servings:
½ recipe medium egg soup (2 eggs, 1 cup dashi, *⅓ teaspoon salt, ½ teaspoon soy sauce, and ½ teaspoon mirin)*

Garnishes:
⅓ cup cubed kamaboko
3 tablespoons okra slices (parboiled)

Clear Soup: (to pour over the chilled custard)
1½ cups dashi
1 teaspoon soy sauce
⅓ teaspoon salt
1 tablespoon sake
A dash of MSG

1. Divide the garnishes and egg soup into 6 glass cups or bowls. They will be only half filled. Add cubed *kamaboko*.
2. Steam as for custard soup, but only for 5 minutes.
3. Cool and chill in the refrigerator several hours or overnight.
4. Make the clear soup by heating the *dashi* with the seasonings until they dissolve. Cool and chill in a tightly covered jar.
5. Carefully pour the well-chilled clear soup over the custard in bowls, float okra slices and serve.

CUSTARD SOUP WITH NOODLES   ★ *page 69*
(*Odamaki Mushi*)

Place boiled noodles in the bowls, arrange garnishes over and cover with the medium egg soup. Steamed in larger bowls, this becomes a meal by itself. Steam in a pot, following directions on page 113. Allow extra time.

For 6 servings:
Clear Sauce Glaze (gin-an):
  Mix all together and boil.
1 cup dashi
1 teaspoon soy sauce
¼ teaspoon salt
1 teaspoon mirin

Add to thicken:
1 tablespoon cornstarch
  Mixed with a little water

CUSTARD SOUP WITH *TOFU* (*Kūya Mushi*)
                                          ★ *page 69*

Cut soft *tofu* into squares to fit into bowls, and thick enough to come half way up the side of the bowls. Pour in the medium egg soup and steam. Steaming will take longer because of the cold *tofu*. Serve with clear glaze "*gin-an*" poured over, and add a bit of *wasabi* paste for flavor.

EGG TOFU (*Tamago Dofu*)

The name comes from its similarity to soft *tofu* in shape and texture. It can be served hot or cold or in soup as a garnish. This makes 4 servings as a side dish or 10–12 servings as a soup garnish.

Use a bread pan 4″ × 8½″ (10 × 22 cm). Cut plastic wrap to fit the pan and line it. This makes unmolding easy.

1. Start heating water in a pot. Place a shallow dish in the bottom so that the custard in a mold does not get the direct heat. Water should come up to one third of the side of the mold.
2. Break eggs into a bowl, stir well, trying to cut the whites. Mix in the seasoned, warm *dashi*. Strain into the lined pan and cover with aluminum foil or plastic.
3. When the water comes to a boil, place the custard in boiling water. Cover and lower the heat to low.
4. Steam about 10–12 minutes. Slow steaming is essential for a satiny smooth egg *tofu*.
5. When the custard is set, take the pan out of the hot water. Then the custard can be lifted out of the pan by holding the plastic wrap. If serving cold, let it cool and chill in the pan.
6. To serve, cut into 4 squares. To serve hot, pour *"gin-an"* (see page 114) over. To serve cold, pour the milder dipping sauce on page 35 over. A small mound of *wasabi* paste or ginger is good with both.

1 recipe firm egg mixture (page 113)

TWO-COLOR EGGS (*Nishiki Tamago*)

This looks and tastes almost like a dessert, but it is not. It is one of the sweet things served in the course of a dinner.

1. Peel the eggs while they are still warm. Separate whites from the yolks.
2. Put the egg whites through a sieve or whirl in a food processor. Mix in half the sugar and a pinch of salt.
3. Using the same sieve, put the yolks through it. Mix in the other half of the sugar and a pinch of salt.
4. Line a rectangular pan or dish which will hold 1½–2 cups with a sheet of plastic wrap. Spread the egg whites evenly in the pan. Flatten and press with the back of a spoon.
5. Spread the sieved yolks on the egg whites. Lightly press with the back of a spoon.
6. Steam for 10 minutes. When it is slightly cool, take it out of the mold by lifting it by the plastic wrap.
7. When completely cold, remove the plastic wrap and cut into bars.

6 hard boiled eggs (boil 12 minutes after water comes to a boil.)
3–4 tablespoons sugar
A dash of salt

Beef

At Matsuzaka near Ise, there is a restaurant which serves the famous Matsuzaka beef completely raw as *sashimi*! Here is Beef *Tataki* (rare-broiled *sashimi*) similar to Bonito *Tataki*, which has become very popular in the last few years in Japan.

RARE-BROILED BEEF *SASHIMI*
(Beef *Tataki*)

For 3-4 servings:
1-1½ lb. lean beef such as tenderloin, top round, eye of round, or steaks 1¼" (3 cm) thick.

Condiments:
2 tablespoons chopped chives, scallions, or green onions
1 tablespoon grainy Dijon mustard

Dipping Sauces: (Choose one of the two)

Lemon soy sauce:
1-1½ tablespoons lemon juice
2 tablespoons sake
4 tablespoons soy sauce
½ teaspoon sugar
Mix all together.

Sesame Sauce: (see page 104—*Chicken* Sashimi)

Garnish:
Lettuce, shredded cucumber or carrot, radish, sliced tomatoes.

Oven Method:
1. Take the meat out of refrigerator a few hours before cooking to bring it to room temperature.
2. Brush the meat with oil and place in a baking pan and put it on the middle shelf of oven.
3. When using tenderloin, top round or eye of round, broil 10 minutes (550°F.-290°C.), turning once. Broil 15 minutes for meat 2½" (6.5 cm) thick. When using steaks, brown in a skillet, about 1½ minutes on each side.
4. Cool and slice against the grain.
5. Arrange on plates with the garnishes, and serve with sauce and the condiments.

Pan-Fry Method:
1. Heat 1 tablespoon oil in a heavy skillet. Brown the meat on all sides.
2. Pour in ¼ cup sake and cover the pan.
3. Steam on low heat for 10 minutes for a roast 3 inches thick—less for thinner pieces of meat. The meat should be very soft and pliable when pressed with your finger.

Note: Grated garlic or ginger, prepared horseradish and *wasabi* paste are also good as the condiments.

BEEF TERIYAKI (*Gyūniku Teriyaki*)

Unmarinated:
Rub steaks with cut garlic pieces and sprinkle with freshly ground pepper. Barbecue or broil, just like regular steak. Brush with *Teriyaki* Glaze (page 94) and dry over low heat. Serve with a hot glaze poured over.
Marinated:
See Chicken *Teriyaki* (page 105). Follow the directions except shorten the cooking time.

PAN-FRIED BEEF *TERIYAKI*
(*Gyūniku Nabeteriyaki*)

This is the easiest and quickest *teriyaki*, if you have only two
or three steaks to do at a time. This makes 2–3 servings.

1. Rub the meat with the garlic and sprinkle with pepper.
2. Heat a heavy skillet and add 1–2 tablespoons oil.
3. Arrange the steaks in the hot skillet and quickly brown one
   side—takes about 2 minutes.
4. Turn the steaks over and brown the other side.
5. When the bottoms are nicely browned, pour in the *mirin*
   and soy sauce. Cover and lower the heat to medium to boil
   down the sauce. Shake the pan and watch carefully so it does
   not burn.
6. Serve immediately with the sauce poured over.

*2–3 steaks (these must lie flat
in the skillet without
overlapping)*
*⅓–½ cup mirin (or ⅓–½ cup
sake with 2–3 tablespoons
sugar)*
5–6 tablespoons soy sauce
1 clove of garlic plus pepper.

BROILED BEEF WITH *MISO* GLAZE
(*Gyūniku Misoyaki*) ★ *page 70*

If you like *miso*, you will like this! Serves 3–4.

1. Arrange half of the beef slices on a platter or a board.
2. Spread all the *miso* paste over the slices with a spatula.
3. Place the remaining beef slices on the *miso*-covered slices.
4. Let these stand for about 1 hour.
5. Barbecue over charcoal, or broil in the oven very close to
   the heat. Since one side is spread with *miso*, these brown
   very easily. Broil very quickly, turning once.

*1–1½ lb. beef, cut into thin
steaks, about
¼″ (7 mm) thick.*

Miso *Paste:*
*Mix all together to make a
smooth paste:*
*¼ cup (3.5 oz. or 100 g)
red, salty miso*
2–3 tablespoons sake
1–2 tablespoons sugar

BROILED ROLLED BEEF WITH PICKLES
(*Gyūniku no* Pickle *Maki*) ★ *page 70*

My good friend Fay Kramer served this many years ago. I liked
it very much and so do our friends. It is just right when you need
something light as one of the courses, or for an appetizer.

1. Cut the pickles lengthwise into thin strips about ⅓″ × ⅓″
   × 3″ (1 × 1 × 6 cm).
2. Lightly sprinkle the beef slices with salt and pepper.
3. Place one pickle strip on one end of a slice and roll up. Secure
   it with a toothpick.
4. Broil in the oven, 2–3″ (5–8 cm) from the heat until just
   lightly brown. Turn once. Or they may be pan-fried.
5. Brush with soy sauce. Remove the toothpick. Cut crosswise
   into bite-sized pieces.
6. Arrange in a dainty pile on dishes. Add some green garnish
   such as boiled string beans, snow peas or Sweet Pickled
   Ginger and serve.

For 2–4 servings:
*8 slices beef, very thinly sliced
(I use sukiyaki meat)*
1–2 sweet cucumber pickles
Salt and pepper, or soy sauce
Soy sauce

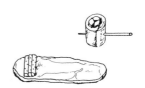

POACHED BEEF AND POTATOES ★ *page 71*
(*Niku Jaga*)

A small quantity of meat is cooked with potatoes (and optional vegetables). The ingredients are similar to stew, however here they are cooked until almost all the liquid has evaporated and the tasty flavors are in the vegetables. This is an economical, family-style dish. This makes 2–4 servings.

For 4 servings:
½ lb. beef for pot roast or
flank steak
2 tablespoons oil
About 1½ lb. boiling
potatoes

Optional:
2 medium sized onions
1 carrot

Cooking Liquid:
About 3 cups water (to cover
the ingredients in a pot)
2–3 tablespoons sugar
3 tablespoons mirin (or 3
tablespoons sake with 1
tablespoon sugar)
5–6 tablespoons soy sauce

1. Cut the beef into squares about 1¼″ (3 cm) wide and ⅓″ (1 cm) thick. Slice meat which requires longer cooking thinner.
2. Peel potatoes and carrots and cut into chunks like pieces for stews. Cut the onions into strips ½″ (1.3 cm) wide following the grain.
3. Heat a heavy stewing pot and add the oil. Quickly stir-fry the meat.
4. When the color of the meat becomes white, add the potatoes and the optional vegetables. Stir to coat with the oil.
5. Pour in water just to cover and bring to a boil. Skim to remove any scum. Lower the heat to medium or medium low.
6. Add ⅔ of the seasonings. Cover with a drop-lid and cook about 20 minutes.
7. Taste and add more seasonings if needed.
8. Continue to cook 10–20 minutes longer, until the liquid is almost evaporated.

MISO FLAVORED MEAT LOAF ★ *page 71*
(*Matsukaze Yaki*)

Foods with poppy seeds sprinkled over them are called by the imaginative name of "*matsukaze*" (wind that blows through the pines). This dish is also good cold. Cut into neat, rectangular pieces and pack attractively into boxed lunches or in "*jūbako*" (stacked, lacquer boxes) for the New Year celebrations.

For 6–8 servings:
2 lb. lean beef, ground twice.
(Or 1 lb. each of beef and
pork for a milder flavor)
2 eggs
2 slices bread

½ teaspoon grated ginger
¼ cup salty red miso
¼ cup sake
¼ cup dashi or water
2 tablespoons sugar
Mix all well.

2 teaspoons poppy seeds
1 tablespoon mirin

1. Soak the bread slices in water to soften. Squeeze out the water.
2. Add the bread, eggs, and the mixed seasonings to the ground meat and mix well.
3. Grease an 8″ × 8″ or 9″ × 9″ (20–23 cm) square casserole or baking pan.
4. Spread the meat mixture flat in the greased container. Smooth the surface. Sprinkle with the poppy seeds.
5. Bake at 350°F. (180°C.) for 30 minutes. If using half pork and half beef, bake for 40 minutes.
6. Remove from the oven. Brush with *mirin* and bake 10 minutes longer.
7. Serve warm or let it cool and cut into rectangles.

Pork

COLD BOILED PORK (*Yude Buta Reisei*)　★ *page 72*
★ *page 72*

This is like lean, pork *sashimi*. Especially good for summer.

1. Blanch the pork by dropping in boiling water for a minute. Drain and rinse with water.
2. In a small, deep pot, bring water with *sake*, green onion and ginger to a boil.
3. Add the meat to the boiling water. The meat should be covered. Remove any scum.
4. Lower the heat to low. Place a drop-lid and the regular lid on top (so the water will not evaporate quickly) and simmer 30–45 minutes until a skewer pierces easily and the liquid coming out of the meat is clear. If the water evaporates, add more boiling water.
5. Remove the pot from the heat and let it cool. If not to be served immediately, remove the lids and cover with plastic wrap letting it rest on the surface of the liquid and refrigerate for several hours. Later, when you remove the plastic wrap, the fat will come away with it.
6. Slice thinly across the grain of the meat and arrange the slices on a bed of lettuce. Add the garnishes. If the pork has been refrigerated, it is better to leave it at room temperature for 20–30 minutes. Cold meat tastes better if not too chilled.
7. Boil equal amounts of the soup and soy sauce in a sauce pan and thicken with cornstarch. The remaining broth will make very good soup.
8. Pour the hot sauce over the pork, add a little bit of mustard paste and serve.

For 4 servings:
1–1½ lb. lean pork such as tenderloin or fresh ham
Water to cover
¼ cup sake
1 stalk green onion
A sliver of ginger root

Sauce:
½ cup broth from the boiled pork
½ cup soy sauce
1 tablespoon cornstarch mixed with 1 tablespoon broth

Garnish:
Lettuce leaves
Sliced tomatoes
Sliced or shredded cucumber
Mustard paste: Mix 1 tablespoon dry mustard with 1 teaspoon water

PAN FRIED PORK WITH GINGER SAUCE (*Buta Shōga Yaki*)　★ *page 72*
★ *page 72*

1. Pound the meat a little to tenderize it. Trim off any fat.
2. Marinate the meat for about 30 minutes.
3. Wash the cabbage leaves. Cut off the hard veins and shred finely. Soak in cold water about 30 minutes and drain.
4. Heat a heavy skillet and add 1–2 tablespoons oil.
5. Pat the pork slices dry with paper towels and place them in the skillet. Brown over high heat. Brown both sides, turning once.
6. Pour in the marinade, cover with a lid and cook over medium

For 4 servings:
4 slices pork steak or 1–1¼ pounds pork sliced ⅓"–½" (1–1.3 cm) thick

Marinade:
⅓ cup mirin (or ⅓ cup sake with 2 tablespoons sugar)
⅓ cup soy sauce
1 teaspoon grated ginger root

Garnish:
Lettuce leaves or finely shred-
ded cabbage
Tomato slices
Boiled asparagus or string
beans, or stir-fried green
peppers

heat for a few minutes—the time depends upon the thickness of the pork.

7. Very soon the sauce becomes bubbly and is easily burned. So shake the pan to coat the meat well and watch carefully.
8. When the sauce is thick and just begins to caramelize, it has reached the optimum stage. Remove from the heat.
9. Transfer the meat to dishes and pour over the sauce.

BREADED PORK CUTLET (*Tonkatsu*) ★ *page 73*

This is very much like Weiner Schnitzel, but it is completely "Japanized" and is one of the most popular common dishes in Japan. Unlike Weiner Schnitzel, it is deep-fried. Serve on a bed of crisped, finely shredded cabbage with soy sauce, Worcestershire sauce or a bottled sauce called "*tonkatsu* sauce."

* The Japanese like coarse-grained breadcrumbs for texture. These are sold in packages at Japanese groceries.

For 4 servings:
4 slices pork tenderloin, loin,
shoulder or fresh ham cut
into pieces about ½" (1.3
cm) thick and about ⅓
pound (150 g) each
Salt and pepper
About 1 cup all-purpose flour
1 egg, lighty beaten to break
the egg white.
About 2 cups breadcrumbs*
Oil for deep-frying

Garnish:
3–4 cabbage leaves, shredded
fine
4 parsley sprigs

1. Soak the shredded cabbage in cold water to make it crisp for about 30 minutes.
2. Pound the pork slices to tenderize and flatten them. Make several pointed cuts at the border lines of fat and meat. This prevents the edges from shrinking and curling up. Pound again to make thinner. Salt and pepper lightly.
3. Arrange a production line of three shallow containers—for the flour, egg and the breadcrumbs—and a tray for the finished slices.
4. Dip each pork slice into flour, the egg, and then coat well with the breadcrumbs. Press breadcrumbs lightly into the meat.
5. Lay the slices on a tray in a single layer and refrigerate half an hour to permit the coating to adhere well.
6. Heat oil to 330°F. (160°C.). Fry one or two pieces at a time, using less than half the surface of the oil. If the temperature is too high, the bread coating browns before the meat is done. Fry between 320°F.–340°F. (160°–170°C.).
7. Turn several times until surface is golden brown and crisp. This will take 2–3 minutes. Keep skimming the oil surface to remove crumbs or scum.
8. Drain on a rack or paper towels. To serve in the Japanese style, cut into strips ¾" (2 cm) wide. Arrange on a bed of well-drained, shredded cabbage and add a parsley sprig.

Home-made Tonkatsu *Sauce:*
¼ cup each catsup and
Worcestershire sauce
2 tablespoons soy sauce
1 tablespoon Chinese
oyster sauce
Mix well.

Serve with soy sauce, Worcestershire sauce or *tonkatsu* sauce.

Tonkatsu Variations: ★ *page 73*
Bite-sized, Breaded Pork (*Hitokuchi Katsu*). Cut the pork into bite-sized pieces and proceed as for regular *tonkatsu*.

BREADED PORK ON SKEWERS (*Kushi Katsu*)

Cut pork into thin, narrow strips so it will cook in the same time needed for the vegetables. Put bamboo skewers through alternately with green pepper, onion, or the root part of green onion strips. Coat and fry like *tonkatsu*. These are good for buffet parties. ★ *page 73*

SOY MARINATED FRIED PORK (*Tatsuta Age*)

See "*Tatsuta Age*" on page 101, but omit the grated *daikon*. Instead of *mirin* and soy sauce marinade, you might try straight soy sauce. Sprinkle the pork slices with soy sauce, pat with your hands and let stand 15–20 minutes. Coat with cornstarch and fry. Because it is preseasoned, this is also good for boxed lunches.

MISO SIMMERED PORK AND VEGETABLES
(*Butaniku no Miso-daki*)

1. Cut the carrots 2½″ (6 cm) long and quarter them.
2. Peel the turnips and quarter. (Peel the potato and cut as for stew)
3. Cut *konnyaku* into pieces 2½″ (6 cm) long and ½″ (1.2 cm) square, and parboil.
4. Blanch the pork in boiling water and drain.
5. Heat 1 tablespoon oil in a heavy frying pan and brown the surface of the pork.
6. Place the pork, carrot, *konnyaku* and potatoes in a pot. (Turnips should be added 30 minutes later because they cook faster.) Cover with water, add ⅔ of the seasonings and the ginger slices and bring all to a boil.
7. Remove any scum. Lower the heat and cover with a drop-lid. Simmer for 1–1½ hours, until the meat is very tender and the liquid is almost evaporated. Check several times and add more hot water and seasonings if necessary.
8. Parboil snow peas or string beans in salted boiling water. Rinse with cold water and drain.
9. Arrange in individual bowls and add green beans or snow peas and a bit of mustard paste, shredded ginger or lemon rind. Serve.

For 6 servings:
1 lb. pork shoulder roast, cut like stew meat or 1½ lb. country-style spareribs, cut 1½″ (4 cm) long with bones
2 medium carrots
2 medium or 1 large turnip, or 1 large potato
A handful of green vegetables such as snow peas, string beans or green onions.

Optional: ½ loaf konnyaku

Cooking Liquid:
Water to cover (about 3 cups)
2 tablespoons sugar
2–3 sweet white or light mellow miso
1–2 tablespoons soy sauce
1 tablespoon toasted white sesame seeds, ground (or creamy peanut butter)
2–3 slices of ginger

Condiment:
Mustard paste (Mix 1 tablespoon dry mustard with 2 teaspoons water), ginger or lemon rind shredded needle-thin

SIMMERED PORK AND *DAIKON*
(*Buta to Daikon no Kakunifū*)

This is a simplified version of the well known "*Buta no Kakuni*" from Nagasaki, Kyushu. Nagasaki was the only open port during the Tokugawa Period and therefore was the source of all international influence. People in Nagasaki enjoyed meat long before the average Japanese did.

Make one day ahead, chill and remove fat.

For 8–10 servings:
1½ lb. (700 g) fresh bacon or shoulder roast, cut into cubes 1½"–2" (4–5 cm)
2–3 lb. (1–1.2 kg) daikon (or potatoes or turnips)
2 quarts water
2–3 slices of ginger
2–3 tablespoons sugar
1 teaspoon salt
4–5 tablespoons soy sauce
Mustard paste (Mix 1 tablespoon dry mustard with 2 teaspoons water)

1. Blanch the pork in boiling water. This will reduce scum.
2. Slice the *daikon* 1¼" (3 cm) thick. If it is large, cut the slices in half. With potatoes or turnips, add them during the last 30–40 minutes of cooking.
3. Place the pork and *daikon* in a large stewing pot and add 2 quarts of water. Bring to a boil and remove scum.
4. Reduce the heat to low and cover with a drop-lid. Simmer about one hour until the meat is tender.
5. Cool. Cover with plastic wrap letting it rest on the surface and refrigerate overnight.
6. Remove the plastic wrap, peeling away with it any congealed fat on the surface. Spoon out any remaining fat.
7. Place on the heat, add seasonings (and now add potatoes or turnips if you are using one of them instead of *daikon*). Continue to simmer 40 minutes to 1 hour longer. Watch the liquid and add more hot water if necessary.
8. When everything is fork tender and a little sauce is left, it is ready to serve. Add a dab of mustard on the top and serve.

Tofu(Bean Curd)

Ten years ago who would have guessed that *tofu* would be sold at practically every market in the USA? With this popularity, there are all kinds of new recipes in Western or Chinese manner being introduced. But here are some traditional, old-fashioned, Japanese *tofu* recipes.

The commonest Japanese *tofu* dishes are very simple, such as "Chilled *Tofu*" and "Simmering *Tofu*." More complicated dishes came from the vegetarian menus in Buddhist temples, where no efforts were spared to transform *tofu* into many shapes and tastes.

Several kinds of *tofu* are now sold in American markets. Of the Japanese types, there are regular *tofu* and soft *tofu* (*kinugoshi*), which is softer and smoother. Chinese *tofu* is firmer than the Japanese regular *tofu*. Regular *tofu* can be used for any *tofu* dishes, while soft *tofu* is used when its custard-like, smooth texture is preferred. See page 17 for more information.

CHILLED *TOFU* (*Hiya Yakko*)   ★ *page 74*

This is utterly simple—just squares of *tofu* served well-chilled with some sauce and condiments. But the simplicity itself appeals to real *tofu* connoisseurs, as well as to busy housewives. When chilled, silken morsels slide down the throat, you will understand why it is so popular!

The Japanese name for this *tofu* dish has an interesting history. The word "*yakko*" in Japanese cooking terminology means cutting food into squares. It is said that it derives from the big, white square of family crests on the sleeves of *kimonos* worn by "*yakko*"—the lowest ranking retainers in *samurai* households. "*Yakko*" paraded through the streets of *Edo* (present day Tokyo) when their feudal lords made their procession to the *Shogun's* castle.

Soft *tofu* sold at the markets is coagulated in its fluted, polyethylene container, and it is very difficult to get it out of the container neatly. Try pulling and squeezing the container to loosen the *tofu* cake before turning it out onto the cutting board.

1. Remove the *tofu* from the container. Place on folded paper towels on a dish to drain, and chill it in the refrigerator for 1 hour.
2. Cut into bite-sized pieces and arrange on individual dishes. Top with condiments and serve with sauce.

For Chilled Tofu:
4–6 oz. (110–170 g) soft tofu per serving

Sauce:
Straight soy sauce, Bonito-Flavored Soy Sauce (page 90) or Lemon Soy Sauce (page 90).

Condiments: The commonest combination is:
Green onion or chives, thinly sliced
Bonito flakes
Grated ginger

Other good condiments are:
Nori (dried seaweed sheets) cut needle thin
Lemon rind, grated or cut needle thin.
Shichimi tōgarashi (seven-taste pepper) or cayenne pepper
Wasabi paste
Shiso leaves (perilla) shredded
Myōga (bud of ginger family plant), shredded

Innovative sauces and condiments:
Catsup
Catsup and soy sauce, mixed half and half
Catsup, soy sauce and Chinese oyster sauce, mixed
Chopped parsley
Prepared mustard
Horseradish
Finely crumbled fried bacon

POACHED TOFU (Ni Yakko) ★ page 75

In winter, when it is too cold to serve "Chilled *Tofu*," this is the answer. Boil cubed *tofu* in the Standard Cooking Liquid (*happō dashi*) on page 36 until the *tofu* is heated through. Arrange in individual dishes, pour over the liquid and top with some condiments from the list above.

Use 4–6 oz. (110–170 g) regular or soft *tofu* per serving.

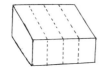

PAN-FRIED TOFU (Yaki Yakko) ★ page 75

For 4–5 servings:
1 cake of regular tofu (21 oz. *or 590 g)*
3–4 tablespoons oil

Sauce:
¾ cup milder dipping sauce on page 35, made from ½ cup dashi *boiled with 2 tablespoons soy sauce and 1½ tablespoons* mirin

Condiments:
Thinly sliced green onions, grated ginger and bonito flakes

This is a simple, but satisfying, dish.

1. Cut a *tofu* cake crosswise into 4 or 5 slices, each ¾–1″ (2–2.5 cm) thick. Drain the slices and pat dry with a paper towel.
2. Heat a heavy skillet until very hot. If it is not heated well, the *tofu* will stick. Add the oil and tilt the pan to coat the bottom.
3. Place the *tofu* slices in the skillet. Cover and sauté slowly over medium heat until the bottom is nicely browned. Turn over and brown the other side.
4. Meanwhile, prepare the sauce and the condiments.
5. Arrange the *tofu* in dishes with a little depth. Pour over the hot sauce and top with the condiments. Serve.

DEEP-FRIED TOFU (Agedashi Dofu) ★ page 76

With sizzling hot *tofu* with a crisp fried surface and mellow and smooth inside, this is a real treat. Even though soft *tofu* is a little harder to handle than regular *tofu*, it is worth the effort for this dish.

4–6 oz. (110–170 g) regular or soft tofu *per serving*
Cornstarch
Oil for deep-frying

Sauce: The same as for pan-fried tofu

Condiments: Grated daikon, *grated ginger and thinly sliced green onions.*

1. Cut the *tofu* into rectangular pieces about 1″ (2.5 cm) thick.
2. Arrange the layers on paper towels and leave for 10–15 minutes to drain. Change the paper and turn over the slices.
3. Sprinkle cornstarch on a plate. Arrange the *tofu* slices on it. Sprinkle more cornstarch over the *tofu*. A powdered sugar shaker does a good job here.
4. Heat oil for deep-frying. The temperature should be high—355°F. (180°C.).
5. Pat any excess cornstarch off the *tofu* slices and slide them into the hot oil, one by one. Do not add too many slices at once, because *tofu* lowers the oil temperature. Fry until golden, turning once.
6. Drain on paper towels.
7. Arrange in a compote-type dish, pour over the hot sauce. Top with a mound of grated *daikon*, a bit of grated ginger, sliced green onions and serve piping hot.

TOFU WITH GROUND CHICKEN SAUCE
(*Tofu no Tori An-Kake*)   ★ *page 76*

This *tofu* is simmered in chicken broth and served with a thickened sauce.

1. In a pot big enough to hold the *tofu* slices, bring the cooking liquid to a boil.
2. Add the drained *tofu* slices. Lower the heat and simmer about 5 minutes until the *tofu* is heated through. Overcooking *tofu* will coarsen its texture.
3. With a slotted spoon, transfer the *tofu* slices to fairly deep dishes, like small cereal or soup plates.
4. Place the ground chicken in a pot. Measure 1½ cups broth in which the *tofu* was cooked and add it to the pot. Season and cook, stirring to break up the ground chicken which tends to stick together.
5. When the chicken is cooked, taste the sauce and adjust the seasoning. Thicken with cornstarch and water mixture.
6. Pour the hot sauce over the *tofu*. Place a small mound of grated ginger on it and serve.

For 4 servings:
1 cake regular tofu, *16–18 oz. (450–500 g), cut into 4 slices*

Cooking Liquid:
2 cups chicken broth, unseasoned
1 teaspoon soy sauce
1 teaspoon salt
1 tablespoon sugar

Sauce:
⅓ lb. (150 g) ground or chopped chicken
1½ cups liquid in which the tofu *was cooked*
1 tablespoon sugar
2 tablespoons soy sauce
2 tablespoons cornstarch mixed with 2 tablespoons water

Condiment:
1 tablespoon grated ginger

GRILLED *TOFU* ON SKEWERS WITH *MISO* GLAZE (*Dengaku*)   ★ *page 76*

This is old-fashioned country fare which is served at some street stalls, or at restaurants, barbecued over a charcoal fire. You can also grill *tofu* on the stove top by placing a brick at the two sides of the burner. These serve as supports for the skewers, suspending the *tofu* over the burner. Since *tofu* does not drip like fish or meat, this direct heat method works well. Broiling in the oven makes *tofu* leather-like because the heat is not strong enough.

Use thin, pointed metal skewers placed parallel, so that the *tofu* slices do not roll or tip. (Thick skewers tear *tofu*). After the *tofu* is grilled, remove the metal skewers and insert bamboo skewers.

For the *miso* glaze, three varieties are given. You may use just one kind, or two or three for the color contrast. This cooked *miso* keeps 2–3 weeks in the refrigerator and is very useful as a sauce or dressing by diluting with *sake* or *dashi* (or water with MSG).

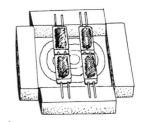

For 4–8 servings:
1 lb. (450 g) regular tofu
32 bamboo skewers 5″ (12 cm) long

1. Cut one pound *tofu* into 16 rectangular pieces about ¾″ (2 cm) thick.
2. Arrange on double thicknesses of paper towels and let stand 20 or 30 minutes.
3. Carefully insert two metal skewers parallel through two pieces of *tofu*.
4. Put the ends of the skewers on the two bricks and grill the *tofu* over high heat until brown speckles appear.
5. Turn it over and grill the other side. Spread *miso* glaze on the browned side with a spatula.
6. Turn it over again to grill the glazed side lightly.
7. Invert the skewered *tofu* onto a cutting board. Remove the metal skewers and insert bamboo skewers. Insert two short, straight skewers to make a "V" shape. Sprinkle on condiments you are using and serve.

Miso Glazes
The following recipes make ½ cup of thick sauce—enough for 4–6 servings. Make ahead of time and dilute with either *sake* or *dashi* (or water with MSG).

⅓ *cup* aka-dashi miso *(or red, salty* miso)
¼ *cup* mirin *(or ¼ cup* sake *or sherry with 4 teaspoons sugar)*
3–4 *tablespoons sugar*
2 *tablespoons* sake
1 *egg yolk**
* *May be omitted, however, 1 yolk or ⅓ whole egg makes a smoother more mellow glaze.*

Red *Miso* Glaze (**Aka Nerimiso**)
In a small pot, mix all the ingredients and cook over low heat until smooth and velvety. When cool, the sauce should be thick enough not to drop from a spoon held upside down.

⅓ *cup sweet white* miso
3 *tablespoons* mirin *(or 3 tablespoons* sake *or sherry with 1 tablespoon sugar)*
1 *tablespoon* sake
1 *tablespoon sugar**
1 *egg yolk*
* *Amount of sugar depends on the sweetness of the* miso.
A *suitable condiment for topping—lemon rind*

White *Miso* Glaze (**Shiro Nerimiso**)
Mix all ingredients in a small pot and cook over low heat until glossy.

Green *Miso* Glaze (*Kinome Miso*)
In spring to early summer, ground fresh new leaves of "sansho," the aromatic leaves of prickly ash, are mixed together with white *miso* glaze and green essence made from spinach to make it green-colored and fragrant. "*Kinome Dengaku*," grilled *tofu* with green *miso*, is usually topped with a *sansho* leaf. Here it is replaced by parsley.

One recipe of White *Miso* Glaze
Color white *Miso* Glaze with the green essence. In place of *sansho* leaves, sprinkle chopped parsley on the green *miso* glaze after it is grilled.

1 tablespoon natural green coloring (aoyose) *(page 21)*
1 tablespoon chopped parsley

TRANSFORMATION OF *TOFU*
Buddhism came to Japan from China, bringing with it Chinese vegetarian cooking in which *tofu* was used in many forms. It was cooked in complex methods, such as deep-fried and simmered, mashed and fried. The results are remarkably rich tasting, almost like meat.

DEEP-FRIED *TOFU*

Fried Soybean Puffs (*Age* or *Aburage*)
Pressed, thin slices of *tofu* are fried until golden and puffed. There are thinner, flat ones and puffy ones. Rinse with boiling water before simmering to remove excess oil.
Uses include:
As a soup garnish—especially good in *miso* soup.
Simmered with vegetables and mixed in rice. See Rice with Five Garnishes (*Gomoku Meshi*) on page 236.
Simmered soybean puffs, cut in half and opened, filled with *sushi* rice (see *Inari Zushi* on page 248).
Age pouch stuffed with vegetables and simmered with other vegetables and fish cakes, as in *Oden* on page 230.

Inari Zushi

Fried *Tofu* Cutlet (*Atsu Age* or *Nama Age*; Thick Soybean Puffs)
Atsu Age or *Nama Age* is skin-fried and the inside is still *tofu*. Rinse with boiling water before simmering.
Uses include:
Bake or pan sauté until hot. Serve with *Tempura* Dipping Sauce (page 35) and grated *daikon*.
Meat-stuffed *Tofu* Cutlet. Cut in half, diagonally. Stuff with meatloaf mixture (beef, chicken or pork). Bake or deep-fry. Serve with soy sauce.
Braised with Vegetables. Replace chicken with *Atsu Age* or *Nama Age* in Braised Chicken with Vegetables (*Iridori*) on page 107.

FROZEN AND DRIED *TOFU* (*Kōya Dofu*)

The word "*tofu*" becomes "*dofu*" when it is used with an adjective or a noun. The name "*Kōya*" comes from the *Kōya-san*, a mountain southeast of Osaka. Here Buddhist monks made this frozen and dried *tofu*. Cakes of *tofu* were hung outdoors in the severe cold of winter. The cakes would freeze and melt in the sun, leaving them shrunken and completely dried. It was an ideal food with high protein content preserved before the days of refrigeration.

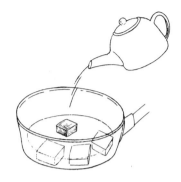

To reconstitute frozen and dried *tofu*:
1. Place frozen and dried *tofu* cakes in an ample sized pot, cover with a drop-lid and pour over hot (but not boiling) water to cover.
2. Let stand 3 to 5 minutes until the cakes are swollen and softened throughout. If the inside is still hard, leave it a little longer. However, if left too long, it will disintegrate.
3. Gently squeeze out the water. Soak in cold water and squeeze out the water again. Repeat this several times until the water is clear.

Homemade Frozen *Tofu*
Cut regular *tofu* into serving sizes for quicker freezing and defrosting. Freeze overnight in the freezer compartment. *Tofu* becomes light brown-colored when frozen. Pour over boiling water to cover and leave it about 10 minutes to defrost. Squeeze out the water and rinse with water. The texture is not as fine as commercially manufactured *tofu*, but the taste is not bad. Use it in soup, simmered or in stir-fry.

Uses of Dried *Tofu* (*Kōya*)
Because of its spongy texture, *kōya dofu* is extremely good in simmered dishes. It absorbs and holds the seasoned liquids.

For 4 servings:
4 *cakes of frozen dried* tofu, *reconstituted*
4–8 *dried* shiitake *mushrooms*
1 *cake* kamaboko (*white or top-browned, not the tinted type*)

Cooking Liquid:
2½ *cups* dashi (*use water from reconstituting the dry* shiitake *as part of this*)
⅓ *cup* mirin (*or* ⅓ *cup sake or sherry with 2 tablespoons sugar*)
2 *tablespoons sugar*
1 *tablespoon soy sauce*
¾ *teaspoon salt*

SIMMERED DRIED *TOFU* WITH FISHCAKE AND *SHIITAKE* MUSHROOMS (*Kōya Dofu to Kamaboko, Shiitake no Taki Awase*) ★ *page 79*

1. Soak the *shiitake* in lukewarm water for half an hour. Cut off and discard the stems. Cut the caps in half if they are large. Save the water for *dashi*.
2. Cut the softened *tofu* into 3 to 4 pieces.
3. Place all the materials in a pot. Add the cooking liquid and cover with a drop-lid. Simmer on medium heat about 30 minutes until the liquid has almost evaporated.

Note: Some substitutes for *kamaboko* include 1 stick of *chikuwa* (fishcake in a roll) or 2–4 *satsuma age* (deep-fried fishcake), or ¼–⅓ lb. chicken, cut into bites.

DRIED *TOFU* WITH *MISO* SAUCE (*Kōya Dofu Miso-an-kake*) ★ *page 77*

1. Cut each cake into 4–6 pieces.
2. Place them in a pot, cover with the cooking liquid and a drop-lid. Simmer about 20 minutes until the liquid is reduced by half.
3. Transfer the *tofu* pieces to individual dishes.
4. Serve with warm *miso* sauce poured over and top with a small mound of grated ginger or mustard paste.

For 4 servings:
4 cakes reconstituted, frozen-dried tofu

Cooking Liquid:
2 cups dashi
¼ cup mirin (or *¼ cup* sake *or* sherry with *4 teaspoons* sugar)
½ teaspoon each soy sauce and salt

Miso Sauce:
Mix and heat:
3 tablespoons red miso *glaze (page 126)*
1 tablespoon dashi (or *water with* MSG

Condiment: 1 teaspoon grated ginger (or mustard paste from mixing dry mustard with water)

FRIED AND SIMMERED DRIED TOFU (*Kōya Dofu Age-ni*) ★ *page 77*

Softened *kōya dofu* is deep-fried before simmering. This little variation in preparation adds a subtle richness to the taste.

1. Cut the *tofu* into 2 triangles or rectangles.
2. Wrap the *tofu* in a paper towel and gently squeeze out the water.
3. Deep-fry the *tofu* cakes at fairly high temperature 340°F. (170°C.). These fry very quickly. When they are yellow-colored, lift them out and drain on a paper towel. Up to this point, you may prepare several days in advance.
4. Place *tofu* in a pot, pour boiling water to cover, and parboil for a minute to remove oil. Drain and squeeze.
5. Simmer the *tofu* in the cooking liquid, covered with a drop-lid, until the liquid is reduced to one third.
6. Prepare the green vegetable. Parboil in salted, boiling water. Rinse with cold water and cut into 1½–2″ (4–5 cm) lengths. Boil celery until tender but not soft. Peel off the stringy skin, split the wider part of the stalk into two or three pieces.
7. Add the prepared green vegetables to the pot, and cook several minutes longer to season the vegetables.
8. Arrange the simmered *tofu* and vegetables in dishes and pour over the remaining liquid.

For 4 servings:
4 cakes reconstituted, frozen dried tofu
Oil for deep-frying

Green vegetable. Use one of the following:
4–8 green asparagus
4–8 green onions
2 stalks of celery
A handful of snow peas or string beans
¼ bunch of spinach

Cooking Liquid:
2 cups dashi
2 tablespoons sugar
2 taspoons soy sauce
½ teaspoon salt

MASHED *TOFU*

Tofu, when mashed and mixed with a binder, achieves yet another transformation.

Mashed Tofu *Base:*
1 *lb. regular or Chinese firm tofu*
1 *egg*

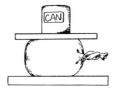

1. Wrap a *tofu* cake in a dish towel and squeeze the bag, twisting the ends tightly. The towel-bag may be pressed between two boards weighted down with a one-pound can for an hour.
2. Grind *tofu* in a food processor or a blender.
3. Add the egg and mix well. To determine the amount of egg binder to use, use at least 10% of the weight of the *tofu* used.

DEEP-FRIED *TOFU* PATTIES (*Ganmodoki*)

"*Gan*" is wild goose, and "*ganmodoki*" means it tastes just like goose. Usually made into patties about 3" (7–8 cm) in diameter, it can also be meatball size or simply dropped from a spoon. This recipe makes 6–8 servings.

1 *recipe Mashed* Tofu *Base:*
½ *teaspoons sugar and salt*
2–3" *(5–7.5 cm) carrot, peeled and shredded thinly (or grated)*
2–3 *tablespoons thinly shredded, softened* shiitake *mushrooms or* ki-kurage *(cloud ear mushrooms, page 23)*

Optional: Use one of the following:
1–2 *tablespoons toasted peanuts, pine nuts or pistachio nuts, roughly chopped.*

1. Mix the seasonings and garnishes into the mashed *tofu*.
2. Shape into patties or balls with oiled hands. Place the patties on an oiled sheet. If the mixture is too soft to shape, it may be dropped from a spoon.
3. Deep-fry until golden.
4. To serve hot, serve with soy sauce and mustard paste or *Tempura* Dipping Sauce (page 35) and grated *daikon*. Fried *tofu* patties also keep well—one week in the refrigerator or frozen. They make a very good simmered dish and in "*Oden*" (page 230).

SIMMERED *TOFU* PATTIES ★ *page 78*
(*Ganmodoki Nimono*)

Rinse the Fried *Tofu* Patties with boiling water. Removing the excess oil in this way makes the patties more absorbent of seasoned liquids. Simmer them in a Standard Cooking Liquid (page 36).

TOFU BURGER (*Tofu* Hamburger-*fū*) ★ *page 78*

Mashed *tofu* mixture is pan sautéed here. It is good with *Tempura* Dipping Sauce (page 35), with grated *daikon*, soy sauce and mustard paste, or catsup and soy sauce mixed half and half.

1. Mix all the ingredients with mashed *tofu.*
2. Shape into patties with oiled hands.
3. Heat a heavy skillet. Add about 2 tablespoons oil to heat. Arrange the patties in the hot pan and sauté like hamburgers.

Variations of *Tofu* Burger
Instead of the crumbled bacon, add ½–¾ cup of one of these: grated cheese of your choice—for *Tofu* Cheeseburger; cooked crab or shrimp meat—for Crab or Shrimpburger; sautéed ground meat—for *Tofu* Meatburger.

For 6 servings:
1 recipe Mashed Tofu *Base*
  (page 130)
½ *teaspoon salt*
1 *additional egg*
1 *tablespoon chopped parsley*
3 *tablespoons fried and*
  crumbled bacon
2–3″ *(5–8 cm) carrot, chopped*
2 *tablespoons chopped green*
  onions
½–1 *tablespoon peppercorns*
  (black or white), cracked

BAKED *TOFU* LOAF (*Gisei Dofu*)   **page 78*

Eggs were not allowed in Buddhist vegetarian cooking, so eggs were hidden in this simulated *"gisei" tofu.* It is very good served either hot or cold and is excellent for boxed lunches.

1. In a small pot, heat the oil and stir-fry the carrots and *shiitake* mushrooms for 1 minute. Add the seasonings and cook, stirring, for one or two minutes.
2. Add one more egg and the seasonings to the mashed *tofu* base. Blend well.
3. Mix all the garnishes and liquid into the *tofu* mixture.
4. Preheat the oven to 325°F. (160°C.).
5. Grease, or spray with a non-stick vegetable spray such as Pam, a regular bread pan measuring 4″ × 8″ × 2½″ (10 × 20 × 6.5 cm). Pour the *tofu* mixture in and spread it out evenly.
6. Bake for about 1 hour, until the top is slightly colored and a bamboo skewer inserted comes out clean.
7. Take it out of the oven and wait a couple of minutes. The puffed-up loaf will shrink a little. With a knife, pull the edges from the pan. Invert onto a plate. Then invert it again onto a cutting board, so that the right side is up.
8. Cut into 1–1¼″ (2.5–3 cm) thick slices and serve.

For 8 servings:
1 lb. tofu *(regular or soft),*
  wrapped in towel and
  squeezed
2 *eggs*
½ *tablespoon soy sauce*
¼ *teaspoon salt*
1 *tablespoon sugar*

Garnishes:
2–3″ *(5–8 cm) carrot, shred-*
  ded needle thin or roughly
  chopped
2–3 shiitake *mushrooms,*
  softened and shredded
1 *tablespoon oil*

Seasonings:
1½ *tablespoons soy sauce*
1 *tablespoon sugar*
2 *tablespoons sake*

2 *tablespoons green peas, par-*
  boiled (or 3–4 string beans,
  shredded and parboiled)

Vegetables, Dried and Manufactured Foods

AVOCADO *SASHIMI*
(Avocado *no Sashimi*)

★ *page 80*

Avocados which are ripe but still firm make interesting *sashimi*. Cut an avocado in half lengthwise. Remove the seed. Peel the skin off. Slice crosswise and squeeze lemon juice over the slices to prevent darkening. Serve well chilled with soy sauce and *wasabi* paste like regular *sashimi*. Also, try *Miso* Sauce with Vinegar (*Sumiso*) with *wasabi* paste or grated ginger as a condiment.

For an unusual *sashimi*, combine avocado and *Konnyaku Sashimi* (page 142) with Red *Miso* Sauce with Vinegar. The velvety texture of the avocado *sashimi* contrasts with the resilient, slippery texture of the *Konnyaku Sashimi*.

2 *tablespoons red* miso
1 *tablespoon mirin (or 1 table-*
spoon sake or sherry with 1
teaspoon sugar)
1½–2 *tablespoons sugar*
1 *tablespoon vinegar*
1–2 *tablespoons water*

Condiment: mustard
paste
1 *teaspoon dry mustard*
mixed with ½ *teaspoon*
water

RED *MISO* SAUCE WITH VINEGAR
(*Sumiso*)

Mix and cook over low heat until well dissolved. If you have Red *Miso* Glaze (page 126), add 1 tablespoon vinegar and dilute with a little water.

BAMBOO SHOOTS

Living abroad, one of the things Japanese miss is the scent of fresh bamboo shoots in spring with their unmistakable fragrance! In Japan, from April to May, one see piles of bamboo shoots in husks, still with dirt on them, at the markets. Bamboo shoots dug up in the morning and sold on the same day are the best. The shoots develop a bitter taste quickly once they are dug from the earth.

To prepare fresh bamboo shoots:
1. Wash the shoots in the husks. Remove two or three outside husks and cut off the hard bottom part.
2. Cut the tips off with a diagonal cut.
3. Make a slit, cutting through the husks, taking care not to cut the core.

4. Place in a deep pot and cover with rice washing water—the white water thrown away when washing rice. Add one red cayenne pepper, and bring to a boil. Lower the heat, put on a drop-lid, and simmer for one hour. Let the shoots cool in the pot.
5. Rinse with water. Peel off the husks. Inner tender skins can be used in salad when finely julienned.
6. The tip is the tenderest part; the bottom is the hardest. Cut or slice across the grain. Slice the harder parts thinner. The bottom part should be cut into julienne strips.

Canned bamboo shoots are water-boiled, referred to as bamboo shoots in the following recipes.

SIMMERED BAMBOO SHOOTS AND CELERY
(*Takenoko to* Celery *no Nimono*) ★*page 80*

Celery is substituted here for "*fuki*" (coltfoot), another spring to early summer vegetable. *Fuki* is a stem vegtetable like rhubarb, but it is green and not tart. It is available in cans, but cooked celery has a similar flavor.

1. Cut the tender parts of bamboo shoots with a rolling cut (see page 48), or slice thick against the grain. Wash and drain.
2. Place them in a pot and add 1 cup (240 ml) cooking liquid. Cover with a drop-lid, and cook over medium heat until the liquid is almost evaporated.
3. Meanwhile, parboil celery stalks 2–3 minutes until tender-crisp. Rinse with cold water. Peel off any stringy outside fibers and cut into pieces 2″ (5 cm) long and ⅓″ (1 cm) wide.
4. Boil ½ cup (120 ml) cooking liquid in a small pot. Add the celery and simmer 2–3 minutes. Turn off the heat and let stand in the liquid.
5. Arrange the bamboo shoots and the celery in serving dishes and pour over some liquid from the pot and serve.

For 4–5 servings:
½ lb. (225 g) bamboo shoots
2 stalks of celery

Standard Cooking Liquid:
1½ cups dashi
2½ tablespoons mirin (or 3 tablespoons sake or sherry with 2 teaspoons sugar)
3 tablespoons soy sauce*
  *If light color is preferred, use light-colored soy sauce or ½ teaspoon salt and 1 tablespoon soy sauce.

Topping: 1 sprig of parsley

In Japan, bamboo shoot dishes are almost always topped with one or two leaves of *kinome* (the aromatic leaves of prickly ash—sansho), adding a nice green touch and the aroma of spring. Substitute a bit of parsley.
  In place of celery, string beans or snow peas may be used, similarly prepared.

SIMMERED BAMBOO SHOOTS WITH BONITO FLAKES (*Takenoko Tosani*) ★*page 80*

Bamboo shoots are poached in water with bonito flakes. For family-style serving, use the flakes as they are. But for a more deluxe preparation, crumble the flakes to coat the simmered shoots.

For 4 servings:
1/2 lb. (225 g) bamboo shoots
1 cup water
1/2 cup (5 g) bonito flakes
2 teaspoons mirin
2 tablespoons soy sauce

Additional: 1 cup (10 g) bonito flakes (for crumble coating)

Topping: 1 tablespoon chopped parsley or sansho leaves

1. Cut the bamboo shoots with the rolling cut described on page 48 or cut into thick slices.
2. Place these in a pot, add the water and the bonito flakes and bring to a boil. Remove any scum.
3. Add the seasonings, cover with a drop-lid and simmer. Shake the pot several times while cooking, and cook until the liquid is almost evaporated. It may be served at this point for a simpler fare.
4. Meanwhile make the bonito crumbs by placing the rest of the flakes into a heavy, ungreased, dry pot over low heat. Stir-dry the flakes for about 5 minutes. Cool and crumble the flakes with your hands.
5. Coat the drained bamboo shoots with the crumbled bonito. Arrange in serving dishes and sprinkle with chopped parsley in place of *kinome*.

GLAZED BAMBOO SHOOTS (*Takenoko Tsukeyaki*)

Skewered bamboo shoot slices are grilled over a stove-top burner like Grilled *Tofu* on Skewers (*Dengaku*) (page 125). Brush with straight soy sauce or *Teriyaki* Glaze (page 94) and grill lightly to dry.

GRILLED BAMBOO SHOOTS WITH *MISO* GLAZE (*Takenoko Dengaku*)

Grill skewered bamboo slices over a stove-top burner. Then brush with *Miso* Glaze (page 126) and grill lightly. Follow the directions for *Tofu Dengaku* on page 125.

STIR-FRIED BURDOCK (*Kimpira Gobo*)

"*Kimpira*" is first stir-fried, then stir-cooked with seasonings. To the Japanese, the vegetable used is always burdock, or burdock combined with *konnyaku*. But *Kimpira* can also be made with other vegetables such as bamboo shoots, celery, carrots, *daikon*, or fresh lotus roots thinly sliced and parboiled.

Since *Kimpira* keeps well in a refrigerator, it is a good idea to make enough for more than one meal. It is also good in a boxed lunch.

For 6–8 servings:
2 cups shaved* burdock (or other vegetables)
    *see page 49 for directions for shaving
1/2 cup konnyaku, parboiled and cut into julienne strips
2 tablespoons oil
1 tablespoon sake or sherry
1 tablespoon sugar
2 1/2–3 tablespoons soy sauce

1. Before shaving the burdock, scrub the root with a wire brush. If the skin is thick and dry, you may have to scrape it with the back of a knife. Soak the shaved burdock in water for 10–15 minutes and drain. If the root was dry, parboil the

shavings for a few minutes after soaking.
2. Heat the oil in a heavy saucepan and stir-fry the burdock with the red pepper for 1–2 minutes.
3. Add sugar and *sake* and stir-cook 1 or 2 minutes. Add soy sauce and stir-cook until the liquid has evaporated. Toasted sesame seeds may be sprinkled over the dish before serving.

CABBAGE ROLL JAPANESE STYLE ★ *page 80*
(*Wafu Kyabetsu Maki*)

The filling can be meat or Mashed *Tofu* Base mixed with vegetables. The rolls are simmered in chicken stock and served with a thickened sauce.

1. Carefully peel off the cabbage leaves. Slice off the hard veins.
2. Parboil the leaves until pliable. Rinse with cold water and drain.
3. Prepare the filling of your choice by mixing the ingredients. Divide the filling into 8 portions.
4. Place one filling portion on each cabbage leaf. Roll up the cabbage leaf. If you fold them carefully, there is no need to tie them.
5. Arrange the rolls in one layer in a flat bottomed pot. Pour the mixed liquid over them and bring to a boil.
6. Remove any scum. Lower the heat to medium and cover with a drop-lid. Simmer until the liquid is reduced by half.
7. Transfer the rolls to a cutting board. Cut each roll into 4 pieces, which are enough for a small serving.
8. Mix the cornstarch with a little water. Add to the pan liquid to thicken it and pour this gravy over the rolls.

Optional: 1 small dried red pepper (seeds removed and sliced) or a dash of cayenne pepper.

Also optional: 1 teaspoon toasted sesame seeds

For 4–8 servings:
8 outer leaves of a cabbage

Filling: Two kinds of filling are given to choose from. Each is for 4–8 servings)

Tofu Filling:
⅓ recipe Mashed Tofu Base (page 130)
¼ lb. (110 g) ground chicken
2" (5 cm) carrot, minced
2 dried shiitake, softened and chopped
1 egg
1 tablespoon each mirin and soy sauce
Optional: ½ cup shirataki (sukiyaki noodles) cut into ⅓" (1 cm) lengths

Meat Filling:
½ lb. (225 g) ground meat (chicken, pork or beef)
1 slice bread, soaked in water and squeezed dry
1 egg
1 tablespoon chopped onion
1 tablespoon each mirin and soy sauce

Cooking Liquid:
1½ cups water
1½ chicken bouillon cubes
3 tablespoons each mirin and sake or sherry
½ tablespoon soy sauce
Mix all together to dissolve.

135

STIR-FRIED CELERY (Celery *Kimpira*) ★ *page 80*

"*Kimpira*" made with celery is quite different from the usual "Burdock *Kimpira*," but it is very good.

3 cups shredded celery
2 tablespoons oil
1 tablespoon sake or sherry
1–2 tablespoons sugar
2½–3 tablespoons soy sauce

Optional Spice:
1 small dried red pepper seeded and chopped, or a dash of cayenne pepper
1 teaspoon toasted sesame seeds

1. Wash celery stalks, remove stringy fiber, and cut into julienne.
2. Heat oil in a heavy saucepan, and stir-fry celery and red pepper 1–2 minutes.
3. Add sugar and *sake*, and stir-cook 1 or 2 minutes. Add soy sauce and stir-cook until the liquid has evaporated. Toasted sesame seeds may be sprinkled over before serving.

POACHED CELERY (Celery *Fukume-ni*)

This simple celery dish is good either warm or well-chilled. It is also fine as a garnish for poached fish.

For 4 servings:
6–8 stalks of celery
Light-colored Cooking Liquid
(page 36)

1. Prepare celery stalks by parboiling and cutting into strips, as in Celery with Peanut Sauce.
2. Bring the Cooking Liquid to a boil. Add the celery and cook about 2 minutes. Turn off the heat and let stand until cool.
3. To serve warm, heat up in the pot. To serve cold, put the cooked celery into a container with a cover and refrigerate from several hours to overnight. Serve with the liquid.

DAIKON

Daikon, the giant white radish, is one of the most basic vegetables in Japan. It is good eaten raw or cooked. On the West Coast, *daikon* is now being discovered as an ideal low-calorie diet food.

BRAISED *DAIKON* WITH FRIED *TOFU*
(*Daikon to Age no Itame-ni*)

This is one of the typical, old-time family dishes that was cooked in quantity to last for a few days, and to be eaten with a lot of bland white rice. You can adjust the amount of seasonings to your liking, and also replace fried *tofu* with julienned or ground pork, chicken or beef.

1. Heat the oil in a pot, add *daikon* and stir-fry over high heat for 4–5 minutes until translucent.
2. Mix in Fried *Tofu* strips, add *dashi* and sugar, cover with a drop-lid and cook about 10 minutes on low heat.
3. Add soy sauce and continue to simmer until all the liquid is gone.
4. Add a dash of cayenne pepper and serve. Good hot or cold.

For about 8 servings:
4–5 cups daikon *(about 1 lb. or 450 g), shredded*
1–2 Fried Tofu *(puffs or cutlets) cut into strips*
2 tablespoons oil
1 cup dashi
2–3 tablespoons sugar
3 tablespoons soy sauce
A dash of cayenne pepper

MORE *DAIKON* RECIPES

POACHED *DAIKON* WITH GROUND CHICKEN (Page 108)
SIMMERED PORK AND *DAIKON* (Page 122)
BOILED *DAIKON* WITH *MISO* SAUCE (follow directions for Boiled Turnip with Miso Sauce on page 151)

DRIED *DAIKON* (*Kiriboshi Daikon*)

Sun-dried *daikon* in strips or in disk forms is sold in small packages. These are light brown and don't look appetizing, but when cooked, they have a subtle, sweet taste and are a very convenient material to keep as a standby. They are versatile as a garnish in *miso* soup, and can be simmered or pickled. However, they are now forgotten by the younger people in Japan. Therefore we were pleasantly surprised when our American friends liked the braised, dried *daikon*.

BRAISED DRIED *DAIKON* (*Kiriboshi Daikon Itame-ni*)
★*page 80*

This is similar to Braised *Daikon* with Fried *Tofu*. But the dried *daikon* has a nutty flavor and a crunchy texture.

1. Quickly rinse the dried *daikon*. Place in a big bowl and cover with plenty of water. Soak for 40 minutes to one hour. The *daikon* will expand about three times in volume.
2. Drain the *daikon* and cut into 2″ (5 cm) lengths. Cut the fried *tofu* into strips.
3. Follow the directions for Braised *Daikon* with Fried *Tofu* on page 136.

For 6–8 servings:
1 package dried daikon *strips (3 oz. or 85 g)*
2 Fried Tofu *(puffs or cutlets)**
2 tablespoons oil

Cooking Liquid:
1 cup dashi *(or ½ cup* dashi *and ½ cup water in which the* daikon *was soaked)*
2–3 tablespoons sugar
3–4 tablespoons soy sauce
A dash of MSG
*In place of Fried Tofu, *you may use ½ cup pork, chicken or beef cut in strips.*

EGGPLANT

Eggplant is a very versatile vegetable which can be grilled, fried, poached or steamed. Japanese and Chinese eggplants are smaller and more slender than the American variety, with fewer seeds. Japanese eggplants are now sold at more markets on the West Coast, summer through winter. But unfortunately, they are not always fresh. Fresh ones have shiny, unblemished skin with a beautiful purple color. When an eggplant is cooked whole, soaking is not necessary. However, when cut, the surface of eggplant turns dark and develops a bitter taste. So soak the slices in water. (For American eggplant, in salted water: 1 teaspoon salt in 1 cup water) for 15–30 minutes before cooking.

BAKED EGGPLANT (*Yaki Nasu*)

Eggplant can be grilled on a stove-top burner or barbecued over charcoal, but baking in the oven at 350°F. (180°C.) is the easiest method.

For 4 servings:
4 Japanese eggplants, or one small American eggplant

Condiments:
1 teaspoon grated ginger or 1 tablespoon bonito flakes
Soy sauce to drizzle over at the table

1. Prick the eggplant skin with a skewer at several points to prevent the eggplant from exploding in the oven. (Cut an American eggplant into two lengthwise. After soaking in salted water, wipe dry and brush the cut surface with oil.)
2. Place the eggplants on a rack in the oven. Turn the heat to 350°F. (180°C.).
3. Bake 15–20 minutes until tender. You can press them or put a skewer through to test whether they are done. American eggplant halves will take 20–30 minutes.
4. Dip the hot eggplants into cold water and peel off the skin. Cut into long wedges or slice crosswise.
5. Arrange on individual dishes, top with grated ginger or bonito flakes, and serve with soy sauce.

For 4 servings:
4 Japanese eggplants, baked whole and peeled

Cooking Liquid:
1 cup dashi
2 tablespoons mirin (or 2 table-spoons sake or sherry with 2 teaspoons sugar)
1 tablespoon soy sauce
⅔ teaspoon salt
A pinch of MSG

Condiments:
1 teaspoon grated ginger or 2 tablespoons bonito flakes

POACHED BAKED EGGPLANT (*Nasu Ni-bitashi*)

★ page 81

If you poach baked eggplants they will become a delightful side dish, especially when well chilled.

1. Place the baked and peeled eggplant in a pot, add the liquid, cover with a drop-lid, and bring to a boil.
2. Lower the heat and simmer for 5 minutes.
3. Remove from the heat and let the eggplants cool in the liquid.
4. Refrigerate the pot with eggplants for several hours or overnight.
5. Slice each eggplant into three or four pieces. Arrange in a small bowl or dish, pour some liquid over and top with the condiment of your choice.

TORTOISE SHELL EGGPLANT
(*Nasu Kikko-Yaki*)

★ *page 81*

This dish uses *kamo nasu* from the Kyoto area which is round and similar to an American eggplant, although smaller. Cross-diagonal scoring is called *"kikko"*—tortoise shell.

1. Cut the whole eggplant (with the stem and cap intact) in half lengthwise.
2. Using a pointed knife, about ¼″ (6 mm) in from the edge on the cut side, make an incision ½″ (1.2 cm) deep all around the edge of the eggplant. Then make cross-diagonal scores.
3. Soak in salted water for half an hour.
4. Preheat the oven to 350°F. (180°C.).
5. Pat the eggplant halves dry and brush the scored surface with oil.
6. Place them on a baking dish with the cut side up and bake for 15 minutes.
7. Spoon a little of the soy sauce mixture over the scored surface and continue to bake. Repeat this two or three times at 5 minute intervals. Bake until tender. The baking time is 30–40 minutes in total.
8. Serve hot topped with bonito flakes or chopped parsley.

For Westernized variation, when the eggplants are done, sprinkle the surface with grated Cheddar or Gruyere cheese and broil for a few minutes.

For 4 servings:
2 *Italian eggplants or small American eggplants*
2 *tablespoons salad oil*
2 *tablespoons soy sauce* ⎫
2 *tablespoons dashi* ⎭

Topping:
2 *tablespoons bonito flakes or chopped parsley*

GRILLED EGGPLANTS WITH *MISO* GLAZE
(*Nasu Shigi-Yaki*)

Slice an eggplant crosswise ½″ (1.3 cm) thick. Soak (see page 138) and pat dry. Skewer the slices and brush with oil. Follow the directions for Grilled *Tofu* (*Dengaku*) on page 125.

STIR-FRIED EGGPLANT WITH *MISO*
(*Nabe Shigi-Yaki* or *Nabe Shin*)

★ *page 81*

Simple and quick to make, but a delicious family dish.

1. Slice eggplant ⅓″ (1 cm) thick. Soak in water for 15 minutes. Drain and pat dry.
2. Heat oil in a heavy skillet. Add eggplants and stir-fry over high heat, turning the slices with a wooden spatula so they are all coated with oil. Stir-fry until eggplants are tender.
3. Add the mixed seasonings and stir well. Sprinkle on a dash of cayenne pepper if you like.
4. Arrange on serving dishes and if you wish, sprinkle on the toasted sesame seeds.

For 4 servings:
4–6 *Japanese or 2–3 Chinese eggplants*
3–4 *tablespoons oil*

Seasonings:
3 *tablespoons red* miso ⎫
2½ *tablespoons sugar* ⎬
3 *tablespoons water* ⎭
Mix all together.

Optional:
A *dash of cayenne pepper and* ½ *tablespoon toasted sesame seeds or lemon rind cut needle-thin*

DEEP-FRIED EGGPLANT (*Nasu no Agedashi*)

★*page 81*

Cooking eggplant with oil seems to enhance the flavor. Serve this eggplant dish piping hot with *tempura* dipping sauce and grated *daikon* and ginger.

For 4 servings:
4 Japanese or 2 Chinese
  eggplants or 1 small
  American eggplant
Oil for deep-frying
Tempura Dipping Sauce
  (see page 35)
½ cup grated daikon
1 teaspoon grated ginger

1. Cut eggplant lengthwise into halves and soak in water for 15 minutes. Slice American eggplant crosswise 1¼″ (3 cm) thick and soak in salted water.
2. Meanwhile, prepare the sauce and grate the *daikon* and ginger.
3. Heat oil to 335°F. (170°C.).
4. Dry the eggplant halves and fry, turning several times.
5. Drain the eggplant on paper towels. Arrange them in individual dishes and pour some sauce over. Top with a mound of grated *daikon* with a bit of grated ginger on it. Serve immediately.

POACHED FRIED EGGPLANT (*Nasu no Age-ni*)

Poach the deep-fried eggplants in Standard Cooking Liquid (page 36) for 5 minutes and serve with grated ginger as a condiment.

STEAMED EGGPLANT

Steam whole eggplants over high heat. Slender eggplant takes about 10 minutes to become tender. Do not overcook or it will become too soft. Steamed eggplant can be served in various ways. See Eggplant with Mustard Dressing (page 218) and Eggplant with Peanut Dressing (page 219).

EGGPLANT *SASHIMI* (*Nasu no Sashimi*)

Press the steamed whole eggplant between two cutting boards with a 1-pound weight (use a can of food) until completely cool and firm. Chill in the refrigerator and slice like *sashimi*. Serve with grated ginger or *wasabi* paste and soy sauce.

SOY GLAZED GRILLED ASPARAGUS
(Asparagus *Tsuke-Yaki*)   *page 81*

This is a nice accompaniment with any barbecued food. Skewer asparagus spears on two or three metal skewers, brush with oil and grill over a stove-top burner or charcoal until tender-crisp. Brush with soy sauce and lightly dry.

GRILLED GREEN ONIONS WITH *MISO* GLAZE
(Negi no Miso-Yaki)   ★ *page 81*

"*Negi*" (Japanese leek) is thinner than Western or European leeks and thicker than green onions. It has a sweet taste and is indispensable in *sukiyaki*, but it is also good when grilled. Use the root parts of thick green onions or thin leeks as a substitute.

1. Cut green onions into 2" (5 cm) lengths.
2. Put one or two skewers through the onions. If the skewers are round, use two skewers to prevent the onions from rolling.
3. Brush onions with oil and grill or broil in the oven until lightly browned.
4. Brush with *miso* glaze and brown lightly.
5. Arrange nicely on dishes, removing the skewers.

For 4 servings:
2 bunches thick green onions
2 tablespoons oil

Miso *Glaze:*
3 tablespoons red miso
2–2½ tablespoons sugar
2 tablespoons sake
A pinch of cayenne pepper
Mix all together and cook until dissolved.

POACHED GREEN PEAS *(Endō no Fukume-ni)*

Freshly shelled green peas, poached and cooked in the liquid, are a nice side dish to bring Spring to the table.

1. Bring the cooking liquid to a boil. Add the peas and cook until the peas are tender.
2. Remove from the heat and let stand until completely cool.
3. Serve the peas in a dainty cup or bowl with the juice and a spoon.

For 4–6 servings:
1 cup fresh green peas

Light Cooking Liquid:
 1 cup dashi
 ½ teaspoon salt
 1 tablespoon sugar

BRAISED *KONNYAKU* *(Konnyaku no Iri-ni)*
     ★ *page 82*

Konnyaku is a curious food. Refer to "Japanese Ingredients" for a description (page 23)

1. Prick *konnyaku* with a fork all over so it absorbs the seasonings better.
2. With your hands, break it into irregular, bite-sized pieces.
3. Heat a heavy saucepot. When it is hot, add *konnyaku* pieces. They will make an awful crackling noise! Stir-cook to let the moisture evaporate.
4. Add the oil and stir-fry.
5. Add *dashi* and the seasonings and cook, stirring constantly until the liquid is gone.
6. Sprinkle with sesame seeds and serve. A little cayenne pepper may be sprinkled on if you like it hot.

For 4 servings:
2 slabs of konnyaku
 (preferably the darker kind)
1 tablespoon oil
½ cup dashi
2 tablespoons sugar
3 tablespoons soy sauce
1 tablespoon mirin or sake
A pinch of MSG
2 tablespoons toasted white sesame seeds

141

KONNYAKU SASHIMI (Konnyaku no Sashimi)

Light-colored *konnyaku* is parboiled and sliced like *sashimi*. Chill well before serving. Serve with Red *Miso* Sauce with Vinegar (page 132) and mustard paste.

POACHED LOTUS ROOT (Hasu Shiro-ni)

For 6–8 servings:
1½ cups sliced and parboiled lotus*
*Canned lotus root is already parboiled. If using fresh lotus, as soon as it is peeled and sliced, drop the slices into vinegared water (1 tablespoon vinegar to 1 cup water) and parboil in the same water.

Cooking Liquid:
1 cup dashi
3 tablespoons sugar
½–¾ teaspoon salt

Lotus roots are being discovered by Western cooks. They have an interesting, crunchy texture and taste, and make beautiful slices because of the holes. (See page 51, for cutting directions.) A simple vegetable dish like this makes a nice addition to a lunch box, or as a garnish for meat or fish.

Cook the lotus slices in the liquid covered with a drop-lid for 10 minutes. Let them cool in the liquid.

VINEGARED LOTUS ROOT (Subasu) ★ page 82

1½ cups lotus root thinly sliced and parboiled.

Sweet Vinegar:
½ cup each vinegar and dashi
3–4 tablespoons sugar
¼ teaspoon salt
Mix all together and cook until dissolved.

Optional: One small, dried cayenne pepper, seeded and sliced.

Pickled in sweet vinegar, it will keep for a long time and is very useful as a garnish for *Chirashi Zushi* (Mixed *Sushi*) or for broiled fish or meat.

Place the lotus slices in a jar, pour the hot vinegar over, add the red pepper, and cover with a lid. This is better after standing one or two days, and will keep serveral weeks in the refrigerator.

MUSHROOMS

There are now many varieties of cultivated mushrooms available at the markets—*shiitake*, abalone or oyster mushrooms, and delicate white *"enoki"* mushrooms. *Shiitake* and abalone mushrooms are grilled, sautéed, fried and poached. *Enoki* mushrooms are blanched and used in salad and are also marvelous cooked briefly in *"nabemono."*

ABALONE MUSHROOMS WITH SESAME SAUCE (*Shimeji Goma-ae*) ★ *page 82*

1. Pour boiling water over the *tofu* puff to wash out some oil. Rinse and squeeze out water. Cut into strips 1¼–¼" (3 × 0.6 cm).
2. Place the strips in a pot, cover with the cooking liquid and cook for 5 minutes.
3. Meanwhile, wash the mushrooms and cut off the roots. If some are too big, cut into halves or thirds to make the size uniform.
4. Add the mushrooms to the cooking pot, cover with a drop-lid and cook 2 to 3 minutes.
5. Prepare the sesame sauce, then mix in the drained mushrooms, *tofu* puff strips and the spinach stems.

Note: For other combinations, use shredded, boiled or roast chicken instead of *tofu* puff, or cooked carrot matchsticks in place of spinach stems. Grilled or broiled fresh *shiitake*, cut into strips, are very good in place of poached oyster mushrooms.

For 4 servings:
¾–1 cup abalone or oyster mushrooms
1 fried tofu puff (age)
¼–⅓ cup parboiled spinach stems, cut into 1" (2.5 cm) lengths. (Save the stems for this when you use spinach leaves)
Standard Cooking Liquid (page 36)

Sesame Sauce:
4 tablespoons toasted white sesame seeds
1 tablespoon soy sauce
½–1 teaspoon sugar

POACHED MUSHROOMS (Mushroom *Fukume-ni*) ★ *page 82*

Regular mushrooms, poached, may be served as hors d'ouevre or with other poached foods.

1. Wash the mushrooms and cut off the dark end of the stems. Leave them whole if they are small. Cut into halves or quarters if they are large.
2. Poach them 10 minutes in the boiling cooking liquid. Let them cool in the liquid.

½ lb. (225 g) mushrooms
Standard Cooking Liquid: See page 36.

SIMMERED *SHIITAKE* (*Shiitake Fukume-ni*)

Simmered in their own juice, *shiitake* mushrooms are always a good addition to any kind of "*nimono*" (poached food).

1. Soak the *shiitake* for half an hour in enough lukewarm water to cover. Place a small dish over them to keep them submerged.
2. Remove the stems from the reconstituted mushrooms. Leave the small ones whole, cut the larger ones into two or four pieces.

1 oz. (28 g) dried shiitake (15–20 medium-sized mushrooms)

Cooking Liquid:
1½ cup liquid in which the shiitake were soaked

143

For Regular Poaching:
2 tablespoons sake *or* sherry
2 tablespoons soy sauce
3 tablespoons sugar

3. Place the mushrooms in a pot, add the liquid and half the seasonings. Cover with drop-lid and simmer until the liquid is reduced by half.
4. Taste, add more seasoning, and continue to simmer until almost all the liquid is gone.

Note: If you are serving the *shiitake* by themselves, sprinkle with poppy seeds for added interest.

GRILLED SHIITAKE (*Shiitake Tsukeyaki*)   ★ *page 82*

Fresh *shiitake* grilled over charcoal or a stove-top burner, or broiled in the oven, brushed with soy sauce, are very good served with wedges of lemon. Cut into strips, they make an interesting addition to salads. Abalone or oyster mushrooms or regular mushrooms may be used in the same manner.

SIMMERED PUMPKIN (*Kabocha Nimono*)   ★ *page 82*

Even though any kind of pumpkin may be prepared this way, the hard-skinned *"Kuri Kabocha"* (page 27), or buttercup pumpkin are the tastiest.

For 4–5 servings:
1½ lb. (225 g) "kuri kabocha"
   or buttercup pumpkin
1½ *cup* dashi
3 tablespoons mirin (*or just
   add 1 tablespoon sugar*)
1–2 *tablespoons sugar*
½ *teaspoon salt*
½ *tablespoon soy sauce*

1. With a heavy cutting knife, cut the pumpkin in half. You may have to hammer on the knife. Remove the seeds and cut into chunks 1½″ × 2″ (4 × 5 cm). Cut off the hard part of the skin. If you want to be like the professional chefs, trim the sharp edges.
2. Place the pumpkin pieces, skin side down in a pot with the thicker pieces at the bottom of the pot. Pour in *dashi* until it comes up ⅔ of the height of the pumpkin. Add half the seasonings. Cover with a drop-lid and bring to a boil.
3. Lower the heat to medium low and cook 15–20 minutes.
4. Taste and add more seasonings. Continue to cook until the pumpkin is tender and there is about ⅓ the liquid left.
5. Turn off the heat and let the pumpkin absorb the liquid.

Note: Poached snow peas or string beans (page 53) would be a nice addition to this dish.

DEEP-FRIED AND POACHED PUMPKIN VARIATION (*Kabocha Age-ni*)

Deep-fry pumpkin pieces until golden. Then cook in the same liquid described above, but use only half the sugar.

SESAME TOFU (*Goma Dofu*)   ★ *page 82*

This is a special dish in a Buddhist vegetarian dinner because it takes hours to prepare in the traditional way. It is served in place of *sashimi*. However, using an oven for toasting the sesame seeds and a food processor for grinding, it is much faster. *"Kuzu"* (arrowroot starch) is used. Cornstarch may be used, but the result will be heavier. *Kuzu* is sometimes difficult to find, so I have used gelatin as a substitute, and the result was very good—lighter, easier, and lower in calories!

The only drawback is that you cannot serve it warm or as a garnish in a soup.

Gelatin Method:

1. Spread sesame seeds on a baking sheet and bake at 300°F. (150°C.) for 6 minutes.
2. Place sesame in a food processor and process several minutes. At first the seeds will fly around, but eventually will settle down and become like peanut butter.
3. With the processor running, gradually add the dissolved gelatin and the seasonings.
4. Strain the mixture into a wet mold. Cool and refrigerate several hours until set.
5. Unmold and cut into serving pieces. Arrange on individual dishes, pour the sauce over it and place a small mound of the condiment of your choice on it.

Kuzu Method:

1. Follow steps 1 and 2 above in Gelatin Method.
2. With the processor running, gradually add *kuzu*, water and the seasonings.
3. Strain into a heavy pot and cook over medium low heat, stirring all the time. When it starts to thicken, lower the heat and continue cooking until translucent. This takes about 30 minutes.
4. Turn into a wet mold. Flatten the surface and immerse the mold in cold water to cover. This permits quick cooling and prevents formation of a film. Cover with a well-wrung cloth and chill in the refrigerator.
5. Unmold and cut into serving pieces. Serve with sauce and condiment.

Note: Sesame *tofu* is usually served cold, but during cold weather it is sometimes served warm (after steaming), or in soup as a garnish. Only Sesame *Tofu* made with *kuzu* can be used in warm dishes.

The following recipes make 4–6 servings.

Gelatin Method:
½ cup white sesame seeds

2 envelopes (2 tablespoons) unflavored gelatin
2 cups water
Soak in water and cook until dissolved.

⅓ teaspoon each sugar and salt

Dipping Sauce:
Tempura *Dipping Sauce (page 35)*
or

Miso Sauce:
1 tablespoon each red salty miso, mirin and dashi
1–2 teaspoons sugar
Mix all and cook until well blended.

Condiment: 1 teaspoon of your choice:
Grated ginger, mustard paste, wasabi paste, or lemon rind needles.

Kuzu *Method:*
½ cup white sesame seeds
½ cup kuzu (arrowroot starch), or cornstarch if kuzu unavailable.
2 cups water
⅓ teaspoon each sugar and salt

SESAME *TOFU* VARIATIONS

Follow the basic recipe, but replace the ½ cup of sesame seeds called for with the following:

PEANUT *TOFU*:
   Replace sesame seeds with creamy peanut butter—half the amount of sesame called for in the recipe—and omit sugar and salt.

WALNUT *TOFU* (*Kurumi Dofu*):
   Use ⅔ cup blanched walnuts instead of the sesame seeds.

GREEN SOYBEAN *TOFU* (*Edamame Dofu*):
   Use shelled, fresh soybeans boiled in hot salted water until tender—⅔ cup soybeans.

GINGKO NUT *TOFU* (*Ginnan Dofu*):
   Replace sesame with ⅔ cup canned, (boiled) gingko nuts.

AVOCADO *TOFU* (Avocado *Dofu*):   ★ *page 83*
   Use one large ripe avocado. Cut it in half, remove the seed, squeeze on lemon juice. Scrape out the pulp—don't miss the green part near the skin. Use only the Gelatin Method with avocado, because it doesn't require cooking.

SNOW PEAS (OR STRING BEANS) WITH PEANUT DRESSING
(*Kinusaya* or *Ingen no* Peanut-*ae*)   ★ *page 83*

For 4–6 servings:
½ lb. (225 g) snow peas or
   string beans
1 recipe Peanut Dressing
   (page 219)

1. Trim string beans and slant-cut into 1½″ (4 cm) pieces. Soak in water for half an hour.
2. Cook the beans in salted boiling water until tender crisp. Drain and plunge them into cold water for keeping bright green color. Drain in a colander.
3. Mix with the dressing just before serving.

MARINATED SPINACH (*Hōrenso Ohitashi*) ★ *page 83*

This is perhaps the most frequently served vegetable dish in Japanese family dinners. Other mild and tender green leaf vegetables can be prepared the same way. Try mustard greens, Chinese cabbage, "*shungiku*" and watercress..

146

1. Wash well and cut off the roots from the spinach.
2. Boil plenty of water with salt. When it is at the full boil, add a handful of spinach, stir and when the water is at full boil again, lift out the spinach and plunge it into a bowl of cold water. Drain and rinse with cold water until the spinach is completely cold. Repeat this process until all the spinach is cooked. (Boil mustard greens 1 minute, Chinese cabbage just until tender).
3. Squeeze out the water, then cut into 1½″ (4 cm) lengths. The stems and leaves may be mixed, or they may be separated and used in different dishes. Sprinkle 1 teaspoon soy sauce over the spinach and let it stand a few minutes.
4. Squeeze out the water again, and marinate in the sauce 10–30 minutes.
5. Pile into small individual bowls, top with bonito flakes or toasted sesame and serve.

For 4 servings:
1 bunch spinach
1 teaspoon soy sauce

Marinating Liquid:
¼ cup dashi
¼ cup soy sauce

Topping:
1 tablespoon bonito flakes or
  1 tablespoon toasted sesame seeds

SPINACH WITH MUSTARD SAUCE *page 83
(*Hōrenso no Karashi-ae*)

1. Boil spinach or other greens the same as directed in Marinated Spinach recipe above, 1, 2, and 3.
2. Toast *tofu* puffs golden in the oven about 2–3″ (5–7 cm) below the broiler. Cut into thin strips.
3. Make the sauce in a bowl by mixing mustard, sugar and soy sauce.
4. Add the green vegetables and *tofu* puffs and mix well.

This is delicious as a side dish, or served in a small quantity as an appetizer. Mustard greens, collard greens or watercress are also good for this recipe. Instead of "*age*" (fried *tofu* puff), boiled or steamed chicken, leftover roast beef, ham or "*kamaboko*" would be excellent substitutes.

For 4 servings:
1 bunch spinach
1 teaspoon soy sauce
2 fried tofu puffs

Mustard Sauce:
2 teaspoons mustard mixed
  with water
1½ tablespoons soy sauce
1 teaspoon sugar
Mix well.

SPINACH WITH SESAME SAUCE (*Hōrenso Goma-ae*)

Prepare the spinach as in recipes above. Mix with Sesame Sauce (page 143).

SPLIT PEA SWEET PURÉE ★ page 83
(*Midori Kinton* or *Green Kinton*)

"*Kinton*" is a sweet mash served in the course of a traditional Japanese dinner to provide a flavor contrast. It is almost dessert-like. Although it is usually made from sweet potato and chestnuts or from white beans, in an experiment I used split peas—a purely Western ingredient—and it turned out beautifully! This is simple to prepare, has a nice green color and good flavor.
   Serve small quantities, one or two tablespoons per serving,

in dainty cups or dishes. Or it could be piled into a serving bowl and passed around to the guests. It is always a good addition to a boxed lunch.

For 1 cup:
½ cup split peas
2½ cups water
¼–⅓ cup sugar
⅛ teaspoon salt

1. Wash the split peas and cover with 2½ cups water.
2. Bring to a boil. Skim and simmer until tender. All the water will be absorbed and it will become like mashed potatoes.
3. Add the sugar and salt and mix well over low heat. Remove from the heat and cool. It will thicken when it is cool.

CHESTNUT KINTON (*Kuri Kinton*) ★ *page 83*

Makes 10–12 servings: (keeps in refrigerator 5–6 days)
1 lb. (450 g) sweet potato or yam (the yellow-colored one is good)
20 chestnuts, canned in syrup
1 teaspoon alum*
2 quarts (8 cups) water
6 tablespoons syrup from the canned chestnuts
½–¾ cup (150 g) sugar
3 tablespoons mirin
2 tablespoons white corn syrup
½ teaspoon salt

1. Wash the sweet potatoes or yams. Slice them ⅜″ (1 cm) thick and drop into 1 quart of water with alum. Peel the skin off each slice deep enough to cut away the inner circle line which makes the potato dark when exposed to the air. Soak in the water 30 minutes.
2. Boil 1 quart of water with alum. Add the potatoes and cook until half tender.
3. Boil another quart of water in a separate pot. Transfer the sweet potatoes from the first pot. Boil the potatoes until fork tender.
4. Drain and put through a sieve while still hot. Or process in a food processor for a second or two to make a mash.
5. Place the mash in a thick pot, add the syrup and a part of the sugar. Cook over low heat, stirring constantly. Add more sugar to your liking. When it is thick enough for you to see the bottom of the pot for a second or two, add the *mirin*, corn syrup and the chestnuts. Cook a few minutes more until glossy and heated through.

* Alum is optional in this recipe. It helps to produce a better color from the sweet potatoes.

WHITE BEAN KINTON (*Shiro-Ingen Kinton*)

For 10–12 servings: (keeps 5–6 days in the refrigerator)
12 oz. (340 g) dried white lima beans
1–3 cups sugar
¼ teaspoon salt

1. Wash the beans and remove any beans that float. It is not necessary to soak beans before cooking.
2. Add plenty of water to cover the beans and bring to a boil. Lower the heat to medium and cook for 5 minutes.
3. Drain the beans in a colander.
4. Repeat steps 2 and 3, four or five times. This repetitive process produces whiter cooked beans.
5. Add water three times the volume of the beans to the pot and simmer until tender. From this point, the beans may be cooked in a crockpot.
6. When the beans are quite tender, add a pinch of salt to prevent breaking. Keep simmering until they are extremely tender.
7. Drain the beans in a colander.

8. Put ⅓ of the beans through a sieve or process in a food processor.
9. Place the rest of the beans in a pot, add sugar and cook.
10. Add the strained bean mash and stir gently, making a coating for the beans. Add the rest of the salt (to your taste) at the last minute.

APRICOT KINTON (Anzu no Kinton) ★ page 83

This is a California style *kinton*, using dried apricots with the base of white bean *kinton*.

1. Cover the apricots with water and cook until tender.
2. Add sugar and simmer to season the apricots. Cut each apricot into 4 pieces.
3. Cook white beans as in the recipe above. Sieve all the beans, or process in a food processor.
4. Put the sieved bean mash into a pot, add the apricot syrup and sugar to your liking, and cook until thickened, stirring constantly.
5. Combine with the apricots.

For 10–12 servings: (will keep in refrigerator for 5–6 days)
1 recipe White Bean Kinton
1 cup dried apricots
1 cup water
½ cup sugar

DEEP-FRIED AND SIMMERED SWEET POTATO (Satsuma-imo Age-ni) ★ page 83

Deep-frying before simmering makes the sweet potatoes in this dish rich tasting.

1. Slice potatoes ¾" (2 cm) thick. Peel off the thick skin, cutting out the inner line on each slice that is about ¼" (6 mm) inside the skin. See Chestnut *Kinton* page 148, 1.
2. Drop the potatoes into the water with alum and soak half an hour.
3. Drain and wipe the potato slices dry.
4. Heat oil to 335°F. (170°C.) and fry the potato slices quickly—about 30 seconds to 1 minute—until they are golden colored. Drain on paper towels.
5. Place the slices in a pot, add water, half the sugar and salt, and bring to a boil. Lower the heat and cover with a paper drop-lid, vented. See page 39.
6. Simmer slowly until the liquid is almost gone. Half way through the cooking, taste and add more seasoning. Unless you use the lowest heat, the potatoes may crumble.

For 6 servings:
1 lb. (500 g) sweet potatoes or yams
½ teaspoon alum (optional. See note on page 148)
4 cups water
Oil for deep-frying

Cooking Liquid:
1 cup water
3–4 tablespoons sugar
⅔ teaspoon salt

TARO POTATO (Sato Imo)

Japanese taro potatoes are smaller than Hawaiian or Chinese taro. They are harvested at the end of summer, and are offered for the September full moon, called "Imomeigetsu—beautiful moon in potato harvest time."

Like Cherry Blossom Viewing, Moon Viewing is a delightful Japanese custom that has been observed for a long time— probably as early as the 10th century. On a balcony or corridor where the moon can be viewed, an offering table is set with some pampas grass in a vase, rice dumplings about the size of ping-pong balls to resemble a round, full moon set on an unstained wooden stand, and steamed taro potatoes in their skins. Early in September it is still quite hot. The cool evening breeze is very pleasant, and people enjoy looking at the full moon, particularly people with a literary bent who write poems.

STEAMED TAROS IN THEIR JACKETS
(*Sato-imo Kinukatsugi*) ★ *page 84*

Choose small sized young taro potatoes. Wash well, but do not peel. You may cut both ends off for neater appearance and easier eating. Boil plenty of water in a steamer. (See steaming instructions on page 54). When the steam is high, place the taros on a rack and steam 10–15 minutes until a bamboo skewer goes through a taro easily.

Serve piled on a platter or a basket, with small dishes for soy sauce and grated ginger.

To eat them, pull back the skin from one end, dip into the soy sauce mixed with grated ginger, and bite into it. Since taro potatoes are slippery, the skin comes off easily.

SIMMERED TAROS FAMILY STYLE
(*Sato-imo no Nikorogashi*)

For 4 servings:
1 lb. (450 g) taro
1 tablespoon salt

Cooking Liquid:
1 cup dashi
3 tablespoons sugar
¼ teaspoon salt
1 tablespoon soy sauce
A sprinkling of grated lemon rind

1. Wash the taros.
2. Cut off each end and peel the skin.
3. Place in a basket and sprinkle with 1 tablespoon salt. Let stand 5 minutes.
4. Shake the basket and wash the taros under running water to remove any sliminess.
5. Put the taro potatoes in a pot and add *dashi* and the seasonings. Bring to a boil.
6. Lower the heat and cover with a drop-lid and simmer until almost all the liquid is gone. At the last stage, shake the pot often to coat the potatoes with the liquid.
7. Pile them into a serving bowl and grate some lemon rind over them to add aroma.

TURNIPS (*Kabura*)

Turnips are available almost anywhere and year round. They can be cooked or pickled and they can substitute for *daikon*. Choose smooth-skinned ones.

150

BOILED TURNIPS WITH *MISO* SAUCE
(*Kabura Furofuki*) ★ *page 84*

If you like turnips in pot-au-feu, you know how good boiled turnips can be. Try serving this dish piping hot with *miso* sauce. In Japan it is more commonly done with *daikon* in winter, when it is at its prime.

1. Cut off the top and bottom of each turnip.
2. Peel the skin like an apple, or peel down the sides to make a hexagon or octagon.
3. On the bottom, make a cross incision for quicker cooking.
4. Place the turnips in a pot, cover with the rice washing water (or plain water) and simmer until slightly tender. Drain and rinse.
5. Put the optional *kombu* in a pot. Place the turnips over and cover with water. Simmer with a drop-lid until a bamboo skewer goes through easily.
6. While the turnips are cooking, prepare a *miso* sauce and the condiments.
7. Transfer each turnip with a slotted spoon to individual bowls. Pour over the hot sauce and top with condiment. Serve immediately.

Note: When using *daikon* in place of turnip, slice 1¼″ (3 cm) thick. Peel and make a cross incision on the back and cook like turnips.

For 4 servings:
4 small turnips
2–3 cups rice washing liquid* (the white colored water from washing rice)
3″ (8 cm) square kombu (kelp) (optional)
Miso *Sauce (dilute any of the miso glazes on pages 126).*

Condiment: Lemon rind sliced needle-thin.

* *The rice washing liquid removes some harshness of taste, tenderizes, and makes the vegetables whiter.*

STEAMED TURNIPS (*Kabura Mushi*)

Here is a favorite dish for winter. Turnips are transformed into a delicate, cloud-like topping over fish or chicken and served with a hot glaze. The most delicious combination is broiled eel (*unagi*) or conger eel (*anago*) with parboiled lily bulbs. But you can use chicken breast, white-meat fish, shelled prawns, and precooked vegetables.

1. Sprinkle 1 teaspoon salt and 1 tablespoon *sake* over the white fish and let stand 15 minutes. Then pour boiling water over. This salting and rinsing with hot water removes any fishy smell. Remove the heads and shells from the prawns, leaving the tails on. Remove the black veins with a toothpick. Butterfly the prawns.
2. Sprinkle the seasoning mixture over the fish, prawns and chicken. Let stand for 10–15 minutes.
3. Sprinkle a mixture of 1 teaspoon each soy sauce and *sake* over the fresh mushrooms. If using dry *shiitake*, soften in lukewarm water, remove the stems and quarter the caps. Cook in ½ cup soaking water with 1 teaspoon soy sauce

For 4 servings:

Turnip Topping:
1 lb. (450 g) turnips
1 small egg (or 1 egg white of a large egg, or 2 yolks)
A pinch each of salt and MSG

Ingredients to steam:
An assortment like this, or just one or two kinds in larger quantities:
½ lb. (225 g) white fish (halibut, red snapper, rock cod, sea bass, sea bream, etc.)
4 prawns
2 oz. (60 g) chicken breast, thinly sliced

Seasoning for fish, prawns and
   chicken:
2 tablespoons soy sauce
1 tablespoon each mirin
   and sake (or 2 table-
   spoons sake with
   1 teaspoon sugar)

2–4 dried or fresh shiitake*
8 snow peas or 2 tablespoons
   green peas parboiled
* Instead of shiitake, regular button mushrooms, abalone or
   oyster mushrooms may be used.

Condiment:
1 teaspoon grated ginger or
   wasabi paste

Thickened Sauce (An):
1 cup dashi
2 tablespoons soy sauce
1½ tablespoons mirin (or 2
   tablespoons sake with 1
   teaspoon sugar)
1½ tablespoons cornstarch
   mixed with 2 tablespoons
   water

1 medium turnip (or 3 slices
   daikon) cut 1″ (2.5 cm)
   thick

Sweet Vinegar Liquid:
½ cup each vinegar and dashi
4 tablespoons sugar
¼ teaspoon salt

For the stamen:
1 dried, red cayenne pepper,
   seeded and cut into rings, or
   2 teaspoons sieved, hard-
   boiled egg yolk, lemon
   rind, red caviar, or tobiko.

Garnish:
Chrysanthemum leaves

and ½ teaspoon sugar.
4. Divide the ingredients into small serving bowls. Start a
    steamer (refer to page 54) with plenty of water. When
    steam is high, place a rack with the bowls in it and steam
    for 10 minutes until the fish or chicken is cooked. Place a
    towel under the lid of the steamer to prevent moisture
    dripping.
5. Meanwhile, prepare the topping. Peel the turnips and grate
    them into a bowl. Pour boiling water over the turnips to
    cover, stir, and drain in a colander which is lined with dou-
    ble thickness of cheese cloth. Squeeze out water, but leave
    some moisture.
6. Mix in an egg, salt and MSG.
7. Spoon the turnip topping into bowls and steam for 4–5
    minutes.
8. Boil dashi, mirin and soy sauce in a pot. Add ¼ cup boil-
    ing dashi to the cornstarch mixture, blending well. Remove
    the pot from the heat, add diluted cornstarch, mix well and
    return to the heat to make a clear glaze.
9. Pour the sauce over the steamed bowls, top with grated
    ginger or wasabi paste and serve covered (if the bowls have
    lids).

CHRYSANTHEMUM TURNIPS   ★ page 84
(Kikuka Kabu)

Raw turnips or daikon, cut like chrysanthemums and pickled in
sweet vinegar, are very handy as a garnish for broiled fish or meat,
or as an addiion to appetizers, because it keeps for weeks in the
refrigerator.

1. Cut the turnip crosswise 1″ (2.5 cm) thick and peel off the
    skin.
2. Put the slice between two bamboo skewers or thin chop-
    sticks. With a sharp, thin cutting knife, cut from right to
    left as thin as possible (¹⁄₁₆″ or 2–3 mm apart). The
    skewers of chopsticks prevent your cutting through to the
    bottom.
3. Turn the slice 90 degrees and cut again from right to left,
    holding the slice with your thumb and middle finger.
4. Turn the slice upside down. Cut from the uncut side into
    squares measuring ¾–1″ (2–2.5 cm).
5. Soak the turnip pieces in salted water (2 teaspoons salt in
    1 cup water) for 30 minutes to one hour, until they are
    pliable.
6. Prepare sweet vinegar liquid. Place the drained and lightly
    squeezed turnips in a jar and cover with the vinegar mix-
    ture. Marinate at least 2 hours. These may be prepared days
    in advance.

7. Drain the turnips and fluff up to make them look like chrysathemum flowers. Put red pepper ring (or sieved yolk) in the center and garnish with chrysanthemum leaves.

Note: Success in simulating a flower depends on how thin you cut and how pliable you are able to make it. *Daikon* can be worked exactly like turnips for these flowers.

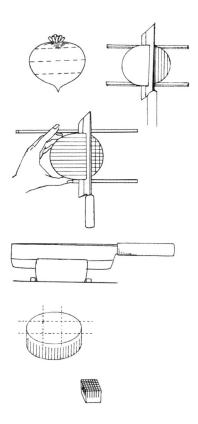

VEGETABLE *TEMPURA* (*Shōjin Age*) ★ *page 84*

Without any seafood, all-vegetable *tempuras* are equally as good and as pretty to look at. Almost any vegetables that are not watery may be used. Read pages 97 to 101 for cooking instructions for *tempura*.

Garnishes:
Leaves of celery, chrysanthemum, Japanese maple, persimmon, *shiso* (parilla), spinach, etc.
Shiso seedpods
Small *nori* sheets (come in packet) or larger sheet cut into pieces 2″ × 3″ (5 × 8 cm)
Dried apricots, softened in water and drained
Seeded olives, drained and skewered one or two to a toothpick

Suitable Vegetables:
Carrots, sliced thin
Eggplant, sliced, soaked in salted water for 30 minutes, and dried
Green asparagus
Green peppers, cut into strips
Fresh regular mushrooms, sliced.
Fresh shiitake mushroom caps
Lotus root slices, cut ⅜″ (1 cm) thick and soaked in vinegared water (1 tablespoon vinegar to 1 cup water)
Onions, sliced
Pumpkin slices cut ⅜″ (1 cm) thick
Snow peas or string beans, strings removed
Sweet potato or yam, sliced ⅜″ (1 cm) thick, peeled and soaked in water.

Batter: See page 100
Leaves and *nori* sheets. Dip in batter just on one side, float on
    the frying oil.

Frying Temperature:
Root vegetables take longer to cook, so they should be fried at
a lower temperature than seafood—320–340°F. (160–
170°C.) Leaves and *nori* sheets should be fried at around 340°F.
(170°C.) just for a minute or so until crisp.

Dipping Sauce:
Use dipping sauce on pages 35, 97

Condiments:
Grated *daikon*

SPOON-DROPPED MIXED *TEMPURA*
(*Kaki Age*)

Suitable Vegetables:
Carrots, shredded
Burdock, shredded and soak-
    ed in water for 20
    minutes and drained
Onions, thinly sliced

See page 101 which explains Seafood *Kaki Age*.

You may use just one kind of vegetable, or two or three mixed.
Cut them into similar sizes in order to have the same cooking
times.

PART-III
Appetizers
Soups
Salads
Casseroles
Rice
Pickles
Desserts and Japanese Sweets

A Basket of Fall Leaves with
Dry Tidbits, pages 199–200.
Fried Kelp Leaves, Gingko Leaf Potato Chips, Red Leaves, Noodles Pine Needles, Fried Gingko Nuts and Roasted
Chestnuts.
Persimmon Cups, page 265.

158   Top: Caviar on Endive Leaf Boats, page 189.   Boat-Shaped Ice Container: Right: Smoked Salmon Cucumber
Rolls, page 193. Center: *Nori*-Rolled Tuna, page 191. Left: Sesame Coated *Sashimi*, page 191. Bottom:
Bottled Seasoned *Wuni* on Grated Cucumber, page 195., Fried Smelts, page 194.

Top right: *Enoki* Mushroom Snow Salad, page 218.   Left: Caviar on *Tofu*, page 188.   On the tray: Broiled
Shrimp, page 192., Vinegared Lotus Root Snow Flakes, pages 50, 142., Nandina Caviar, page 189.

◁
1

◁
2

◁
3

◁
4

160 Clear Soups, pages 201–204. Top to Bottom: 1. Flower-Shaped Hard-Boiled Eggs, *Daikon* Sprouts, Dried *Shiitake* and Pricky Ash 2. Flower-Shaped *Kamaboko*, Wheat Gluten Cake, Bean Threads and Watercress. 3. *Chikuwa*, Cucumber, Wheel Macaroni and *Yuzu*. 4. *Tofu, Shimeji*, Maple-Shaped Carrot and Lime.

1: Cucumber with Sweet Vinegar Dressing, page 215. 2: Crab meat with Vinegar Dressing, page 215. 3: Scallops and *Shiitake* with Vinegar Glaze, page 217. 4: Shrimp, Avocado and Cucumber with Yellow Dressing, page 218. 5: *Daikon* Salad, page 216. 6: Persimmon and *Daikon* Salad, page 216. 7: Arricot and *Daikon* Salad, page 216.

161

Top: Avocado and Papaya with Tart *Tofu* Dressing, page 221.
Above: Japanese Salad Platter with Sesame *Miso* Dressing, page 223.

Right: Assorted Casserole, page 228.

Left top: *Tofu*, Fish and Vegetable Casserole, page 226.
Bottom: Chinese Cabbage Casserole, page 226.
Above: *Shabu Shabu*, page 227.
Below: Chopped green onions, grated ginger and minced lemon rind.

Above: Boiled Chicken Casserole, page 228.
Right top:　Seafood Casserole, page 229.
Bottom:　*Oden*, page 230.

168 Top: Chicken *Miso* Casserole, page 234.
Bottom: Oyster *Miso* Casserole, page 234.

Sukiyaki, page 230.

Above: Iron Griddle Cooking, page 232.
Below: Chopped Chives.
Right: Pancake Snack, page 233.

170

171

Green Pea Rice, page 235.

Ginger Rice, page 236.

Green Leaf Rice, page 236.

Soy-Seasoned Rice Dishes

Rice with Five Garnishes, page 236.

Chestnut Rice, page 237.

Oyster Mushroom Rice, page 237.

▽ Steak Rice Bowl, page 239.

△ Crumbly Chicken Rice Bowl, page 238.

△ Chicken and Egg Rice Bowl, page 238

▽ Breaded Cutlet Rice Bowl, page 239.

△ *Tempura* Rice Bowl, page 239.

175

Top: Steamed *Sushi*, page 246.   Bottom: Mixed *Sushi*, page 245.

Top: Pressed *Sushi*, page 246.   Bottom: Stuffed *Tofu* Puff *Sushi*, page 248.

Top: Thin *Nori* Rolls (*Hoso Maki Zushi*), page 250.
178 Bottom: Dew Drops Thin Rolls, page 250.

Top: *Nori* Roll, page 249.
Middle: Three-Colored Striped *Sushi* and Two-Colored Striped *Sushi*, page 248.
Bottom: Smoked Salmon Roll, page 248.

179

Make-Your-Own-*Sushi*, page 251.

Nigiri Zushi, page 252. Vinegared mackerel, boat-shaped *sushi* with salted flying fish roe, cuttlefish, yellow tail, tuna, halibut, boat-shaped *sushi* with red caviar, broiled eel, baked egg and boiled prawn. Sweet pickled ginger *"gari,"*

Pickles, pages 257–259.   Top to Bottom: Celery Pickles, Thousand Slice Turnip Pickle, Refrigerator Chinese
Cabbage Pickle, Green Pickle and Sweet-Sour Pickled Dried *Daikon.*

Desserts, pages 260–266.   Top to Bottom: Rosé Wine Sherbet, Snow Jelly with Strawberry Sauce, Floating Ice, Sesame Crisps, Chestnuts with Chocolate Sauce, Cantaloupe Ice with Green Grapes and Lemon Cream Sauce, Persimmon Ice Cup and Ripe Persimmon with Lemon Cream Sauce.

184　Top: Round Tray: Chestnut Pastry, page 270. Japanese Waffles, page 269. Steamed Chestnut-Bean Paste Squares, page 268. Middle: Japanese Waffle cut and Chestnut Pastry cut. Bottom: Plum Wine Jelly, page 264.

Appetizers

Although called by many names such as *"otōshi,"* *"sakizuke,"* *"tsukidashi,"* *"ma-e hassun,"* these are all appetizers to be served with *sake.*

They may consist of only one item or an assortment of many. Main dishes may also be served as *zensai*, prepared as small morsels. The rules to keep in mind for *zensai* are:

1. Serve small pieces so they are not filling;
2. Awaken the taste buds, but keep them eager for the courses which will follow;
3. If there is an assortment of *zensai*, consider contrasts and varieties in materials, colors, tastes and textures.

EGG APPETIZERS

AMBER EGGS (*Ran-oh Misozuke*)

These are *miso*-pickled egg yolks. When *miso*-pickled, raw egg yolks become firm, amber-colored, and acquire a very interesting taste. Prepare this 3 days before you plan to serve it.

1. Mix the two kinds of *miso*.
2. Spread half the mixed *miso* in a plastic or ceramic container large enough to hold the 4 yolks.
3. Cover the *miso* with a layer of cheese cloth. Make indentations using the pointed end of an egg.
4. Slip the yolks into the holes.
5. Cover with another layer of cheese cloth and with remaining *miso*.
6. Cover and refrigerate for 3 days.
7. The yolks are now ready to serve. If left longer they will become too salty. To serve, cut each yolk into four pieces. Serve as is, or sprinkle with toasted sesame seeds or chopped parsley. They may also be wrapped in a small piece of *nori* or *shiso* leaf (perilla).

4 egg yolks
½ cup red miso
½ cup mellow, white miso
Cheese cloth

EGG WHITES WITH ANCHOVY
(Ranpaku Anchovy-ae).

For 8–12 servings:
4 egg whites
6 spinach stems
Anchovy paste to taste
Garnishes: Chopped parsley or
lemon rind, cut thread-thin

1. Oil a medium sized custard cup or a bowl. Pour in the unbeaten egg whites. Cover with aluminum foil.
2. Pour about 1″ (2.5 cm) of water into a pot. Place the cup or bowl in the water.
3. Cover the pot and boil over medium heat for about 10–15 minutes, until the egg whites are set. Take the cup or bowl out of the water and cool it.
4. Blanch spinach stems 30 seconds in salted boiling water. Drain and rinse with cold water.
5. Cut the egg whites and the green stems into julienne 1″ (2.5 cm) long.
6. Add anchovy paste and mix. To serve, make dainty piles in small individual dishes or in scooped out cherry tomatoes. Slice the bottoms off the cherry tomatoes to stabilize them. Or pile into scooped out lemon cups. Sprinkle with the garnish.

CHICKEN APPETIZERS

Yakitori (page 105) and Soy Marinated Fried Chicken (*Tatsuta Age*) (page 106) make fine *zensai* if made on a smaller scale.

FRIED NORI WRAPPED CHICKEN
(Tori no Isobe Age)

Half of a chicken breast, cut
into strips 2¼″ × ⅓″ × ⅓″
(6 × 1 × 1 cm)

Seasoning Mix:
1 tablespoon soy sauce
1 teaspoon sake
¼ teaspoon grated ginger

2–3 sheets of nori, each sheet
cut into 8–12 pieces. Or
use small yakinori measur-
ing 2½″ × 2½″ (6.5 × 5.7
cm), sold in packages
Cornstarch glue made from 1
teaspoon cornstarch mixed
with ½ teaspoon water
Oil for frying

1. Mix the chicken with the seasoning mix and let stand for 30 minutes.
2. Place one strip of chicken on a squre of *nori*. Roll it up and seal with the cornstarch glue.
3. Heat the oil to 350°F. (175°C.). Fry the rolls one handful at a time until they are crisp. Drain on paper towels.

SHISO ROLLS (Tori no Shiso Maki)

1. Wash the leaves and dry them on paper towels.
2. Spread about ½ teaspoon *miso* on a leaf, place one strip of chicken on it and roll up and seal with cornstarch glue. If necessary, fasten with a toothpick.
3. Sauté in a heated frying pan over medium heat with a little oil. Turn once. Serve with a toothpick.

Note: Instead of chicken, this can be made with strips of *kamaboko* or strips of raw jicama.

Half of a chicken breast cut into strips 2" × ⅓" × ⅓" (5 × 1 × 1 cm)

12–20 shiso leaves (perilla) or substitute spinach leaves. You need as many leaves as pieces of chicken.

3 tablespoons mellow white, Hawaiian type miso or 3 tablespoons aka miso mixed with ½ tablespoon sake and 1 tablespoon sugar

1 teaspoon cornstarch glue (1 teaspoon cornstarch mixed with 1 teaspoon water)

CHICKEN AND CUCUMBER WASABI SOY SAUCE (Tori to Kyuri Wasabi Jōyu)

1. Peel the cucumber if the skin is hard. Cut into two lengthwise, remove the seeds and slice.
2. Sprinkle with a little salt. Let stand 10 minutes. Squeeze out the juice.
3. Mix with shredded, cooked chicken and the sauce.

Note: Other shredded ingredients to use include blanched squid or scraps of *sashimi*. Substitutes for the greens include boiled string beans or spinach stems and blanched *mitsuba* (trefoil). Also, dried seaweed (*wakame*), soaked and shredded with the vein removed, give an interesting texture.

¼ lb. cooked chicken, shredded (may be steamed, boiled, sautéed or roasted).
1 small cucumber

Wasabi Soy Sauce:
½ to 1 teaspoon wasabi powder (or paste)
3 tablespoons soy sauce
1 tablespoon dashi
Mix all together.

SEA FOOD APPETIZERS

ANCHOVIES

Anchovies have much in common with Japanese delicacies such as "shio wuni" (salted sea urchin roe) and "shio kara" (salted and fermented sea food). Since anchovies are salty, combine them with something bland and adjust the amount of salt or soy sauce in the dressing.

ANCHOVY SALAD (Anchovy Sunomono)

1. Roughly chop the anchovy fillets. Wash with 1 tablespoon *sake* and add the *sake* to the vinegar.

3–4 anchovy fillets
1 tablespoon sake
½ cup cucumber, sliced or in fine julienne, sprinkled with ¼ teaspoon salt
1 tablespoon rice vinegar mixed with ⅛ teaspoon MSG
½ teaspoon grated ginger

2. Squeeze out the juice from the cucumber. Mix with anchovy and the vinegar.
3. Pile into *sake* cups or very small dishes. Top with a bit of grated ginger.

Note: In place of cucumber, shredded *daikon*, jicama, turnip or boiled potato may be used.

ANCHOVY IN SNOW (Anchovy *Mizore-ae*)

3–4 anchovy fillets
1 tablespoon sake
½ cup grated daikon or turnip, lightly squeezed*
1 tablespoon lemon juice
1 teaspoon soy sauce

1. Cut the fillets crosswise. Wash with *sake*. Add this *sake* to the lemon juice.
2. Add the soy sauce to the lemon juice and mix with grated *daikon* and anchovy bits. Do not add salt since anchovies are salty.
3. Serve piled into small cups or on lemon slices.

* If you use grated cucumber instead, this is called Anchovy in Green Jade Snow (*Hisui-ae*).

ANCHOVY PASTE

Anchovy paste is a very handy material to have on hand. It can be mixed with a variety of things and can be used as a glaze.

ANCHOVY COATED SEAFOOD (Anchovy *Shiokara*)

¼ cup raw squid, abalone or scallops, shredded or cubed
1 teaspoon anchovy paste

This is an instant "*shiokara*"—a salted and fermented seafood delicacy.
Mix the seafood with the anchovy paste. Pile about 1 teaspoon into small serving cups or dishes.

ANCHOVY GLAZE

1 egg yolk
2 teaspoons anchovy paste
Mix:

Spread mixture onto lightly broiled *shiitake* mushrooms or squid and broil lightly.

4 slices tofu, preferably the soft type, cut 1½" square × ¾" thick

CAVIAR

CAVIAR ON *TOFU* (*Tofu* Caviar Mori)   ★ *page 159*

Here is a wonderful combination! The sharp color contrast of black and white carries through in taste and texture as well. Place a slice of *tofu* on a small dish, spread caviar over, sprinkle with grated ginger and add a lemon slice. Serve with a small spoon. Squeeze lemon juice over before eating.

Note: Instead of caviar, red caviar or *"tobiko"* (salted flying fish roe) is also very good.

4 tablespoons black caviar
¼ teaspoon grated ginger
4 slices lemon

NANDINA CAVIAR *(Ikura Nanten)* ★ *page 159*

1. Place the *nandina* sprigs on a plain dish and arrange the red caviar like berries in two or three clusters on it.
2. Add the grated *daikon* to look like snow.

4 sprigs of nandina shrub, washed and wiped dry
6 tablespoons red caviar

CAVIAR ON ENDIVE LEAF BOATS ★ *page 158*

Caviar, red caviar or flying fish roe *(Tobiko)* piled on small leaves of Belgian endive make lovely and easy to make appetizers. A bit of sour cream may be added.

6 tablespoons grated daikon ⎫
1 tablespoon lemon juice ⎬
¼ teaspoon salt ⎭
Mix:

RED CAVIAR IN SNOW OR GREEN JADE SNOW
(Mizore-ae/Hisui-ae)

1. Taste test the grated *daikon*. If it is too hot, soak it in water for a minute and squeeze out.
2. Mix with the seasoned vinegar, and then mix in the red caviar.
3. Pile onto lemon slices or into the cherry tomato cups.

½ cup daikon *or cucumber, grated and lightly squeezed*

1 tablespoon rice vinegar ⎫
⅛ Teaspoon salt ⎪
1 tablespoon dashi ⎬
½ tablespoon sugar ⎭
Mix.

3 tablespoons red caviar
Lemon slices or scooped out cherry tomatoes with bottoms sliced off so they will stand up.

MINI *SUSHI* (Mini Zushi)

Sushi is becoming so popular, why not serve ingredients for "Hand Rolled *Sushi*" for your guests to assemble and roll themselves?

1. Prepare *sushi* rice according to directions.
2. On a tray arrange the rice in a bowl, with a spoon or two. Surround the bowl with *nori* sheets, garnishes and *wasabi*. Since the garnishes are all salty, there is no need for soy sauce, and the absence of soy sauce makes it safer to serve in the living room!
3. Place about ½ teaspoon rice on a *nori* sheet, add dab of *wasabi* paste, add garnish of your choice, roll up and eat.

Small, toasted nori *sheets, sold in packets of 10 pieces. Or toast a large sheet (see page 241) and cut into 8 pieces.*
Sushi *rice (page 240) for* Nigiri

Garnish Suggestions:
  Caviar
  Red caviar
  Tobiko *(salted flying fish roe)*
  Smoked salmon, cut into strips
Condiment: Wasabi *paste*

FISH CAKES

There are several varieties available, all ready to eat:

Kamaboko: White, red-tinted, or top-browned, packaged on a piece of wood.
Chikuwa: A round stick with a hole in the center, with browned skin.
Kani kamaboko (crab stick):   Colored and shaped like crab legs.
Hanpen: Square or round, light, spongy-textured fish cake.

RAW FISH CAKE WITH *WASABI* SOY SAUCE

Use any one of the fish cakes, sliced. Accompany with *wasabi* paste and soy sauce. Serve like *sashimi*.

BOILED FISH CAKE

Kamaboko, *crab sticks, or* chikuwa, *sliced*
Grated ginger or wasabi *paste*
Soy sauce

Place the sliced fish cake in a pot, cover with water and bring to a boil. Drain and serve with grated ginger or *wasabi*. Eat with soy sauce.

BROILED FISH CAKE

Use any one of the fish cakes, cut into thick slices.

Broil until lightly browned. Brush with soy sauce. Then broil just enough to dry.

FRIED FISH CAKE

Use any one of the fish cakes, cut into ¾" (2 cm) cubes
Oil for frying
Salt

Heat the oil to 350°F. (180°C.) and fry the cubed fish cake to a golden color. Sprinkle with salt. Serve with toothpick.

CHIKUWA WITH CHEESE (*Chikuwa* Cheese *Ikomi*)

Chikuwa
Cheese spread (cheddar cheese is good)

Fill the hole with the cheese spread. Wrap and refrigerate. Slice about ⅓" (1 cm) thick and serve.

SASHIMI TIDBITS

Seasoned, raw fish cut into small cubes or sticks makes an excellent appetizer. See next 3 recipes.

SESAME COATED SASHIMI (Sashimi Goma Mabushi)

★ page 158

1. Toast sesame seeds in an unoiled, covered frying pan over medium heat until several seeds pop.
2. Marinate the fish in the soy sauce-*sake* mixture for 15 minutes. Roll in the toasted sesame seeds. Serve with toothpicks.

Raw fish such as tuna or albacore, cut into ²/₃" (1.5 cm) cubes
Black or white sesame seeds, toasted
Soy sauce

ROE-COATED SASHIMI
(Sashimi Tarako/Tobiko Mabushi)

1. Broil or boil the salted roe. Remove the skin and loosen the tiny eggs. *Tobiko* comes as loose eggs—use as is.
2. Dip the fish in *sake* and roll in the loose eggs. Serve with toothpicks.

Raw fish such as halibut, cut into small slices
1 tarako (salted codfish roe) or tobiko (salted flying fish roe)
Sake

NORI-ROLLED TUNA (Maguro Isobe Maki)

★ page 158

Marinate the fish in the soy sauce for 5 minutes. Place on the *nori*, add a smear or *wasabi* and roll up. Secure with a toothpick.

Red tuna or albacore, cut into stickes 2" × ¹/₃" × ¹/₃" (5 × 1 × 1 cm)
Soy sauce
Wasabi *paste*
Nori *sheet cut into pieces* 2" × 2¹/₃" (5 × 6 cm) (One nori *sheet makes 12*)

SAUTÉED SCALLOPS (Kai-bashira Butter Yaki)

Heat the butter in a frying pan. Quickly brown scallops on both sides. Add soy sauce. Coat well. Sprinkle with *sansho* or cayenne pepper.

¼ lb. (150 g) scallops, sliced crosswise ½" (1.2 cm) thick
1 tablespoon butter
1 tablespoon soy sauce
Sansho *powder or cayenne pepper*

SCALLOPS AND GREEN ONION MISOYAKI
(Kai-bashira to Negi no Misoyaki)

1. Cut thicker part of green onions the same length as the scallops.
2. Skewer the scallops alternately with green onions. Brush with salad oil.
3. Broil both sides.

¼ lb. scallops, cut into strips (following the grain) about 1" × ¹/₃" × ¹/₃" (3 × 1 × 1 cm)
1 bunch green onions

191

Mix:
3 tablespoons *red* miso
1½ tablespoons *mirin*
A *dash of cayenne pepper*

1 teaspoon *poppy seeds*
Salad oil
Short bamboo skewers

4. Spread mixed *miso* on one side and brown lightly. Sprinkle with poppy seeds and serve.

BROILED SHRIMP (*Ebi Tsukeyaki*) ★ *page 159*

Shrimp with shells
Soy sauce and mirin, *equal parts mixed*
Short bamboo skewers

1. Remove the black vein from the shrimp, leaving the shells on.
2. Put the skewers through the shrimp.
3. Broil both sides.
4. Brush with the sauce and broil again lightly.

FRIED SHRIMP (*Ebi Kara-age*)

¼ lb. *shrimp with shells*
½ teaspoon *salt*
Cornstarch
Oil for frying

1. Remove the black vein from the shrimp, but leave the shells on.
2. Sprinkle with ¼ teaspoon salt. Let stand for 10 minutes.
3. Coat shrimp with cornstarch. Shake off the excess.
4. Bring the oil to frying temperature and deep-fry shrimp until crisp and golden.
5. Drain and sprinkle with ¼ teaspoon salt and serve.

SMOKED SALMON IN SNOW OR GREEN JADE SNOW (Smoked Salmon *Mizore-ae/Hisui-ae*)

Prepare like Red Caviar in Snow (page 189)

½ cup grated daikon or cucumber
1 tablespoon vinegar
⅛ teaspoon salt
½ tablespoon sake
Mix all together.

2 oz. (60 g) smoked salmon, cut into small cubes
1 teaspoon lemon juice

Sprinkle the salmon with lemon juice and mix with seasoned "snow." Cubed cucumber is a pretty addition to grated *daikon*.

SMOKED SALMON CUCUMBER ROLLS (Smoked Salmon *Yasai Maki*)

Thin slices of lox type smoked salmon
Vegetable sticks (daikon, cucumber or jicama) *cut into sticks 1½″ × ⅓″ × ⅓″ (4–5 × 1 × 1 cm)*

Place one stick on a salmon slice. Roll up and secure with a toothpick.

SMOKED SALMON CUCUMBER ROLLS
(Smoked Salmon *Kyūri Maki*)   ★ *page 158*

1. Cut cucumber into 2 pieces about 3″ (8 cm) long. Peel the skin if it is hard.
2. With a thin, sharp knife, peel cucumber like unrolling rolled paper. Soak in salted water to make it pliable. Discard the center.
3. Spread the cucumber and place thin slices of smoked salmon to fit. Roll them tightly. Wrap with plastic sheet and refrigerate 1–2 hours.
4. Unwrap and cut into slices.

6″ (16 cm) long straight cucumber
2–3 oz. (60–80 g) lox type smoked salmon

TUNA AND GREEN ONION *TSUKEYAKI*
(*Maguro to Negi Tsukeyaki*)

Tuna and green onions on bamboo skewers may be broiled like Broiled Shrimp, or sautéed in a pan.

1. Skewer tuna alternately with green onions.
2. Heat the oil in a frying pan. Arrange the skewers in pan and sauté both sides over medium heat. Pour the oil out of the pan.
3. Add the mixed sauce. Cover and cook 3–4 minutes, turning once.
4. Uncover and boil down the sauce, shaking the pan, and coating both sides.
5. Sprinkle with *sansho* powder or black pepper and serve.

¼ lb. tuna cut into strips 1″ (2.5 cm) long
1 bunch green onions, cut 1″ (2.5 cm) long
3 tablespoons soy sauce and 2 tablespoons mirin, mixed
2 tablespoons salad oil
Sansho powder or black pepper
Short bamboo skewers

MARINATED FRIED FISH (*Kisu Nanbanzuke*)

1. Cut the belly of the fish and remove entrails. Rinse with water.
2. Sprinkle with a little salt and let stand 10 minutes. Rinse again and wipe dry with a paper towel.
3. Boil the marinade. Add red pepper and onion slices and cool.
4. Fry the fish, starting at lower temperature of 320°F. (160°C.). to make the fish crisp to the bones. Drain.
5. Place the hot fried fish in a container and pour over the marinade. Let stand for 30 minutes. Serve with lemon slices.

¼ lb. white bait or smelt
1 small onion, sliced thin to make rings
1 red cayenne pepper, seeded and cut into small rings
3 slices of lemon, each slice cut into quarters
Oil for frying

Marinade:
2 tablespoons soy sauce
1 tablespoon mirin
3 tablespoons dashi or sake
3 tablespoons vinegar
Boil and cool

FRIED SMELTS (*Kisu Kara Age*)   ★ *page 158*

¼ lb. smelt or white bait
Oil for frying
Salt

1. Split the bellies and remove entrails. Rinse and wash with water.
2. Sprinkle with a little salt and let stand 10 minutes. Rinse with water and wipe the fish dry with paper towels.
3. Deep-fry the fish, starting at lower temperature of 320°F. (160°C.) to make the fish crisp to the bones. Drain on paper towels.
4. Sprinkle some salt over the fish and serve.

SEA URCHIN (*Wuni*)

This curious shellfish, considered an utter nuisance by many, offers us a delicacy much appreciated by the Japanese. The yellow morsel is like the coral of crab or lobster.

RAW SEA URCHIN ROE (*Nama Wuni*)

Eat raw like *sashimi* with soy sauce and *wasabi* paste. Or with soy sauce and lemon juice. Also used for topping of *Nigiri Zushi*.

BOTTLED SEASONED *WUNI*
(*Neri Wuni*)   ★ *page 158*

This *wuni* paste is seasoned with salt and alcohol. It may be served as is, in a very small quantity, or make a small mound of grated cucumber or daikon seasoned with Vinegar Dressing (page 212) in a dainty cup and top with *wuni* paste.

WUNI DRESSING (*Wuni-ae*)

Grind the bottled seasoned *wuni* in a mortar with a pestle. Dilute with a little *sake*.

Use as a dressing with mixed materials such as abalone, scallops, squid (raw or blanched), raw halibut or sea bass. Vegetables good with *wuni* dressing include boiled bamboo shoots, avocado, jicama, etc.

WUNI GLAZED EGGS (*Tamago Wuni-yaki*)

1. Cut the eggs into 5 or 6 slices. If using quail eggs, just halve them and cut a slice off ends of eggs so they will stand up.
2. Arrange the slices on a baking dish and spread the cut surfaces with the glaze.
3. Place in the upper shelf of the oven and broil a couple of minutes just to dry the glaze but not to brown.

Note: Other suitable materials are slices of fish cake and bamboo shoot. Also, *shiitake* mushroom caps, butterflied prawns and sliced scallops (already broiled) are good.

Wuni Glaze:
2 tablespoons bottled seasoned wuni
1 egg yolk
Mix all together.

3 hard-boiled eggs (or 8 boiled quail eggs, canned)

MISO-MARINATED TOFU (*Tofu Misozuke*)

Make a *miso* bed and follow the directions for pickling given in the recipe for Amber Eggs (page 185).

1. Place the whole *tofu* in a pot, cover with water.
2. Bring to a boil. Simmer for 10 minutes. Drain.
3. Place on a board, cover with another board to press it down. Let this stand for 1 hour to drain the water from the *tofu*.
4. Pickle in mixed *miso* on a double thickness of cheese cloth for 2 to 3 days in the refrigerator. Cut into slices 1″ × 1″ × ⅓″ (2.5 × 2.5 × 0.8 cm). If left longer in the *miso*, it will become too salty, so remove from the *miso* bed and keep in the refrigerator.

1 loaf of regular tofu

VEGETABLE APPETIZERS

RAW VEGETABLES WITH *MISO*
(*Nama Yasai to Miso*)

This is "finger food." The raw vegetables sticks are dipped into *miso* and eaten.

Three to five kinds of assorted vegetables, choosing from carrots, celery, cucumber, daikon, jicama, green onions, radishes with small leaves, etc.

Dipping Sauce:
½ tablespoon per person "moromi"—grainy miso sold in jars, or miso paste.
To make miso paste, mix 3 tablespoons miso, white or red; 3 tablespoons sake, and 1 teaspoon—1 tablespoon sugar. Heat over low heat until dissolved and cool.

MARINATED VEGETABLES

Suitable vegetables are carrots, celery, cucumber daikon, *jicama. Cut vegetables into sticks about 2″ × ⅓″ × ⅓″ (5 × 1 × 1 cm)*

Marinade:
2 tablespoons vinegar
2 tablespoons sake or dashi
½–1 teaspoon sugar
½ teaspoon salt
Mix all and boil to dissolve. Cool.

Marinate the vegetable sticks for 10–15 minutes. Drain and serve.

MARINATED *DAIKON* WITH GREEN SEAWEED (*Sudaikon Aonori Mabushi*)

Marinated daikon *(jicama is also good). See recipe above.*
Green seaweed, crumbled or chopped parsley

Roll drained *daikon* or jicama in *aonori* just before serving. Chopped parsley may be used in place of *aonori*.

VEGETABLES WITH *NORI WASABI* SOY SAUCE

Nori Wasabi *Soy Sauce:*
2 tablespoons soy sauce (may add 1 tablespoon dashi)
1 teaspoon wasabi *paste (to make, mix* wasabi *powder with water)*
1 sheet of nori, *toasted and crumbled*

Choose one from:
Avocado, cubed
Daikon *or* jicama, shredded
Potato, blanched *(page 198)*

1. Toast the *nori* sheet over medium heat, turning often to toast evenly all over, until it is crisp and the color is slightly lighter with a greenish tinge. Crumble in a paper bag. Take care not to burn the *nori*, but if it is not toasted long enough it will not crumble.
2. Just before serving, mix the sauce with one of the following vegetables and serve:

VEGETABLES MIXED WITH LEMON *MISO* (*Lemon Miso-ae*)

2 tablespoons white miso *paste*
¼ teaspoon grated lemon rind

Grated lemon rind resembles the Japanese citrus fruit called *yuzu* and adds a similar flavor.

Mix with cubed avocado or shredded *daikon* or jicama.

BOILED VEGETABLES

BOILED FAVA BEANS OR BOILED FRESH SOY BEANS

These simple, salt-boiled beans are a favorite snack at home and as an appetizer at restaurants in Japan. From May to June fava beans (*soramame*) are served, and from July to August fresh soy beans (*edamame*) are served.

FAVA BEANS (*Soramame*)
Shell the beans. Cook in boiling, salted water until tender. Drain and rinse with cold water. Sprinkle with salt. Squeeze the beans out of their skins when you eat them.

FRESH SOY BEANS (*Edamame*)
Cut off both ends of the shells. Cook in boiling, salted water until the beans inside are tender. Drain and rinse with cold water. Sprinkle with salt. Serve with the shells and eat them by squeezing out the individual beans.

BOILED ASPARAGUS OR BROCCOLI WITH *MISO*

Cook asparagus or broccoli in boiling salted water until just tender but still crisp. Serve with *miso* glaze, either white or red (page 126.)

ENOKI MUSHROOM MARINATED SALAD
(*Enoki Dake Su-bitashi*)

These delicate white mushrooms with stems like bean sprouts are now cultivated on the West Coast. Always wash and blanch first.

1 *bag* enoki *mushrooms*

Marinade:
2 *tablespoons vinegar*
1 *tablespoon each* sake, *soy* sauce *and* dashi
Boil together and cool.

1. Wash the mushrooms. Cut off the yellowed root part.
2. Drop into boiling water and drain immediately.
3. Rinse with cold water. Cut into 1½" (4 cm) lengths.
4. Marinate for 30 minutes in the refrigerator. Serve with the sauce.

CHILLED WHITE WATERFALL (*Hiyashi Shirataki*)

Thin, white *konnyaku* noodles (*sukiyaki* noodles) are called white waterfall—"*shirataki*" in Japanese. Serve them well chilled in small glass cups with cold soup when the weather is hot. This has no calories and is very cooling.

For 4 servings:
1 cup konnyaku *noodles, parboiled and cut 3" (8 cm) long*

Soup:
1 cup dashi
2 tablespoons soy sauce
1 tablespoon lemon juice

Condiment:
½ tablespoon chopped parsley

1. Parboil *konnyaku* noodles for a few minutes.
2. Chill the drained noodles and the soup.
3. Divide the noodles into cups, pour over the soup, top with the condiment and serve.

Note: Beanthread vermicelli, "*harusame*" (page 20), is also good served like this.

BLANCHED POTATO (*Yutōshi Jagaimo*)

Peel and shred potato into matchsticks. Boil for 2–3 minutes—just long enough to tenderize a little but still crunchy. Drain and rinse with water. This most ubiquitous vegetable now becomes something else. Mix with *Nori Wasabi Jōyu* or Lemon *Miso* (page 196).

BROILED MUSHROOMS (*Yaki Kinoko*)

Mushrooms, *shiitake*, or *shimeji* (abalone or oyster mushrooms) are broiled, brushed with soy sauce, and then broiled dry. To serve, thread on pine needles.

MISO-MARINATED ASPARAGUS
(*Asparagus Misozuke*)

Boil green asparagus until half tender in salted boiling water. Rinse with water and drain. Pickle for 1 hour in *miso* bed, following directions on page 185. Broccoli stems, peeled and boiled, can be pickled the same way.

MISO-MARINATED CELERY (Celery *Misozuke*)

Pickle raw celery in *miso* for 30 minutes. Left any longer, the celery will become soggy.

DRY TIDBITS ★ *page 157*

Deep-fried tidbits can be made ahead and kept in cans. If you make several kinds in leaf shapes, you can make a picturesque basket of fall leaves (*fukiyose*), suitable for fall.

FRIED KELP LEAVES

1. Wipe the kelp with a well-wrung cloth to soften a little. Cut into leaf shapes, like chestnut leaves. Or cut into 1″ (2.5 cm) square or strips ½″ × 4″ (1.3 × 10 cm) following the grain, and tie to make knots. Soften the kelp by wiping with a well-wrung cloth.)
2. Deep-fry at 325°F. (165°C.) until crisp but not browned. Dry on paper towels. Take care not to burn.

Dashi Kombu (kelp)

Knot

GINGKO LEAF POTATO CHIPS

1. Slice ⅛″ (2 mm) crosswise and soak in water for 30 minutes.
2. Drain and cut into gingko leaf shape, using a round biscuit cutter slightly larger than the potato slice.
3. Dry and deep fry until crisp. Drain on paper towels and sprinkle with salt.

Yellow colored yam or potato

RED LEAVES (*Momiji*)

Use carrots. If they are not very thick, cut on the slant and then cut them into leaf shapes with a vegetable cutter. Deep-fry and sprinkle with salt.

Fried

NOODLE PINE NEEDLES (*Soba Matsuba*)

1. Cut noodles into 2–3″ (5–7.5 cm) lengths, depending on the size you want.
2. Hold two noodles together, roll one end with the *nori* strip, and seal with a bit of paste.
3. Deep-fry at high temperature for a few seconds. Noodles will open to look like pine needles.

Green tea noodles (cha soba)
  or spinach vermicelli
Nori *sheets cut into strips*
  ¼″ × ½″ (6 × 12 mm)
Paste made by mixing flour
  with water

FRIED GINGKO NUTS (*Age Gin-nan*)

Drain the nuts. Dry with paper towel and deep-fry. Sprinkle with salt. To serve, thread them on pine needles.

1 jar boiled gingko nuts

ROASTED CHESTNUTS (*Yakiguri*)

Make a slit on the shells and roast the chestnuts in 400°F. (210°C.) oven for 25 minutes. Crack and remove the shell and skin when they are cool.

TOASTED SWEET CHESTNUTS
(*Kuri Amani Yakime*)

1 jar chestnuts in syrup

Drain and wash the chestnuts. Wipe them dry and arrange on a baking sheet. Broil to brown lightly.

ASSEMBLING A BASKET OF FALL LEAVES

Arrange the leaves and nuts in a large basket for a table centerpiece or in small baskets for individual servings.

Soups

At a Japanese dinner, the moment I love best is when, with expectation, I lift the lid of the soup bowl and sniff the aroma of some seasonal herb while my eyes feast on the picture of garnishes set off by the deep color of a lacquer bowl! A formal Japanese soup bowl always comes with a lid, not only to keep the soup hot, but also to seal in the aroma and to provide an element of surprise!

It is said that a good chef is known by the excellence of his soup. *Suimono*, the clear Japanese soup, is very light, yet it has a distinct flavor which comes only from good and fresh materials. It looks so simple and natural, yet one gets a very rich feeling from the multiple effects of aroma, color, taste and the seasonal message of this soup.

Bonito *dashi* is the base. For clear soup it is preferable to use *dashi* made from bonito flakes and *kombu* (page 42) rather than instant *dashi*. Or use unseasoned, degreased chicken broth which has been chilled in the refrigerator and strained. Seasonings for clear soups are salt and soy sauce. The darker the color of the soup (which means it contains more soy sauce), the more country-style it is. The lighter the color (meaning less soy sauce), the more elegant. If you have "*usukuchi*," light colored soy sauce, use it. Also, in summer, one should use less soy sauce than in the winter.

There are infinite varieties and combinations of garnishes. It is a challenge, but also fun, to create combinations—almost like making "*Ikebana*"—a Japanese flower arrangement.

Of the aromatic herbs or spices added to the soup bowl at the last moment before it is covered, the ones used most often in Japan are "*kinomé*"—the fresh leaf of *sansho* (prickly ash), used from spring to summer, and the rind of "*yuzu*" (a citrus fruit), used from the end of summer to winter. There is no substitute for "*kinomé*." In California there are Japanese nurseries which have the prickly ash tree (page 30). Lemon rind, especially from home grown lemons, is very good. Lemon flowers can also be a nice addition. Some decorative cuts of lemon rind are shown on page 51.

Use your creativity for spices to add to the soup.

BASIC CLEAR SOUP (*Suimono*)

For 4–6 servings
4 cups dashi *(page 42)*
(First Soup Stock)

For Lighter Soup:
  ¾ teaspoon salt
  1 teaspoon soy sauce
  A dash of MSG

For Darker Soup:
  ½ teaspoon salt
  2 teaspoons—1 tablespoon
    soy sauce
  A dash of MSG

1. Add the salt to the *dashi* and heat.
2. When it comes to a boil, add soy sauce and MSG and immediately lower the heat. Taste, and if it is right, pour into serving bowls containing pre-warmed garnishes. Add herbs or spices. Cover and serve immediately.

Note: For cooking or warming garnishes, use second *dashi* (page 43) or *dashi* made with instant *dashi*. Greens like *mitsuba* (trefoil), spinach, green onions or celery leaves to add aroma are added to the soup at the last minute.

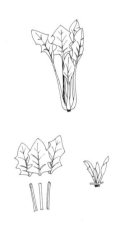

Easy Garnishes:
Tofu, kamaboko (fishcake), *kani kamaboko* (crab fishcake) can all be cut into many shapes and warmed in the soup. Cubed, cut into sticks, made into knots, or cut with a vegetable cutter into flower or leaf shapes all produce varied looks. Kosher fish balls sold in jars can also be used. Eggs are used in many ways also. Wheat gluten cakes (*fu*) come in dainty shapes. There is a mushroom-shaped kind called "*matsutake fu*" with the aroma of pine mushrooms. Soak in water to soften. Squeeze water out and add to soup.

Green Garnishes:
Spinach can be separated, leaves from stems, using just the stems for the soup and the leaves for "*aemono*," or vice versa. Or use the tiny center part of a bunch for soup.
Cucumber slices, Cucumber rings: Cut off ends, remove seeds, slice

Okra: Whole, or sliced to make stars.

Pasta:
Tiny shells, spinach ribbons, spinach spaghetti, wheel macaroni etc.
These are very good. Cook until tender (not al dente).

SAMPLE COMBINATIONS FOR *MISO* SOUP

MAIN GARNISH	SHAPE	SECOND GARNISH	THIRD GARNISH	SPICE
Poached eggs. Drop into soup and cook		Spinach or Watercress		Pepper
Egg *Tofu* (page 115)		Boiled shrimp	Cucumber rings	Grated ginger
1) Flower-shaped hard-boiled eggs (page 204)		Simmered *shiitake* lightly seasoned	*Daikon* sprouts	*Kinome* or lemon rind

MAIN GARNISH	SHAPE	SECOND GARNISH	THIRD GARNISH	SPICE
2) Stirred Egg Soup (page 204)		Toasted crumbled *nori* or chopped parsley		
Kamaboko Flower cut with vegetable cutter		Wheat gluten cake or shell macaroni	Spinach small center leaves (page 202)	Lemon rind or *kinome*
Kamaboko cubes		Wheat gluten cakes	Green onions, shredded	*Wasabi* paste
Chikuwa slices		Wheel macaroni	Cucumber rings	Lemon slices
Crab fishcake		Snow peas or string beans	*Mitsuba* or celery leaves	Lemon rind
Tofu squares in chicken broth		Green onions, chopped		Pepper
3) *Tofu* "Hazy Full Moon" Thickened Soup (page 204)		Crab meat	String beans, shredded	*Wasabi* paste
4) Chicken slices coated with cornstarch (page 205)		Mushrooms	*Mitsuba* or celery leaves	Lemon rind or *kinome*
Chicken, shredded		*Enoki* mushrooms	Cucumber slices	Lemon rind
5) Chicken meatballs (page 205)		Vermicelli or *harusamé* (page 20)	Watercress	Grated ginger
Chicken livers, parboiled		*Tofu* cubes	Green onion, shredded	Parsley, ginger juice**
Prawns or shrimp shelled & parboiled		Mushrooms	Snow peas or *daikon* sprouts	*kinome* or lemon rind
Tofu cubes		Carrot maple leaves cut with vegetable cutter	Abalone mushrooms	Green lemon rind
Scallops, large or small		Pine mushroom wheat gluten cakes	Spinach leaves	Lemon rind or lemon flowers
6) White-meat Fish "Shinjo" (page 205)		Spinach spaghetti or ribbon	*Shungiku* or watercress	Lemon slice or *kinome*
7) Clams in shells, Clam Seawater Soup (page 205)				Ginger juice**
8) White-meat Fish Seawater Soup (*Ushio Jiru*) (page 206)				Lemon slice, ginger juice, or *kinomé*
9) Sardine balls (page 206)		Green onions, shredded		Ginger juice**

(Slice of potato or *daikon*)

For 4 servings:
4 cups basic clear soup
  (page 202). Make the darker
  soup and increase the salt
  $1/4$–$1/2$ teaspoons since eggs
  absorb it.
2 tablespoons sake
A pinch of MSG
2 tablespoons cornsarch mixed
  with 2 tablespoons water
2 eggs
$1/2$ sheet toasted crumbled
  nori (or chopped parsley)

For 4 servings:
4 cups basic, clear dark soup
  (increase salt to 1 teaspoon)
2 tablespoons sake
2 oz. (60 g) crab meat
2 tablespoons cornstarch, mixed with 2 tablespoons dashi
  or water
4 rounds of soft tofu cut with
  a biscuit cutter 2" (5 cm)
  diameter
4 string beans or snow peas,
  thinly cut and parboiled
$1/4$ teaspoon wasabi paste (mix
  $1/4$ teaspoon wasabi powder
  with $1/4$ teaspoon water)

MAIN GARNISH	SHAPE	SECOND GARNISH	THIRD GARNISH	SPICE
10) Winter Melon (or cucumber) Thickened Soup (page 207)		Chicken, bite sized		Grated ginger ..
11) Vegetable Medley Soup (*Sawani Wan*) (page 207)		Shredded burdock, carrot, bamboo shoot, *shiitake*, celery, *mitsuba* stems, pork fat		Pepper

*Toast *nori* until crisp and crumble.   **Add *sake* to grated ginger and squeeze.

CHART NUMBER EXPLANATIONS: ★ *page 160*

1)   Flower-Shaped Hard-Boiled Eggs (Egg Plum Flowers)

Crack hot eggs in cold water and peel. While eggs are still warm, press 5 chopsticks around eggs, as shown. Press ends of chopsticks into a slice of regetable such as potato or *daikon*. Bind the ends of the chopsticks and let the eggs cool. Slice into 5 or 6 pieces. One egg makes 2 servings.

2)   Stirred Egg Soup (*Kakitama Jiru*)

Heat the soup with additional seasonings and thicken with cornstarch. Lightly beat the eggs to break, pour into a gently simmering soup in a slow stream, stirring with a wire whisk. Turn off the heat immediately.

   Pour into soup bowls; add crumbled *nori* or chopped parsley and serve.

3)   HAZY FULL MOON SOUP
(*Mangetsu Dofu Kani Surinagashi Jiru*)

Warm the *tofu* rounds in salted simmering water. Process the crab meat in a food processor and gradually add *dashi*. Heat the crab meat soup gradually, stirring. Add the string beans, and add the cornstarch to thicken. Carefully transfer the warmed *tofu* to serving bowls, pour the soup over, drop in a bit of *wasabi*, cover the bowl and serve.

Note: White-fish meat or chicken may be used in place of crab.

4) CHICKEN COATED WITH CORNSTARCH
(*Tori no Kuzutataki*)

Slice chicken breast very thin, diagonally. Salt lightly, sprinkle with cornstarch and tap slices to coat them evenly. Shake off any excess cornstarch and add to the simmering soup. Cook for one minute, add green garnish and serve.

For 4 servings:
8 thin slices of chicken breast
Salt
Cornstarch

Note: Thinly sliced chicken cooks very fast; when overcooked it becomes less succulent. White meat fish slices may be treated the same way.

5) CHICKEN MEATBALLS (*Tori Dango*)

Chop and pound the chicken on a cutting board. This does not take very long. Mix with green onion and egg white. Gradually add the cornstarch-water mix to make a soft mixture. With a food processor, the chicken will become smoother and more solid, so add more liquid (*sake* or *dashi*).

To make the meatballs family style, drop by teaspoonsfuls into the simmering soup, skim and serve. For serving company, cook in salted water and then add to the soup.

For 4 servings:
4 cups basic clear, light soup
½ cup chicken breast, skinned (½ of a chicken breast)
¼ teaspoon salt
1 tablespoon green onion, chopped
1 egg white (or 2 yolks, or ½ whole egg)
2 tablespoons cornstarch mixed with 2 tablespoons water

6) WHITEMEAT FISH DUMPLINGS
(*Shiromi-zakana Shinjo*)

Preparation for these is similar to the chicken meatballs above. These can be made with chicken, shrimp, scallops, etc. A food processor does the work!

Process fish meat with salt in a food processor until smooth. Add egg white and mix. Gradually add cornstarch water with the machine running. Then add enough *dashi* to make a soft mixture that drops easily from a spoon.

Line custard cups or teacups or a larger mold with plastic sheets. Spoon in the fish mousse and flatten and smooth the top.

Steam for about 10–15 minutes, depending upon the thickness and size of the molds, until set. Test with a bamboo skewer.

For 4 servings:
½ cup white-fish meat, boned, skinned and chopped
¼ teaspoon salt
1 egg white
2 tablespoons cornstarch mixed with 1 tablespoon water and 1 tablespoon sake
1–3 tablespoons dashi

7) CLAM SEAWATER SOUP
(*Hamaguri Ushio Jitate*)

Do not make this soup unless the clams in shells are absolutely fresh and alive! To test for freshness, the shells may be slightly open, but if you touch them, they will close if alive. Even one bad clam will spoil the entire soup. Another way to test for

For 4 servings:
8–12 small clams
4 cups water
1 tablespoon sake
Salt to taste
Few drops of soy sauce

Optional: 2″ (5 cm) square of
   kombu
2 teaspoons ginger juice

freshness is to hit two clams together. If they make a clean, hard sound, they are fresh.

Spread clams in one layer in a pan. Mix one cup water and 1 teaspoon salt and pour over the clams to barely cover them. Leave in a cool dark place for 2–3 hours. The clams will excrete any sand they contain. Wash and scrub the shells.

Heat the water with the optional *kombu*. Soak for half an hour and remove the *kombu* when small bubbles start to rise.

Add the clams to the water and cover. When the liquid comes to a boil and all the clams have opened, add the *sake* and salt. Strain the soup. Add soy sauce, taste and correct the seasoning. Divide the clams into bowls, add the strained soup, drop in ginger juice and serve.

8) WHITE FISH SEAWATER SOUP
(*Sakana Ushio Jiru*)

"*Ushio*" means sea water, and "*ushio jiru*" means fish soup made without *dashi* and seasoned with salt. Good fish for this soup are striped bass (*suzuki*), sea bream (*tai*) and red snapper. The soup is made using the head, back bones and bellies, reserving the better parts of the fish for *sashimi* or broiling.

For 4 servings:
½ lb. (225 g) white fish bones,
   bellies and head
¼ cup sake
1 teaspoon salt
Few drops or soy sauce

Optional: 2″ (5 cm) square of
   kombu
4 Prickly ash leaves (kinome,
   page 30) or 2 slices lemon
   quartered

1. Sprinkle cut up fish liberally with salt to draw out the fishy juices and let it stand half an hour. Place the fish in a basket tray and pour boiling water over it. Rinse with cold water and wash well. Treated this way, fish soup will not be fishy.
2. Cover the fish with water and *sake*. Add the optional *kombu* and bring to a boil. When small bubbles start to rise, remove the *kombu* and discard. Skim and simmer for 15 minutes.
3. Add salt, soy sauce and taste. Strain the soup and serve with some fish. Float "*kinome*" or two quarters or lemon slices as the garnish.

For 4–6 servings:
½ lb. (225 g) sardines,
   heads and bones removed
1 egg
2 tablespoons wheat flour
1 tablespoon cornstarch
3 tablespoons red, salty
   miso
½ teaspoon ginger juice
   (to make, mix 1 teaspoon
   grated ginger with ½ tablespoon water and squeeze)
2–3 tablespoons dashi
Mix all together.

4 cups basic dark soup

9) SARDINE BALL SOUP
(*Iwashi Tsumire Jiru*)

This is a family style soup. Other blue fish such as jack mackerel or mackerel, are also good.

In a food processor, work the sardines until the mixture sticks together. Add the other ingredients and mix well.

Drop by spoonfuls into simmering, dark *dashi*. Skim. When fishballs rise to the surface, add shredded green onions. Taste the soup and add salt and soy sauce to your taste.

10) WINTER MELON SOUP
(*Tōgan Yoshino Jitate*)

Boil the winter melon with water to cover and a little salt until translucent and tender. Drain, add fresh water and soak for 10 minutes and drain.

Boil the soup, add chicken and melon and reduce to simmer for 15 minutes. Remove scum and taste. Correct the seasoning if necessary. Thicken by mixing in the cornstarch mixture.

Pour soup into serving bowls and add a bit of grated ginger. This soup is also good served well-chilled.

"*Tōgan*" (winter melon) is so called because of its frosty appearance, even though it grows only in summer. It has a very bland taste, but the translucent look and the texture is interesting. Use a rich *dashi* or chicken broth.

For 4 servings:
½ lb. (225 g) winter melon, peeled and cut into chunks
¼ lb. (110 g) chicken, cut into bite size

For the Soup:
4 cups dashi or chicken broth, degreased
1 teaspoon salt
1 teaspoon soy sauce
A dash of MSG
1 tablespoon ginger, grated
2 tablespoons cornstarch mixed with 2 tablespoons water

11) VEGETABLE MEDLEY SOUP
(*Sawani Wan*)

This is an unusual soup using pork fat and pepper. The key point here is not to overcook the vegetables. They should retain some crunchiness.

1. Cut the pork fat into matchsticks. Sprinkle with salt and let it stand 5–10 minutes. Meanwhile, shred all the vegetables into fine matchsticks.
2. Wash the pork fat and blanch for a second or two in boiling water and drain.
3. Boil the *dashi* with the pork fat and the salt for 1 minute and remove pork. Add vegetables (except *mitsuba*) in the order listed. Skim.
4. When the vegetables are slightly cooked and still crisp, add the *mitsuba* stems and soy sauce, and turn off the heat.
5. Pour into bowls, sprinkle with pepper and serve.

Note: A missing ingredient here is "*wudo*" which is similar to asparagus but has a unique aroma and flavor that spells spring. Here celery is substituted, but fennel may also be used.

4 servings:
1 oz. (30 g) fat from pork loin
½ teaspoon salt
¼ cup each shredded
    Burdock (soaked in water)
    Carrot
    Bamboo shoots
    Daikon
    Celery
    Green onion
    Shiitake *mushroom*
2 tablespoons mitsuba (trefoil), stems cut into pieces 1″ (2.5 cm)
4 cups dashi or chicken broth
1½ teaspoons salt
1 teaspoon soy sauce
Pepper

CUSTARD SOUP

Custard Soup (*Chawan Mushi* page 113) and Chilled Custard Soup (*Hiyashi Chawan Mushi* page 114) are also served as soup.

MISO SOUP (*Miso Shiru*)

In a traditional Japanese breakfast *miso* soup is the main item eaten with rice, eggs, fish and pickles. But it is also served for lunch or dinner. The difference is that for breakfast, the garnishes are usually light and simple like *tofu*, vegetables or seaweed, while for lunch or dinner they may be richer and more varied.

Formal dinners often have two soups, one at the beginning after hors d'ouevres (*zensai*) and another soup at the end of the entrée courses served with rice and pickles. Usually the first one is a clear soup (occasionally this may be *miso* soup), and the second one is a *miso* soup. A simpler dinner has one soup either at the beginning or end of the meal.

See pages 37 for the various kinds of *miso*. In wintertime more white *miso* is used—perhaps because it is mild and rich tasting. In summer more red *miso* is used because it has a clean, sharp taste to perk up lagging appetites. Try several kinds of *miso* and decide which ones you like best. If you have red *miso* and mild, white *miso*, you can mix the two in various proportions to suit the garnishes and your menu.

While clear soup is delicate and elegant, *miso* soup is robust. So it can handle stronger spices. Experiment with various spices in *miso* soups—you may discover something new! But be careful never to use so much spice that the soup and garnishes are overpowered.

BASIC *MISO* SOUP (*Miso Shiru*)

1. Heat the *dashi* and add garnishes to cook in the soup unless the garnish is one that darkens the soup—in that case cook it separately.
2. Place *miso* in a small bowl, add a little *dashi* and stir with a whisk to dissolve.
3. When the garnishes are cooked, add the dissolved *miso*. (Or, using a small colander, you may dissolve the *miso* right in the soup.) Either way, after the *miso* is added to the soup, it should be served immediately. If you boil it longer, the *miso*'s aroma will be lost.

For 4 servings:
4 cups dashi
¼ cup miso (*1 tablespoon per cup of* dashi)

SAMPLE COMBINATIONS FOR *MISO* SOUP

MAIN GARNISH	*MISO*	SECOND GARNISH	THIRD GARNISH	SPICE
Tofu cubes (soft *tofu*)	White	Mushrooms	*Shungiku* or spinach	Mustard*
Tofu cubes	Mixed	*Wakamé* (sea weed) or cabbage		Mustard*
Tofu, crushed	Red	Crab meat		Green onions chopped
Agé (fried *tofu* puffs), cut in strips	Red	Onion, cabbage, or dried *daikon*		Powdered *sansho***
Agé strips	Red	*Daikon* or turnips	Carrot slice, *konnyaku* strips	7-taste pepper***
Chicken, bite-sized	Mixed	Turnips or *daikon*		Powdered *sansho***
Chicken, bite-sized	Red	Green asparagus		7-taste pepper***
Chiken meatballs (page 205)	White	Small white onions (canned)	Okra stars	Mustard*
Beef, bite-sized slices	Mixed	Celery	Snow peas or string beans	7-taste pepper***
Pork, bite-sized slices	*Aka dashi*	Boiled winter melon cubes	Chives or green onion rings	Powdered *sansho***
Egg *Tofu* (p. 115) (This soup may be chilled)	*Aka dashi*	Okra stars		Lemon flower

MAIN GARNISH	MISO	SECOND GARNISH	THIRD GARNISH	SPICE
Avocado, wedges or cubes	Aka dashi	Tofu cubes	Chopped parsley	Nutmeg
White-meat fish (chunk size) or fish cake squares	Aka dashi	Mitsuba or watercress or green onions		Lemon rind
Baked eggplant (page 138) wedges or slices	Aka dashi	Cucumber rings		Mustard*
Chicken, boiled and shredded	Aka dashi	Enoki mushroom		7-taste pepper***
Taro, thick slices	Mixed	Parboiled celery		Toasted white sesame
Mushrooms (any kind)	Mixed	Shungiku or spinach		Powdered sansho**
Pumpkin, chunks	Mixed	Spinach ribbon pasta		Cloves
Yam, sliced	Mixed	Tomato slices		Cinnamon
Oyster (add milk)	White	Abalone mushrooms	Watercress	Powdered sansho**

*Mustard for dropping into the soup is made by mixing equal amounts of dry mustard powder and water.
**Sansho powder—see page 30.
***Seven-taste pepper—see page 26.

"Aka dashi" means red soup. There are prepared blends of aka dashi miso sold in packages. It makes a delicious soup, but should not be boiled long or the flavor becomes slightly bitter.

STEW TYPE SOUPS

These are more substantial soups with meat or fish simmered along with the vegetables and they make meals by themselves.

PORK MISO SOUP (Buta Jiru)

For 4 servings:
5 cups dashi
1/4 lb. (110 g) pork, cut bite size
(Use pork shoulder or fresh bacon—pork with some fat)

1. Place the pork and ginger in a pot, cover with dashi and bring to a boil. Remove scum.
2. Add the burdock, carrot, daikon, taro and onion and simmer until vegetables are tender about 30 minutes.
3. Blend in the miso. Taste and correct the seasoning.

4. At the last minute, add the green onions. When the soup returns to the boil, remove from the heat, add some seven-taste pepper and serve.

Note: This type of soup tastes better when made in quantity. It is also good the following day reheated.

1 or 2 slices of ginger, chopped
½ cup burdock (gobo), shredded and soaked in water. If unavailable, just omit.
½ cup carrot, sliced
½ cup onion, sliced
½ cup taro, peeled and sliced thick. Salt and wash.
½–¾ cup daikon, quartered and sliced
2–2½ tablespoons each red and white miso
½ cup green onions, cut ½" (1.2 cm) long
Seven-taste pepper

CHICKEN *MISO* SOUP (*Satsuma Jiru*)

Satsuma is the name of an old province at the southern end of Kyushu Island where this soup originated. It is similar to Pork *Miso* Soup, except chicken with bones is used instead of pork. First simmer the chicken in plenty of water or *dashi* until tender, and proceed as for Pork *Miso* Soup. Half a chicken will serve 6–8 people or you may use 6–8 wings, cut up.

MISO SOUP WITH DUMPLINGS
(*Suiton Jiru*)

1. Boil all the vegetables except the green onions and the *tofu* puff in *dashi* until tender. Skim.
2. Mix the flour with water to make a smooth batter.
3. With a wet spoon, drop the batter by spoonfuls into the simmering soup.
4. When the dumplings rise to the surface, add the *miso* which has been thinned and blended with a little soup.
5. When this comes back to a boil., add the green onions and remove from the heat.
6. Serve in generous sized bowls. Pass seven-taste pepper.

For 4 servings:
4 cups dashi or chicken broth
¾ cup daikon, quartered and sliced
½ cup carrot, sliced
½ cup onion, sliced
½ cup taro or potato, sliced thick
1 or 2 fried tofu puffs, cut into strips
2 stalks green onions, cut up
4 tablespoons miso of your choice—one kind or two mixed

Dumplings:
1 cup wheat flour (all-purpose), sifted
½ cup water

Salads

In Japanese cuisine, salad consists of *"sunomono"* (vinegared foods), *"aé-mono"* (foods mixed with dressings), and *"hitashi-mono"* (blanched and marinated foods).

Salads may be served as side dishes or as appetizers at the beginning of a dinner in small, dainty bowls. Or a salad may be passed around in a large serving bowl. However, the popularity of the Western salad in Japan has led to new varieties which closely resemble Western salads.

Seasoned Vinegar Dressing and Sweet Vinegar Dressing are the basic mixes from which many types of dressings are made. Use rice vinegar, available at Japanese markets, for the best results. If not available, substitute wine vinegar.

VINEGAR DRESSING						SWEET VINEGAR DRESSING
For about ¼ cup:	Vinegar	*Dashi*	Soy Sauce	Salt	Optional	
Basic Vinegar Dressing	2 T.	2 T.	1 T.		MSG	Add 1 t. –1½ T. sugar to any dressing.
Light-colored	2 T.	2 T.	½ t.	¼ t.	MSG	
Colorless	2 T.	2 T.		⅓ t.	MSG	
Instant Chicken Bouillon	2 T.	½ t. instant bouillon + 2 T. water	1½ t.			
Lemon Juice	1–1½ T. lemon juice	3 T. *sake**	1 t.	¼ t.	¼ t. *mirin**	

Sake and *mirin* add mellowness to the tart juice.

VINEGAR DRESSING (*Nihai-zu*)

This is used whenever a cleaner and sharper taste is preferred. It is also used to rinse prepared salad materials before mixing with the salad dressing to prevent sogginess.

SWEET VINEGAR DRESSING (*Sanbai-zu*)

Adding a little sugar to the Vinegar Dressing makes it a milder, all-purpose dressing suitable for many salads. Use less sugar for seafood and more for vegetables.

DRESSING MADE WITH VINEGAR DRESSING & SWEET VINEGAR DRESSING

For	To a base of ¼ cup Vinegar Dressing or Sweet Vinegar Dressing. Add	Method
Ginger Vinegar (*Shōga-zu*)	1 t. grated ginger	
Mustard Vinegar (*Karashi-zu*)	1 t. mustard powder	
Wasabi Vinegar (*Wasabi-zu*)	1 t. *wasabi* powder	
Celery Vinegar (*Celery-zu*)	1 T. celery leaves, minced	
Vinegar Glaze (*Yoshino-zu*)	½ t. cornstarch	Mix with 1 t. water and cook with the sauce.
Snowy Dressing (*Mizoré-zu*)	¼ c. *daikon**, grated and lightly squeezed	*May substitute turnips or apple. Light-color basic dressing.
Green Jade Dressing (*Mizoré-zu*)	¼ c. cucumber, grated and lightly squeezed	Use light or colorless basic dressing.
Yellow Dressing (*Kimi-zu*)	2 egg yolks	Beat yolks and gradually add sauce. Cook in a double boiler. Use colorless dressing
Tart Peanut Dressing	2 T. creamy peanut butter	Gradually add warmed dressing to the peanut butter.

OTHER SALAD DRESSINGS

Name	Main Ingredients	Soy Sauce	Salt	Sugar	Vinegar	Other
Mustard Dressing	2 t.–1 T. mustard	1½ T.		1 t.		
Miso Dressing	4 T. miso			1½–3 T.	1 T.	2 T. dashi or sake
Mustard Miso Dressing	4 T. miso 1 t. mustard			1½–3 T.	1 T.	2 T. dashi or sake
Peanut Dressing	3 T. peanut butter	1 T.				1–2 T. hot water
Sesame Dressing	4 T. white, toasted sesame seeds, ground	1–2 T.		½ t.–1 T.		2 T. dashi
Tart Sesame Dressing	4 T. white sesame, ground	½ T.	½ t.	1– 1½ T.	1 T.	1–2 T. dashi
Tofu Dressing (to Prepare see page 220)	½ c. tofu, puréed; 2 T. white sesame* ground		⅔ t.	½–1½ T.		2–3 T. dashi or cooking liquid
Tart White Dressing	Add vinegar to Tofu Dressing				2 T.	

*Sesame seeds are always used toasted. In Tofu Dressings, sesame seeds may be omitted when a smoother texture is preferred. One tablespoon creamy peanut butter may be used in place of sesame seeds.

SALADS

RAW DAIKON WITH BONITO FLAKES AND SOY SAUCE
(Daikon Okaka Jōyu)

When daikon is fresh and succulent, you don't have to do much to enjoy it. Just peel it and julienne finely. Or a shredder or a food processor may be used although the daikon will come out less crisp. Make a small pile in individual dishes and top with bonito flakes and serve. Before eating, a little soy sauce is drizzled on for the seasoning. This is crisp and refreshing.

RAW ONIONS WITH BONITO FLAKES AND SOY SAUCE
(*Tamanegi Okaka Jōyu*)

Slice onions vertically paper thin and soak in ice water for one hour. Drain well and serve like the *daikon* dish above.

CRAB MEAT WITH VINEGAR DRESSING
(*Kani no Nihai-zu*)   ★ *page 161*

Arrange a pile of crab meat, top with grated ginger and garnish with a cucumber fan (see page 49). Serve with a small *sake* cup holding the dressing.

   When you serve a platter of cracked crab, try serving Ginger Vinegar (page 213) instead of the usual melted butter. It is very refreshing.

CUCUMBER WITH SWEET VINEGAR DRESSING
(*Kyūri Momi*)   ★ *page 161*

1. Sprinkle some salt on a board and roll the unpeeled cucumber in it.
2. Rinse with boiling water, then with cold water. This makes the skin a brighter green. If the skin is hard, peel it off but leave some strips of green.
3. If the cucumber is large, cut into two lengthwise. Scoop out the seeds.
4. Slice as thin as possible.
5. Sprinkle the slices with salt and let stand 15 minutes.
6. Knead the softened cucumber slices. Squeeze out the liquid by handfuls. Taste a piece and if salty, rinse with water and squeeze out the liquid again.
7. Sprinkle 1 tablespoon Sweet Vinegar Dressing over. Mix and squeeze out the liquid.
8. Just before serving, mix with the rest of the dressing and serve in small bowls or pass around in a large bowl.

Note: A nice addition is ¼ cup cooked shrimp or crab meat mixed with ¼ teaspoon grated ginger.

For 4 servings:
1 cucumber, thin skinned Japanese or English hothouse variety
¼ cup Sweet Vinegar Dressing

DAIKON SALAD (Daikon Namasu) ★ page 161

"*Namasu*" is an ancient name for vinegared food, and when *daikon* is used, it is called *namasu*. This salad can be made ahead and kept in the refrigerator for a few days. This particular salad is one of the "musts" for New Year's tables.

For 4 servings:
1 cup daikon, *peeled and shredded, or quartered and sliced*
¼ cup carrot, cut the same as the daikon
¼ cup Sweet Vinegar Dressing (Make it sweet with colorless dressing).

Topping: 1 teaspoon lemon rind, sliced needle thin

1. Place the *daikon* and carrot in a bowl and sprinkle with about 1 teaspoon salt. Mix and let stand 15 minutes.
2. Rinse with water and squeeze out the liquid.
3. Mix with 1 tablespoon Sweet Vinegar Dressing and squeeze out the water.
4. Mix with the rest of the dressing. Sprinkle with lemon rind needles.

VARIATIONS OF NAMASU

PERSIMMON AND *DAIKON* SALAD
(*Kaki Namasu*) ★ page 161

To the *Daikon* Salad, add:
¼ cup fresh persimmon, cut into strips. Use the sweet, firm kind, like the "*fuyū*" variety, or the tail pointed "*hachiya*" persimmon treated with alcohol (page 26).

Note: This persimmon salad and the Apricot Salad are nice made with cucumber instead of *daikon*. Served in scooped out persimmons, this salad looks very festive.

APRICOT AND *DAIKON* SALAD ★ page 161
(*Anzu Namasu*)

To the *Daikon Namasu*, add:
4 dried apricots soaked in 2 tablespoons *sake* or sherry, then cut into strips. Add the liquid to the Sweet Vinegar Dressing.

STIR-FRIED *DAIKON* SALAD
(*Itame Namasu*)

This is a cooked salad with the same ingredients and quantities as *Daikon* Salad. Do not soften the vegetables by salting.

1–2 tablespoons salad oil
1 recipe Sweet Vinegar Dressing (page 212)

Heat the oil in a skillet and stir-fry the vegetables until pliable. Pour in Sweet Vinegar Dressing and stir well. Lower the heat to medium-low and cook until the liquid is evaporated. Sprinkle with needle-thin lemon rind.

216

MUSTARD VINEGAR WITH WATERCRESS AND BEEF (Watercress *to Gyūniku no Karashi-ae*)

Parboil the watercress in salted, boiling water. Drain and rinse with cold water. Cut into 1½" (4 cm) lengths and squeeze the water out. Mix with the beef and the dressing just before serving.

For 4 servings:
1 bunch watercress
¼ cup cooked beef (like left-over roast beef), cut into julienne
¼ cup mustard vinegar dressing

WASABI VINEGAR WITH RAW FISH AND CELERY (Celery *Wasabizu-ae*)

1. Parboil the celery in salted, boiling water for 1 or 2 minutes.
2. Rinse with cold water, peel off the outer strings, and cut into julienne.
3. Mix with fish strips, sprinkle with 1 tablespoon sauce and drain.
4. Mix with the rest of the dressing and serve piled into small dishes. Top with needle-thin *nori.*

For 4 servings:
¼ cup raw fish, cut julienne (Use sashimi *scraps)*
1 stalk of celery
¼ cup Wasabi Vinegar (made without sugar, page 213)
1 tablespoon toasted nori *(page 30), cut needle thin*

SCALLOPS AND *SHIITAKE* WITH VINEGAR GLAZE (*Hotate-gai to Shiitake no Yoshino-zu*)

★ *page 161*

1. Shred the scallops following the grain. Sprinkle with cornstarch.
2. Place them in a colander. Swish the colander in salted, boiling water so that the cornstarch turns translucent. Rinse with cold water and drain.
3. Thread the mushroom caps on a couple of thin skewers and grill them over direct heat or broil in an oven. Cut them into strips.
4. Pile the scallops and the mushrooms into individual bowls and pour vinegar glaze over. Top with ginger and add a sprig of parsley for a garnish and serve.

For 4 servings:
¼ lb. (110 g) scallops
4 fresh shiitake (or regular mushrooms)
1 tablespoon cornstarch
1 recipe Vinegar Glaze (page 213)
½ tablespoon ginger, cut needle thin
Sprigs of parsley

GREEN JADE SALAD (*Hisui-ae*)

Chill for 2–3 hours before serving.

1. Pick the grapes off the stems, wash and drain. If they are large, cut into two.
2. Peel the cucumber and remove the seeds. Grate and lightly squeeze out the juice.
3. Add the lemon juice mixture to the cucumber and mix in the grapes.
4. Chill for a few hours and serve in chilled glasses.

For 4 servings:
1 cup seedless green grapes
Green Jade Dressing:
   ⅔ cup grated cucumber, squeezed. (Use 2 small or 1 large cucumber)
   3 tablespoons lemon juice
   ⅓ cup sake or sherry
   2 teaspoons sugar
   ½ teaspoon salt

ENOKI MUSHROOM SNOW SALAD
(*Enoki Dake Mizore-ae*) ★ *page 159*

For 4 servings:
1 bag enoki *mushrooms*
1 recipe Snowy Dressing
  (page 213)

1. Wash the mushrooms. Cut off the yellow root part.
2. Drop into boiling water and drain immediately.
3. Rinse with cold water. Cut into 1½" (4 cm) lengths.
4. Prepare the snowy dressing. Taste the grated *daikon*. If it is too hot, soak it in water for a few minutes, drain and squeeze out water.
5. Mix the mushrooms with the dressing. Serve in small bowls.

SMOKED SALMON AND CUCUMBER SNOW SALAD
(Smoked Salmon *to Kyūri Mizore-ae*)

Mix two parts diced cucumber and one part diced, smoked salmon with Snowy Dressing (page 213). Top with grated lemon rind. It is a colorful salad with red and green mixed with white.

SHRIMP, AVOCADO AND CUCUMBER WITH YELLOW DRESSING
(*Ebi, Avocado to Kyūri no Kimizu-ae*) ★ *page 161*

Mix equal parts of cooked shrimp meat, diced cucumber, and diced avocado which has been sprinkled with lemon juice. Rinse with Vinegar Dressing and squeeze out liquid. Pile onto dishes or into bowls. Pour yellow dressing (page 213) over them.

EGGPLANT WITH MUSTARD DRESSING
(*Nasu Karashi-ae*)

For 4–6 servings:
4 steamed eggplants
½–1 cup steamed, shredded
  chicken (Steam with the
  eggplant.)

Mustard Sauce:
2–3 teaspoons mustard paste
  (Make with dry mustard or
  prepared mustard)
1½ tablespoons soy sauce
1 teaspoon sugar

1. Cut eggplant into strips. Unless the skin is tough, there is no need to peel it.
2. Gently squeeze out the water. The bamboo matchstick mat used for rolling *sushi* is handy for this. Roll the eggplant strips in the mat and squeeze the roll.
3. Mix the ingredients for the dressing.
4. Just before serving, add the dressing to the eggplant and chicken. If mixed too early, it will become soggy.

Note: In place of chicken, fishcake (*kamaboko*) cut into julienne may be used.

CELERY WITH PEANUT DRESSING
(Celery *no Peanut-ae*)

Using peanut butter, this is very easy to prepare.

1. Cook the celery in salted, boiling water (1 teaspoon salt to 2 cups water) until tender-crisp.
2. Rinse with cold water. Peel off stringy fibers and cut into 2″ (5 cm) strips, splitting wider part into 2–4 pieces lengthwise.
3. Make the dressing by gradually adding soy sauce and hot water to the peanut butter. Stir well to make a smooth sauce.
4. Pile celery sticks into serving bowls and pour the dressing over.

For 4 servings:
4 stalks of celery

Peanut Dressing:
3 tablespoons peanut butter (can be either creamy or crunchy)
1 tablespoon soy sauce
1–2 tablespoons hot water

EGGPLANT WITH PEANUT DRESSING
(*Nasu Peanut-ae*)

Mix the steamed eggplant with the dressing just before serving.

For 4 servings:
4 eggplants, steamed (page 140)
A dash of cayenne pepper
1 recipe Peanut Dressing (page 214)

GREEN ASPARAGUS WITH TART PEANUT DRESSING
(*Asparagus Peanut-ae*)

1. Parboil green asparagus in salted, boiling water until tender-crisp. Drain and rinse with cold water. Cut into 1″ (2.5 cm) lengths.
2. Sprinkle over Sweet Vinegar Dressing with lemon and chill in refrigerator.
3. Just before serving, drain the asparagus, coat with the dressing, and serve.

For 4 servings:
12–16 stalks of green asparagus
1 recipe Vinegar Dressing with Lemon Juice (page 212)
1 recipe Tart Peanut Dressing: Add 1 tablespoon vinegar to 1 recipe Peanut Dressing, page 214.

EGGPLANT AND STRING BEANS WITH TART SESAME DRESSING
(*Nasu to Ingen no Gomazu-ae*)

Mix two parts steamed and shredded eggplants with one part cooked string beans thinly sliced, with Vinegar Dressing. (page 214) Chill in refrigerator. Arrange in bowls and top with the dressing.

Tart Sesame Dressing (page 214)

GREEN ASPARAGUS WITH SESAME DRESSING
(Asparagus *no Goma-ae*)

For 4–6 servings:
½–¾ lb. (220–330 g) green
asparagus

Sesame Dressing:
4 tablespoons toasted white
sesame seeds
2 tablespoons soy sauce
½–1 teaspoon sugar
2 tablespoons dashi

1. Cut asparagus into 1″ (2.5 cm) lengths and boil in salted boiling water until tender-crisp. Drain and rinse with cold water.
2. Toast the sesame in a dry skillet and grind with a mortar and pestle. Add the seasoning and dilute with *dashi*.
3. Mix with the asparagus.

Other suitable vegetables are broccoli, carrots, celery, okra, spinach, string beans, watercress and steamed eggplant.

GREEN ASPARAGUS AND CARROT WITH TOFU DRESSING
(Asparagus *to Ninjin no Shira-ae*)

"*Shira-ae*" is a combination of food mixed with a white dressing made from *tofu*. A common combination in Japan is carrot, *daikon*, and *konnyaku*, but green asparagus and carrot make a pretty combination.

For 4–6 servings:
1 cup thin green asparagus
⅓ cup carrot, cut into
julienne
1 recipe light-colored cooking
liquid (page 36)

Tofu *Dressing (Shira-ae*
Goromo):
4 oz. (110 g) tofu, a scant ½
cup
2 tablespoons white sesame
seeds
2–3 teaspoons sugar
¼ teaspoon salt
A pinch of MSG
3–4 tablespoons liquid in
which the vegetables were
cooked

1. Cut asparagus into 1″ (2.5 cm) lengths. Parboil them in salted boiling water for 1 or 2 minutes. Drain and rinse with cold water.
2. Poach the julienned carrot in the cooking liquid for 10 minutes.
3. Add the drained asparagus to the carrot and cook 1 minute. Turn off the heat and let stand until cool. Drain the vegetables, saving some liquid.
4. Parboil *tofu* for a minute or so. Wrap it in double thickness of cheese cloth and squeeze out the water. Or press between two boards with a one pound weight for half an hour.
5. Toast sesame seeds in a dry frying pan over medium heat. Cover with a lid and shake until a few seeds crackle.
6. Grind sesame in a mortar and pestle, or in a food processor (in which the seeds fly around at first, but eventually settle down).
7. Add the *tofu* mash to the sesame and grind until smooth. Add the seasonings and the liquid to make a thick sauce.
8. Mix with the cooked vegetables and serve. It may be mixed ahead and kept chilled.

Other suitable ingredients are broccoli, fried *tofu* puff (*age*), mushrooms (abalone or oyster mushrooms, fresh or dried *shiitake*), string beans, spinach, etc.

CARROT, *DAIKON*, *KONNYAKU*, *SHIITAKE* AND STRING BEANS WITH *TOFU* DRESSING
(*Ninjin, Daikon, Konnyaku, Shiitake to Ingen no Shira-ae*)

This is a more traditional Japanese combination. Follow the previous recipe, but cook the carrot, *daikon*, *konnyaku* and *shiitake* in the standard cooking liquid. Parboil the string beans in salted boiling water. Mix the cooked vegetables with the *Tofu* Dressing and serve.

For 4–6 servings:
¼ *cup each carrot, daikon, konnyaku, shiitake mushrooms (softened), and string beans, all cut into julienne*
1 recipe Standard Cooking Liquid (page 36)
1 recipe Tofu Dressing (page 214)

AVOCADO AND PAPAYA WITH TART *TOFU* DRESSING (*Avocado to Papaya no Shirasu-ae*) ★ *page 162*

Sprinkle the lemon juice over the cubed fruits and chill well. Just before serving, mix with the dressing.

For 4–6 servings:
1 small avocado, cubed
½ *firm papaya (or firm, sweet persimmon), cubed*
1–2 tablespoons lemon juice
1 recipe Tart Tofu Dressing (page 214) without sesame.

KONNYAKU AND GREEN ONION *MISO* SALAD
(*Konnyaku to Negi no Nuta*)

Salad with Mustard *Miso* Dressing is called "*nuta*." Raw or blanched shell fish (clams, scallops) or raw *sashimi* scraps may be used instead of *konnyaku*.

1. Boil *konnyaku* 2–3 minutes. Rinse with cold water and drain.
2. Cut green onions into 1½″ (4 cm) lengths, splitting the thicker parts into halves or quarters. Blanch in boiling water, drain and rinse with cold water. Then rinse with 1 tablespoon vinegar.
3. Mix *konnyaku* and green onions with the dressing. Serve immediately.

For 4 servings:
½ *cup konnyaku in julienne (or cut up konnyaku noodles)*
1 bunch green onions
1 tablespoon vinegar
1 recipe Mustard Miso Dressing (page 214)

221

MARINATED COLD VEGETABLES

These can be made ahead of time and are very refreshing when served well chilled. See Poached Celery (page 136) and Poached Baked Eggplant (page 138).

POACHED SNOW PEAS (OR STRING BEANS)
(*Kinusaya Ao-ni* or *Saya-ingen Ao-ni*)

Green beans which have been parboiled and poached and left in the liquid are good garnishes for other *nimono*, fish or meat.

*½ cup snow peas or string
  beans*

Cooking Liquid:
½ cup dashi
1 teaspoon salt
1–2 teaspoons sugar

1. Pull off the string from the stem, but leave the pointed tip intact. Just remove the pistil. When arranging the beans on a dish, put the pointed tips up.
2. Bring salted water to a rolling boil. Add the beans. Boil snow peas 1 minute—string beans 2–3 minutes.
3. Drain in a colander and rinse with cold water. Fast cooling makes for a brighter green color.
4. Boil the cooking liquid. When it is at a full boil, add the snow peas or string beans and cook for 1 minute. Turn the heat off and let them cool in the liquid.

MARINATED BOILED CELERY SALAD
(Celery *no Mariné Salada*)

Boiled vegetables make a very refreshing salad when marinated in a clear dressing.

For 4 servings:
2 stalks celery

Cooking Liquid:
½ cup water
¼ teaspoon salt
*¼ teaspoon
  chicken bouillon
  cube or instant dashi*

Marinade:
½ cup chicken broth or dashi
3 tablespoons vinegar
¼ teaspoon salt
1 teaspoon soy sauce

Topping:
*Bonito flakes or toasted sesame
  seeds*

1. Blanch celery stalks in salted water for 1–2 minutes.
2. Rinse with cold water and remove strings. Cut into julienne.
3. Bring the cooking liquid to a boil and add the celery. Cover with drop lid and boil until tender-crisp.
4. Drain and place in a container. Cover with the marinade and when is is cool refrigerate for a few hours.
5. Pile into small dishes and top with bonito flakes or toasted sesame seeds.

JAPANESE SALAD PLATTER ★ *page 162*
(*Wafū Salada Mori-awasé*)

Here is a more Westernized salad that goes with any kind of food, Western or Japanese.

* Parboil

Arrange on lettuce leaves on a platter, keeping each pile separate.

For 6–8 servings:
Choose 4–8 ingredients from the list on the left.

White	Green	Yellow Red	Dark
Belgian endive	Cucumber	Carrot*	"Wakame" (Seaweed) page 31
Cabbage	Green pepper	Red sweet pepper	
Celery	Lettuce	Radish	
	Okra	Tomato	Shiitake, grilled page 144
Daikon	Snow peas*	Yellow mum petals, blanched	

Daikon sprouts String beans*
Turnips Green onions
Bean sprouts, Watercress
  blanched
  "*Harusame*"
  (page 20)
Jicama
Lotus root

Mix all the ingredients for the dressing. Let everyone help himself to the salad and pass the dressing.

Sesame Miso *Dressing:*
¼ cup toasted white sesame seeds, ground to paste in food processor or mortar
3 tablespoons mellow white miso
2 teaspoons mustard powder or prepared mustard
1 tablespoon soy sauce
2 tablespoons vinegar
¼ cup dashi
¼ cup salad oil

223

Casseroles

"*Nabemono*" literally means casserole cooking, but it is casserole cooking done at the table. It is probably one of the most popular cooking methods in Japanese homes. There are many good reasons: no elaborate cooking is needed in the kitchen; one can prepare ahead; and platters of beautifully arranged materials appeal to the eyes as well as to the appetite because a great variety of materials is used. They can be meals in themselves! Everyone at the table participates in the cooking and controls the amount of seasoning and length of cooking to suit his own taste. Truly, nothing is like the experience of surrounding a cooking pot and eating together! All the formality is forgotten and friendly conversation is bound to flow in a relaxed mood. Besides, anything tastes best right out of a cooking pot! So this is an ideal company dinner as well as for families.

For a family meal with *nabemono*, plain white rice is served with the casserole, and pickles are served at the end. For company, have some appetizers to fill the time before the casserole is ready—a salad for a soupy casserole, a soup for a drier type of casserole.

There are infinite varieties, but they can be classified into the following categories:

I *Mizutaki* **Group** (Casseroles cooked with water or broth)
Eaten with dipping sauces.
Broth may be drunk as soup by adding seasonings.
II *Yosenabe* **Group** (Casseroles cooked with seasoned broth)
An assortment of ingredients is poached in the seasoned cooking liquid. Eaten with the liquid.
III *Sukiyaki* (Casseroles cooked with very little liquid)
Well-seasoned, to be dipped into bland, raw egg before eating. Use just enough liquid to prevent burning.
IV **Griddle Cooking**
Materials are grilled on a heated iron griddle, earthen board or stone, using oil or butter. Eaten with dipping sauce.
V *Miso Nabe* **Group** (Casserole seasoned with *miso*)

UTENSILS

Electric skillets are very convenient to use. If you have table burners or an electric hot plate, you can use a shallow pot, a sauce pan, a high-heat proof glass casserole, or a Japanese *"donabe"* (earthenware casserole with unglazed bottom). A *donabe* is good for the first and second group of *nabemono* because it heats slowly and keeps hot. If the bottom is curved, use a wok ring under it to collect the heat. The bottom of the *donabe* must be completely dry before cooking.

General Rules for *Nabemono*
1. Use fresh materials. Be especially careful with seafood. Boiling cannot hide a less-than-fresh taste.
2. Do not use materials that have an odor, bitterness, or exude dark juice when cooked. Spinach and *"shungiku"* (page 21) should be parboiled ahead of time or cooked very quickly.
3. Arrange all the materials on a platter as though you are making a picture. This will be the table centerpiece, since with the cooking utensils, the platters and the sauce or broth, there is no room for a flower centerpiece.
4. Have everything you need on the table.
5. First bring the cooking liquid to a boil, add the materials which need longer cooking first, followed by those which cook quickly.
6. Avoid putting too much in the pot at one time. Match the pace of adding things to the cooking pot to that of the diners' removing things from the pot. Continue throughout to remove any scum.

Preparation of Materials
1. Cut everything into bite size.
2. Vegetables, which take longer to cook, should be parboiled beforehand.
3. Seafood: wash and cut fish into chunks, or fillet if the bones bother you. Sprinkle with a little *sake* and salt, and let stand for 20 minutes. Pour boiling water over the fish and then rinse with cold water (not necessary with live fish). This will remove any fishy smell. Shell prawns, leaving tails on, and devein. Cut raw crabs into chunks with the shell still on.

I CASSEROLES WITH WATER OR BROTH

All recipes for 4 servings.

TOFU IN HOT WATER (*Yudofu*)

2 *regular* tofu *cakes, cubed*
Kombu, 6" (15 cm) square

Dipping Sauce:
1/3 *cup soy sauce*
1/3 *cup water or* sake
1/3 *cup bonito flakes*
Combine *and put into a*
  tea cup.

Two or three condiments:
Chopped chives
Bonito flakes
Wasabi *paste*
Nori, *toasted and crumbled*

1. Line a casserole with *kombu*, place the cup with the sauce in the center and fill casserole with water. Add a pinch of salt to water.
2. Add some *tofu* cubes and bring to a boil.
3. When *tofu* is about to float, scoop it out with a slotted spoon into a bowl. Pour on the hot sauce, add condiments and eat.

TOFU, FISH AND VEGETABLE CASSEROLE
(*Chiri Nabe*)   ★ *page 164*

1 *cake* tofu, *cubed*
1 1/2 *lb. (700 g) white-meat fish*
  such as cod fish, halibut, sea
  bass, sea bream, etc.
Kombu, 6" (15 cm) square
Chinese cabbage top
Mitsuba
Spinach or shungiku
Fresh mushrooms
1/2 *cup Lemon Soy Sauce*
  (*page 90*)
Chopped chives
Red grated daikon (*page 89*)

Prepare fish as directed on page 225, item 3. Cook and serve like *Yudofu*, with Lemon Soy Sauce and condiments.

CHINESE CABBAGE CASSEROLE (*Hakusai Nabe*)
★ *page 164*

1. Boil the meat in the water which has been seasoned with salt and MSG.
2. Remove any scum, add the cabbage and mushrooms. The greens are cooked just enough to wilt.

3. Pick up the meat and vegetables and eat with soy sauce and condiments. Drink the broth by adding the seasonings. Save any broth left for later use.

Boiled noodles are a good addition to all soupy casseroles. Add them at the end and serve with the broth.

½ large Chinese cabbage (Use the top part)
1½ lb. (700 g) pork, thinly sliced
1 bunch spinach or shungiku
1 cup fresh mushrooms

Sauce and Condiments:
Plain soy sauce and mustard paste, or Lemon Soy Sauce and red grated daikon.

SHABU SHABU (Swish Swish) ★ *page 165*

Thinly sliced beef is swished through broth for a second or two, dipped in the rich sesame sauce, and eaten.

1. Bring the broth to a boil. Swish each piece of beef through the broth, dip in the sauce and eat.
2. After eating part of the beef, add the vegetables.
3. Add *harusame* at the end. Noodles or *mochi* make it a complete meal.

3 quarts chicken broth
2 lb. thinly sliced beef (Buy rib, delmonico or top round roast and have it sliced paper thin.)
Chinese cabbage
Spinach
Green onions
Fresh mushrooms
Tofu
Harusame *(page 20)*
Boiled noodles or mochi *(page 28)*

Sesame Sauce (Gomadare):
¼ cup toasted, ground sesame seeds
¼ cup sake
2 tablespoons soy sauce
½–1 tablespoon dark, salty miso
½ tablespoon lemon juice
½ teaspoon sugar
¼ teaspoon grated ginger
Drop of tabasco sauce or cayenne pepper
Optional: 1 cube "funyū," Chinese fermented tofu sold in jars.

Mix all and whirl in a blender. Refrigerate one day to blend flavors.

BOILED CHICKEN CASSEROLE ★ *page 166*
(*Mizu-taki*)

1 chicken, 3–4 lb.
  (1.3–1.8 kg), cut into
  chunks with bones
3 quarts chicken broth made
  with backs, necks and any
  chicken bones you have
  saved.
Chinese cabbage
Green onions
Spinach, parboiled
Fresh mushrooms
Mitsuba
Tofu
Harusame
Boiled noodles *or* mochi
  (page 28)

Condiments:
Chopped chives
Red grated daikon (page 89)

Sauce:
⅓ cup Lemon Soy Sauce
  (page 90)
Salt shaker at the table for
  seasoning broth.

1. Rinse chicken pieces with boiling water and simmer in the broth for 40 minutes to 1 hour until tender and the bones separate easily. Overcooking makes the chicken flavorless.
2. Heat the broth and chicken pieces in the table casserole. Eat the chicken with the sauce and condiments.
3. Add other materials and eat as they cook.
4. Drink the broth after adding salt to taste.
5. Finally add the noodles, *mochi,* or make "*zōsui,*" explained below.

Variation: "Shirataki" (white-boiled). Bone the chicken and slice the meat. Cook the raw meat in the broth at the table.

Rice Porridge (*Zōsui*)
Place cooked rice in a colander and rinse with boiling water. Add this to the broth and cook for about 5 minutes. Raw eggs stirred in make it richer. Sprinkle on chopped chives. Use ½ cup of cooked rice per serving to 1–1½ cups broth.

II CASSEROLES WITH SEASONED BROTH

ASSORTED CASSEROLE (*Yosenabe*) ★ *page 163*

Basic Seasoned Broth:
4 cups dashi
¼–½ cup mirin
5 tablespoons–½ cup soy
  sauce

Poultry, sea food, and vegetables are cooked in lightly seasoned broth. Choose from the following:

  Chicken
  Duck
  Clams
  Crab
  Fish
  Fish Cakes
  Prawns
  Scallops
  Squid
  White-meat fish
  "*Fu*" (wheat gluten products)

Tofu
Bamboo shoots
Chinese cabbage
Green onions
Parboiled Chinese cabbage and spinach rolls
Carrot and *daikon* slices, parboiled
Mitsuba (trefoil)
Mushrooms (*enoki*, oyster or *shiitake*)
Snow peas
Spinach or *Shungiku*
Shirataki (*konnyaku* noodles, page 26) or
    Harusame (page 20)
Optional: Lemon wedges as condiment.

NOODLE CASSEROLE (*Udon Suki*)   ★ *page 167*

This is an abbreviation for *Udon Sukiyaki*. Even though the word *sukiyaki*, strictly speaking, means a casserole with very little liquid, it is often used ambiguously for a casserole.

1. Arrange the materials in a casserole, pour in the broth to cover them well, and cook.
2. When the broth has come to a boil, add the cooked noodles and warm them up.
3. Ladle out the noodles, garnishes and the broth into individual bowls and eat like a soup with noodles.

This is a meal by itself. Wonderful for winter because it is so warming.

Boiled noodles
Serveral materials from the list
  for yosenabe above
Basic seasoned broth

Condiments:
Lemon wedges and seven-
  taste pepper

SEAFOOD CASSEROLE (*Uo Suki*)   ★ *page 167*

1. Prepare the fish as explained on page 225. See "Preparation of Materials," item 3. Pour ½ cup of the cooking liquid over the fish and let it stand for 20–30 minutes.
2. Cook the sea food and vegetables in the liquid. Do not overcook.

Cooking Liquid:
2 cups dashi
3 tablespoons mirin
½ cup sake
¼ cup soy sauce

Seafood:
Clams
Halibut
Oysters
Prawns
Rock Cod
Sole
Sea Bass
Scallops
Yellowtail

Any vegetable from the list
  for Yosenabe *on the*
  previous page.

ODEN

★ page 167

Tofu
Fried tofu *puffs* (*rinse with boiling water*)
Konnyaku
Tofu *Patties* (*page 19*)
Hanpen (*soft fishcake*)
Chikuwa *or* Kamaboko
Satsuma age (*fried fishcake*)
Daikon *slices* (*cut 1″ or 3 cm thick and parboil*)
Satoimo (*taro*) *or potato*
Chicken wings *or Beef shanks*
Hard boiled eggs
Cabbage rolls (*page 135*) *tied with* kanpyō *or toothpicks*

Seasoned Broth:
8 cups dashi *or chicken stock*
½ cup mirin
¼ cup soy sauce
1 teaspoon salt

Condiment: Mustard paste

Oden is an exception to *nabemono* because the cooking is done before it is brought to the table. It is one-pot cooking which requires long, slow simmering. In an Americn crock-pot, cook *oden* at "high" for 3–4 hours. In an earthenware pot or heavy metal pot, cook over lowest heat, or bake in an oven at 325°F. (160°C.) for 2–3 hours. Prepare *oden* in quantity, using several ingredients from the *yosenabe* list. This tastes very good when reheated.

III CASEROLES COOKED WITH LITTLE LIQUID

SUKIYAKI

★ page 169

It is said that the name comes from grilling (*yaki*) meat on a heated hoe (*suki*). So it is closer to griddle cooking than to simmering, *yosenabe*-style cooking. Minimal cooking liquid is just enough to cook without burning.

Beef
The best beef for *sukiyaki* is well marbled prime rib slices. Buy a rib roast and have it boned and sliced ⅛″ (2–3 mm) thick. Arrange the slices beautifully on a platter with the other ingredients.

Beef Fat
Searing fat on a sizzling hot skillet followed by pressing out this melted fat from the beef provides the basis for *sukiyaki*'s rich taste. This technique also prevents the meat from sticking to the skillet. If you cannot eat beef fat for health reasons, use salad oil instead for cooking the beef.

Ingredients for 4 servings:
1⅓–2 lb. (600–900 g) sliced beef
2 oz. beef fat
4 raw eggs
4 bunches green onions, cut 2″ (5 cm) long
1 onion, sliced
1 cake tofu, cubed

Raw Eggs
Dipping well-seasoned, hot beef into bland, cold eggs tastes good and cools the meat just enough for eating. However, the eggs may be omitted if you do not care for them raw.

Cooking *Sukiyaki*:

1. Heat a skillet and sear the beef fat (suet), as explained.
2. Add the beef slices to the skillet. Pour 1–2 tablespoons sauce over each slice. Add a little water (2 tablespoons) to the skillet, cover and cook for a few seconds.
3. Uncover and turn the meat over to cook on the other side. Now the first batch of meat is ready to be eaten.
4. Enjoy the first morsels of beef by dipping into slightly mixed raw egg if you like.
5. Add some of the other materials to the empty skillet. Top with some beef slices, pour some sauce over the beef, cover and cook for a few minutes.
6. Uncover and turn the meat over. Beef and spinach are the first items to cook, so help yourself when they are just done. Other items will follow, so pick them up and eat as they are done.
7. Push the cooked things to one side of the skillet and add new materials to the open area of the skillet. Pour on more sauce. Vegetables exude some juice, but when this liquid has evaporated, add a little water. Also, balance the additions of sauce and water to maintain the correct flavor.
8. Adjust the pace of adding new materials to the skillet to match the pace of eating so everyone can enjoy things that have just been freshly cooked.

1 cup shirataki (konnyaku *noodles), (page 26) parboiled*
4 cups Chinese cabbage top, cut 2″ (5 cm) long
1 bunch spinach, cut 2″ (5 cm) long
1 cup any type fresh mushrooms or matsutake fu (page 32)
1–2 potatoes, peeled, sliced and boiled tender
Prepared Sauce
Some water

Prepared Sauce (Warishita)
1 cup mirin
1 cup soy sauce
2 cups sake
If you like it sweet, add 2–3 tablespoons sugar

CHICKEN SUKIYAKI (*Tori Sukiyaki*)

Use boned, sliced chicken in place of beef. Other materials are the same as for regular *sukiyaki*.

Prepared Sauce:
⅔ cup mirin
⅔ cup soy sauce
2 cups sake

SAKE SUKIYAKI (A Variation)

Regular *sukiyaki* is quite sweet. Some people may prefer this non-sweet *sukiyaki*.

Prepared Sauce:
1 cup soy sauce
2 cups sake
Prepare just like sukiyaki, *using this sauce and a little water.*

IV CASSEROLE GRIDDLE COOKING

Nothing can be more certifying than hot seared meat and vegetables grilled to your liking, and eaten with your favorite sauce!

Served with soup and salad, this will be a perfect menu for anybody.

IRON GRIDDLE COOKING (Teppan Yaki)

★ page 170

Sauce Suggestions
Lemon Soy Sauce (page 90)
with grated daikon

Sesame Miso Sauce (⅔ cup):
3 tablespoons toasted white
   sesame seeds, ground
2 tablespoons each light, sweet
   miso, soy sauce, mirin and
   sake, blended and cooked.

Catsup Soy Sauce (⅓ cup):
3 tablespoons catsup
2 tablespoons soy sauce
1 tablespoon Worcestershire
   sauce

Condiments:
Chopped chives or green
   onions
Chopped parsley
Cayenne pepper
Grated garlic and ginger
Mustard paste

1. Slice meat or poultry thicker than for *sukiyaki*—about ¼″ (6 mm) thick. Sprinkle with pepper.
2. Heat an iron skillet well and grease it with salad oil. Sear and sauté the materials. Vegetables take longer to cook. If you are using butter, this is called "butter *yaki*."
3. Dip cooked meat or poultry into the sauce of your choice and eat.
4. At the end of the meal, cook bean sprouts and shredded cabbage to clean up the griddle.

Suitable ingredients to choose from:
  Beef
  Chicken
  Duck
  Pork
  Prawns
  Scallops
  Bean sprouts
  Sliced eggplant
  Green asparagus
  Green peppers
  Shredded cabbage
  Sliced onions
  Mushrooms
  Sliced potatoes or pumpkin
  Snow peas
  String beans
  Corn-on-the-cob (sliced into rounds)
  Sliced zucchini

CHARCOAL GRILL (Ami Yaki)

Similar to the barbecue, except that materials are cut thinner and smaller than for regular barbecuing.

Suitable Materials:
The same materials described for "Teppan Yaki" ex-
cept for bean sprouts and
shredded cabbage which
cannot be handled on a grill.
Small items like snow peas
and mushrooms can be
pierced with toothpicks for
easier handling.

Sauce:
See griddle cooking
(See above)

1. Start charcoal fire half an hour before cooking time. When all the charcoals are red, place the grill over the coals to heat it well. Brush the grill with oil before starting to grill.
2. Place meat in the center of the coals where the heat is most intense. Place vegetables around the sides.
3. When cooked, eat these items by dipping them first into the sauce you choose. Do not overcook.

PANCAKE SNACK (*Okonomi Yaki*—To Your Taste)

★ *page 171*

This is a crepe-like snack with various garnishes of your choice (*okonomi*), either mixed into the batter or sprinkled on as you cook.

In earlier days, cooks just mixed wheat flour (*udonko*) with water and a little salt, and mixed in some dried shrimp and chopped green onions. This batter was then cooked like small pancakes on a heated, greased iron pan placed on a charcoal brazier (*naga hibachi*) which was the center of the family room and on which a kettle of water was always kept boiling for tea. The pancakes were eaten right off the pan with just a little soy sauce drizzled over them. It was a simple children's snack. These days "*Okonomi Yaki*" has incorporated many western ingredients and has become a popular contemporary snack.

1. Make a thin batter with the eggs, water, salt and flour.
2. Pour the batter onto the heated griddle. Sprinkle on some garnishes and cook like pancakes, turning once.
3. Serve with a choice of toppings and sauces.

Batter for 3–4 servings:
2 eggs
1¾–2 cups water or milk
2 cups all purpose flour, sifted
⅛ teaspoon salt

Garnishes to choose from:
Shrimp, raw or cooked
Green onions, thinly sliced
Sausages, sliced or shredded
Ham, shredded or chopped
Leftover roast or steak, cut into strips
Bacon, crumbled
Red caviar
Smoked salmon (use scraps)
Cheese, shredded
Dried fruits
Slightly cooked vegetables such as asparagus, carrots, green pepper, mushrooms and string beans.

Toppings:
Chopped parsley; Green seaweed (page 31), crumbled nori, or shredded red pickled ginger (page 22)
Sauces:
Soy sauce, catsup, Worcestershire sauce
For Dessert:
Jam or "an," a sweet bean paste sold in cans, is used for a filling.

V CASSEROLES WITH MISO

OYSTER MISO CASSEROLE (Kaki Nabe)

★ page 168

This is a perfect dish in which to use small, unsalty oysters. Very large oysters or naturally salty oysters like blue point oysters from the West Coast are not suitable. If you can get very fresh, shelled clams, they are also very good for this dish.

Place the miso in the center of a casserole. Arrange the oysters, tofu, shirataki and the vegetables around them and heat, adding a little dashi. Mix in some of the miso to season to your liking.

For 4 servings:
1½ lb.–1¾ lb. (700–800 g) oysters, shelled
1 cake tofu, *cut into cubes*
2–4 bunches green onions, cut 2″ (5 cm) long
1 can or bag of shirataki (konnyaku *noodles (page 26)*
1 bunch spinach, cut into pieces 2″ (5 cm) long

Miso *Mixture:*
½ *cup* miso
2–4 tablespoons sugar, to taste
2 tablespoons mirin
Mix all together to blend.

3–4 *cups* dashi

CHICKEN MISO CASSEROLE (Tori Miso Nabe)

★ page 168

1. Heat a skillet and add the oil. Add the sliced onions and quickly stir-fry.
2. Add the chicken, green onions and some miso paste with some water or kombu dashi to make a sauce.
3. Chicken cooks very quickly, so do not overcook.
4. Add miso and water or kombu dashi, as needed.

Other good additions are tofu or konnyaku noodles (shirataki).

For 4 servings
1½–2 lb. (700–900 g) chicken, boned and sliced diagonally
2 onions, sliced
2 bunches green onions, cut 2″ (5 cm) long
2 tablespoons salad oil

Miso *Mixture:*
5 *tablespoons* "akadashi miso," dark, salty *miso mixture sold in bags*
2 tablespoons light, sweet miso
3 tablespoons each sugar *and* mirin
2 tablespoons sake
¼ *teaspoon* dashi *essence*
Mix all together well.

3 cups water or kombu dashi (page 43)

Rice

In any culture, important staple foods have many names. In Japanese, raw rice is *"kome,"* the cooked rice is *"gohan"* or *"meshi,"* which also means meals. As a matter of fact, until a generation ago, meals of the common people meant eating mostly rice with a little *"okazu"* (cooked food to go with the rice) and a soup. Now the consumption of rice is rapidly decreasing because people eat more *"okazu,"* but rice is still far more important than the bread in Western meals.

Here on the American West Coast, *"sushi"* has become one of the most fashionable foods. *Sushi* bars are popping up everywhere, and many markets sell small trays of several simple *"sushi."*

Seasoned rice with many garnishes, or *"donburi"* (rice in a bowl topped with some cooked food) can be a nice lunch or supper with a bowl of soup and a salad or even just a tiny dish of pickles.

There is a vast population of rice eaters in the world, however each region has its own way and preference for cooking rice. The Japanese like rice a little sticky and resilient, so the cooking method is different from other countries. Please read "Cooking Rice" in the section on Basic Techniques on page 43.

Rice expands nearly 2½ times in cooking, so 1 cup of raw rice will make about 2½ cups of cooked rice.

SALT-SEASONED RICE DISHES

Standard amount of salt is: ½ teaspoon salt for 1 cup uncooked rice

GREEN PEA RICE (Aomame Gohan) ★ *page 172*

The subtle sweetness and aroma of fresh green peas make this rice a favorite for everyone.

235

2 cups rice
2¼ cups water*
½ cup freshly shelled green
   peas
1 teaspoon salt

1. Prepare rice as explained on page 43. Add the peas and salt.
2. Cook like regular rice—in a rice cooker, on top of the stove, or in the oven. See pages 45–46.
3. When the rice has steamed for 10–12 minutes after the cooking is finished, cut in with a paddle and mix the rice so the peas are well distributed.

GINGER RICE (Shōga Gohan) ★ page 172

2 cups rice
2 cups + 2 tablespoons dashi*
2 tablespoons sake
1 teaspoon salt
2–3 tablespoons ginger
   needles

1. Peel ginger root and cut into fine needles. Soak in water for 10 minutes. Like many vegetables, ginger becomes darkened when peeled and left exposed to air.
2. Cook rice with all the ingredients mixed in.
3. After the rice has steamed, mix with a paddle.

GREEN LEAF RICE (Aona Gohan) ★ page 172

2 cups rice
2¼ cups water*
¼ cup greens such as spinach,
   daikon greens, perilla
   (shiso), parsley.
1 teaspoon salt.

1. Cook the rice.
2. Prepare the greens. *Daikon* greens or spinach should be blanched in salted, boiling water. Plunge them into cold water and squeeze out the water. Chop fine and squeeze again. Mix with salt. If using *shiso* leaves, chop fine, sprinkle the salt on and let stand for 10 minutes. Squeeze out the dark juice. For parsley, just chop it fine and mix with the salt.
3. After the rice is steamed, mix in one of the prepared greens.

SOY-SEASONED RICE

Garnishes:
Choose five from the list:
¼–⅓ cup each
Fine needles of:
   Bamboo shoots
   Carrot
   Dikon
   Gobō
   Shiitake *mushrooms*
   Oyster mushrooms
Chicken, cubed
Agé, *cut into strips*

RICE WITH FIVE GARNISHES (Gomoku Meshi)
★ page 173

This soy-seasoned rice dish with five garnishes is one of the most popular family dishes.

1. Wash the rice, soak it in water and drain in a colander.
2. In small pot, cook all the garnishes with 1 cup *dashi* and the seasonings. When it boils, lower the heat and simmer for 1 minute.

3. Measure the cooking liquid and add water to make 2¼ cups. Add to the rice with the garnishes and cook. For "*kamameshi*," divide into small individual casseroles and bake in the oven (page 46).

"*Kamameshi*" (Rice cooked in a miniature cauldron)

Cooking Liquid for Garnishes:
2 tablespoons sake
1 cup dashi
2 tablespoons mirin
2 tablespoons soy sauce
¼ teaspoon salt

2 cups rice
2 cups + 2 tablespoons liquid*
(Use the cooking liquid from garnishes plus enough water to make this amount.)
2 tablespoons sake

MUSHROOM RICE (*Kinoko Meshi*)

PINE MUSHROOM RICE (*Matsutake Meshi*)

OYSTER MUSHROOM RICE (*Shimeji Gohan*)

★ *page 173*

1. Wash the rice, soak it in water and drain in a colander.
2. Cook the rice with seasoned *dashi* and the mushrooms.

Note: Pine mushrooms (*matsutake*) are available on the West Coast in October. They are very expensive, but have a superb aroma, so Pine Mushroom Rice is a special treat!

2 cups rice
1 cup mushrooms, cut into strips
2 cups dashi*
1 tablespoon sake
1½ tablespoons mirin
2 tablespoons soy sauce
⅛ teaspoon salt

CHESTNUT RICE (*Kuri Gohan*) ★ *page 173*

1. Cook like other rice dishes.

2 cups rice
2 cups water*
3 tablespoons sake
1 tablespoon soy sauce
½ teaspoon salt
¾–1 cup shelled and peeled chestnuts, cut into half. (See direction on page 21)

* The amount of water or liquid to use for cooking rice will change from season to season. In the Fall, right after the harvest, the new rice (*shinmai*) that comes out in October has more moisture. Therefore for a couple of months in the fall, you should decrease the amount of water to equal amount of rice.

RICE BOWLS TOPPED WITH FOOD
(*Donburi*)

Use bowls that are larger than rice bowls.
Western soup bowls may be used. Serve with spoons.

CHICKEN AND EGG RICE BOWL ★ *page 174*
(*Oyako Donburi*)

For 4 servings:
4–6 cups cooked, hot rice
*½ lb. (225 g) chicken, boned
and sliced thin*
1 bunch green onions
4 eggs

Cooking Liquid:
1 cup dashi
¼ cup soy sauce
*3 tablespoons mirin (or ¼ cup
sake and 4 teaspoons sugar)*
*1 sheet nori, toasted and
crumbled or cut into strips*

1. Boil the cooking liquid. Add the chicken slices. Lower the heat to medium and cook for 1 minute.
2. Add green onions and simmer 1 minute.
3. Pour in lightly stirred eggs, cover and turn off the heat. (The eggs should be only half cooked).
4. Ladle onto the rice in bowls, pour in the remaining liquid, top with the *nori* and serve.

Note: In place of green onions, ¼ cup boiled green peas or ½ cup *mitsuba* (trefoil) may be used.

Variation: For Beef & Egg Bowl, use ½ lb. steak cut into thin strips or *sukiyaki* meat cut into bite size in place of the chicken.

CRUMBLY CHICKEN RICE BOWL (*Tori Soboro Donburi*)

★ *page 174*

For 4 servings:
4–6 cups cooked, hot rice
1 lb. (450 g) chicken, ground
⅓ cup mirin
¼ cup soy sauce
*¼ cup green peas or shredded
string beans, boiled*
*1 sheet nori, toasted and
crumbled or cut into strips*
*Optional: Red pickled ginger
matchsticks (sold in jars).*

1. Put the boned chicken through a meat grinder or chop. With a food processor, be careful not to reduce it to a solid mass— use on-and-off processing.
2. Place the chicken in a pot with the *mirin* and soy sauce. Cook, stirring, to make the chicken crumbly.
3. Spoon the chicken with the juice onto the rice in the bowls. Sprinkle with green peas and the optional red ginger, top with *nori* and serve.

VARIATIONS:
HAMBURGER RICE BOWL (*Niku Soboro Donburi*)
Use beef hamburger instead of ground chicken.

THREE-COLOR RICE BOWL (*San-Shoku Donburi*)
Decrease the beef or chicken to half and make the *soboro* with half the seasonings. Make scrambled egg "*iritamago*" (page 110) using 4 eggs. Boil ½ cup shredded string beans in salted, boiling water. Arrange the beef, eggs and string beans on the rice in bowls, divided by colors.

TEMPURA RICE BOWL (*Ten Don*)   ★ *page 175*

Ten Don is an abbreviation of *Tempura Donburi*.
When you do *tempura*, make some extra to serve this way later.

1. While the rice is steaming (that means it will be ready in 10 minutes), make the prawn *tempura*. If the *tempura* is cold, wrap it in aluminum foil and warm for 15 minutes at 350°F. (180°C.) in the oven.
2. Boil the sauce in a small pot.
3. Pour 2 tablespoons sauce over the rice in each bowl.
4. Dip the warmed *tempura* into the sauce and arrange over the rice. Cover and serve.

For 4 servings:
4–6 cups cooked, hot rice
8–16 prawns tempura (page 99). The number depends on the size of the prawns.

Sauce:
³⁄₄ cup dashi
3 tablespoons mirin
¹⁄₄ cup soy sauce

BREADED CUTLET RICE BOWL (*Katsu Don*)
★ *page 175*

"*Katsu*" comes from cutlet, and "*ton katsu*" is pork cutlet that is breaded and fried. "*Don*" is an abbreviation of "*donburi*" (bowl).

1. Boil the cooking liquid in a pot. When it starts to boil, add the pork cutlets and green onions and warm them up for 1 minute.
2. Pour lightly stirred eggs over, cover and turn off the heat.
3. Ladle onto the rice, pour in the remaining juice, cover and serve.

For 4 servings:
4–6 cups hot cooked rice
4 breaded pork cutlets (page 120), cut bite size
¹⁄₂ bunch green onions
4 eggs
Cooking Liquid for Chicken and Egg Bowl (page 238).

STEAK RICE BOWL (*Yakiniku Donburi*)
★ *page 175*

Barbecue Method:
1. Barbecue like regular steak.
2. When nearly done, brush with the sauce and grill both sides.

Pan-Fry Method:
1. Heat a skillet. Add 1–2 tablespoons oil. Brown both sides on high heat.
2. Pour in half the sauce; lower the heat to medium and finish cooking.

3. Slice the steak diagonally.
4. Arrange on the rice and pour some sauce over it. Add some green garnish.
5. Sprinkle on a bit of *sansho* powder and serve.

For 4 servings:
4–6 cups hot cooked rice
1–1¹⁄₂ lb. (500–700 g) of steak, cut about 1″ (2.5 cm) thick
Sauce:
¹⁄₄ cup soy sauce
¹⁄₄ cup mirin
1 tablespoon molasses
1 teaspoon sugar
Boil all together to dissolve.

Sansho powder (see page 30)
¹⁄₄ cup boiled snow peas or string beans for garnish

239

SUSHI

Sushi is vinegared rice topped or mixed with garnishes, or rolled up with fillings inside. It can be a simple picnic food or an elaborate fancy dinner. "*Sushi*" is a general word. With another word before it, it changes to "*zushi,*" like *Chirashi Zushi* or *Nigiri Zushi.*

Rice is the base for *sushi,* so use short grained rice. For the vinegar, if you can get Japanese rice vinegar, it is best. Otherwise use white wine vinegar.

SUSHI RICE

For 4–6 servings:
Yields about 8 cups of sushi
rice—enough to make 3
"futomaki" *(thick rolls) and*
4 "hosomaki" *(thin rolls), or*
about 60 "nigiri"

3 cups rice
3 cups–3 cups + 2 tablespoons
water*
Optional: 4" × 5" (10 × 13 cm)
dashi kombu, *or a pinch of*
MSG
Seasoned Vinegar (recipe
follows)

* *Use less water for* sushi
rice. Water about equal
to the rice will make
it firmer.

1. Prepare rice as explained on page 43–46.
2. *Dashi kombu* imparts a delicate flavor to the rice. If you are using it, place it on the rice with the measured water and remove it when the water begins to boil.
3. Cook the rice and let it steam for 7–8 minutes.
4. Make a pile of the rice in a large baking pan with a rim about 1–2″ (2.5–5 cm) high. An ideal container for this is made of unvarnished wood which will absorb moisture. Pour the vinegar over the rice. Using a cutting and folding motion, mix the rice with a wooden paddle to coat the rice with the vinegar. Fanning the rice at this time and cooling it quickly makes the rice glossy.
5. Spread the rice out and cool it to luke warm. Body temperature is the best to work with. If the rice is colder, it becomes more difficult to mold. Cover with a well-wrung towel to prevent the rice from drying out.

SEASONED VINEGAR FOR *SUSHI* RICE

The right amount of vinegar is about 10% of the uncooked rice. Increase it a little if the *sushi* must be kept longer.

For 3 cups rice (the recipe above):

	Nigiri Zushi not sweet	Mixed *Sushi* (*Chirashi Zushi*) sweet	Pressed *Sushi* (*Bō-Zushi*) well-seasoned
Vinegar	⅓ c.	⅓ c. + 1 T.	⅓ c. + 2 T.
Salt	2 t. – 1 T.	1½ – 2 t.	2 t. – 1 T.
Sugar	2 t.	2 – 4 T.	2 – 3 T.

Heat the vinegar with salt and sugar to dissolve. If you boil this, the flavor of the vinegar will be lost, so just heat.

SWEET PICKLED GINGER (*Gari*)

A small mound of ginger pickle is always served with *"nigiri"* or with other *sushi* to nibble on and to clean the palate. It is available in small packets, but you can make it with fresh ginger root and vinegar.

1. Peel the ginger root and slice it paper thin—thinner than $1/16''$ (2 mm). Thick slices do not absorb the taste and are not pliable enough to make good eating. (I use a Japanese vegetable hand slicer).
2. Place in a pot, cover with water and bring to a boil. Boil 1 minute and drain into a colander. Put into a sterilized jar.
3. Boil the vinegar with the sugar and salt.
4. Remove from the heat and pour over the ginger slices. Marinate at least 1 hour—one day is better. In a refrigerator this will keep indefinitely.

1/4 lb. ginger root

Sweet Vinegar:
1/2 cup vinegar
2 tablespoons sugar
1/4 teaspoon salt

NORI (Dried Seaweed Sheets)

The outside of a folded *nori* sheet is the right side.

Large sheets of *nori* measure $8'' \times 6\frac{1}{2}''$ (20×17 cm). They are sold in packages of 10 sheets. There are "toasted *nori* sheets" (*yaki nori*) and untoasted ones. Toasting makes the sheet dark green-colored and crisp, so it is nice to toast them about 2–3 minutes in oven at 300°F. (150°C.). However, if you are keeping the *sushi* for a whole day, it is better not to toast the *nori* because untoasted *nori* sheets remain stronger and hold the rice better.

WASABI PASTE

This is indispensable with seafood *sushi*. Mix *wasabi* powder with an equal amount of water and stir vigorously to make a firm paste. There is also *wasabi* paste that comes in tubes.

GLAZE (*Nitsume*)

Brush this on boiled squid, octopus, broiled *"anago"* (conger eel) or eel.

Place the soy sauce, sugar, *mirin* and *dashi* in a pot and reduce over heat to two-thirds. Mix a little water with the cornstarch, add to the sauce to thicken it. This can be kept in the refrigerator indefinitely.

1/3 cup soy sauce (or 4 table-
  spoons soy sauce + 2 table-
  spoons "tamari" soy sauce)
1/4 cup sugar
1/4 cup mirin
1/4 cup dashi
2 teaspoons cornstarch

RICE HANDLING VINEGAR (*Tezu*)

Before handling *sushi* rice, this vinegar is used to wet the hands so the rice doesn't stick to you. Dilute vinegar with an equal amount of water.

PREPARATION OF *SUSHI* GARNISHES

EGG CREPE (See page 110)
Use the sweet kind for making wrappers for mixed *sushi* rice.

GOLDEN EGG THREADS (*Kinshi Tamago*, page 111)
Thin egg crepes are cut into thread-like fine strips.

GOLDEN EGG STRIPS

This is used for the center of *"futomaki"* (thick rolled *sushi*)

3 eggs
1 tablespoon sugar
¼ teaspoon salt

1. Mix to stir, trying not to make the eggs bubbly.
2. Strain through a sieve. If it is bubbly, let it rest 15 minutes.
3. Heat a skillet and oil the bottom. Pour in all the eggs.
4. Lower the heat to low. Cover and cook slowly. Turn over once.
5. Turn out onto a cutting board. Cut into strips ½" (1.3 cm) wide.

FLUFFY EGG YOLKS (*Kimi Soboro*)

2 yolks of hard-boiled eggs
1 teaspoon sugar
A pinch of salt

1. Put the egg yolks through a sieve, and place in a small pot.
2. Add sugar and salt and stir over low heat to make it crumbly. Use this for a topping.

THICK BAKED EGGS (*Atsuyaki Tamago*, page 112)

This moist, even-textured, slightly sweet baked egg dish gives one a change of taste from the mostly fish *"nigiri."* The tender texture and rich taste come from a shrimp or fish purée that is incorporated into the eggs. It is said that *"atsuyaki"* is the best test of *sushi* chefs.

If you do not wish to take the trouble to purée shrimp, fish or fishcake for this dish, prepare eggs for Golden Eggs Strips, cut into 1" × 3" (2.5 × 8 cm) pieces, or make *Dashi Maki* (Rolled Egg Omlette) and slice it (page 111).

FLUFFY SHRIMP (*Ebi Soboro*)

1. Chop shrimp meat fine and then pound with the back of a heavy knife or a meat pounder. Or swirl in a food processor to make fine crumbs.
2. Place the shrimp meat in a heavy pot. Cook while stirring over medium heat until fluffy and dry. Add the seasonings, and continue to cook over medium-low heat, stirring all the time, until they are fluffy and dry.

½ lb. shrimp. Boil 1 minute in salted boiling water; cool and shell. (or buy cooked shrimp meat).
1 tablespoon sake *or* sherry
2–3 tablespoons sugar
⅛ teaspoon salt

Soboro has a lovely salmon pink color and is useful as a topping for *chirashi* or a filling for rolled *sushi*. It keeps one week in the refrigerator, and also freezes well.

Note: For a less expensive *soboro*, substitute white meat fish for the shrimp. Color with red food coloring to make it pink. Canned salmon also makes a good *soboro* and does not need food coloring.

VINEGARED MACKEREL (*Shime Saba*)

Salted and vinegared mackerel makes nice topping for *Nigiri* or Mixed *Sushi*. It is also served as *sashimi*. Use a very fresh mackerel.

1. Cut the head off and clean inside.
2. Separate two fillets from the bone. Cut off fins. Pat dry.
3. Salt the fillets generously on both sides. Cover and refrigerate 2–3 hours.
4. Wash the fillets with cold water. Pat dry with paper towels.
5. Marinate the fillets in straight vinegar for 20 minutes until the outside becomes white.
6. Rub the edge of skin to find a transparent outer film and peel it off. The silver blue inner skin remains. Remove bones with tweezers. Slice like *sashimi*.

DRIED GOURD RIND (*Kampyō*)

1. Soak *kampyō* in salted water (1 teaspoon salt to 1 cup water) until soft. Rinse and wash well with water.
2. Place in a pot and cover with water. Bring to a boil. Lower the heat and simmer until *kampyō* is fairly soft. Drain and cut according to your need.
3. Put in a pot, add *dashi* and seasonings, cover with a drop-lid and cook over medium heat.
4. About 10 minutes later, taste and add the saved seasonings if necessary. *Sushi* garnishes should be well-seasoned. Cook until the liquid has almost evaporated.

1 oz. (28 g) kampyō (page 23)

Cooking Liquid:
1 cup dashi
1 tablespoon mirin
3 tablespoons sugar
3 tablespoons soy sauce
Save 1 tablespoon each for adding while cooking.

FOREST OR *SHIITAKE* MUSHROOMS (*Shiitake*)

1 oz. (28 g) dried shiitake
*(about 16 medium-sized
ones)*
*Cooking Liquid: The same as
for* kampyō, *except instead
of* dashi *use 1 cup water in
which the* shiitake *were
soaked.*

1. Soak *shiitake* in enough lukewarm water to cover until tender—about 15 minutes.
2. Cut off the stems and discard. Cut into the size you need.
3. Place in a pot, add the cooking liquid, cover with a drop-lid and cook like *kampyō*.

Note: If you are cooking both *kampyō* and *shiitake*, they can be cooked together, using *shiitake* water.

COOKED VEGETABLES FOR MIXED *SUSHI*

*About 2 cups vegetables cut
into fine julienne. Use one
or two kinds, or mix all of
these.*
   bamboo shoots
   carrots
   celery
   daikon

Cooking Liquid:
1 cup dashi
1½ tablespoons sugar
1½ tablespoons mirin
2 tablespoons soy sauce
¼ teaspoon salt

Cook with a drop-lid over medium-low heat until the liquid has almost evaporated.

BOILED PRAWNS

For *Nigiri Zushi*, medium-sized, headless prawns which are about 30 to the pound (450 g) are good. For other *sushi*, smaller ones would do.

1. Remove black veins with a toothpick, poking at the overlapping sections of the shells.
2. Pierce a toothpick or a short bamboo skewer through the belly. This prevents the prawns from curling up during cooking.
3. Boil in salted boiling water for 1 minute. Turn off the heat and let them cool in the liquid.
4. When completely cool, remove the toothpicks. Shell the prawns, but leave the tails on.
5. Butterfly the prawns by slitting the bellies.

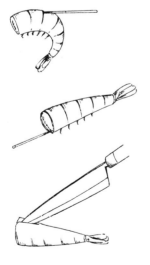

GREEN VEGETABLE GARNISHES

Always some green vegetable is used as a topping for Mixed *Sushi*, or as a filling a Rolled *Sushi*.

Raw Cucumber:
Sprinkle a little salt on a cutting board and roll the cucumbers on it. This salt-rolling makes the skin greener and more tender. Rinse with water and slice thin or cut into strips.

Cooked Greens:
Green peas
Snow peas
Spinach
String Beans

Blanched Green:
Mitsuba *(trefoil) is blanched by pouring boiling water over and rinsing with cold water.*

MIXED SUSHI (*Chirashi Zushi*) ★ *page 176*

Chirashi Zushi is a very popular *sushi* in Japanese homes because it is versatile in materials, can be made ahead and it doesn't require much expertise.

Here the most common garnishes are listed, but you don't have to use them all—just use those you can get easily. Use your imagination to harmonize taste and color.

1. Add the mix-in garnishes to the *sushi* rice and make a mound on a large serving platter or on individual dishes or shallow soup dishes.
2. Sprinkle on the toppings in the listed order: fluffy shrimp, golden thread eggs, green vegetable, and finally the red ginger and *nori*. If you don't have the red pickled ginger, use sweet pickled ginger (page 241).

For 6–8 servings:
1 recipe sushi *rice (page 240) made for "Chirashi"*

Mix-in Garnishes:
½ recipe Kampyō *(page 243)*
½ recipe Shiitake *(page 244)*
½–1 recipe cooked vegetables (page 244)

Toppings:
½ recipe Fluffy Shrimp (page 243) or Fluffy Egg Yolks (page 242)
½–1 recipe Sweet Gold Thread Eggs (page 111)
½ cup green vegetable garnish, raw or cooked
¼ cup red pickled ginger (sold in jars, already shredded)
1 sheet toasted nori *(page 30) cut needle thin or crumbled*

STEAMED SUSHI (*Mushi Zushi*) ★ *page 176*

Mixed *sushi* in bowls may be steamed for 10–15 minutes and served warm. This is good for winter. Add *nori* just before serving.

MORE TOPPING SUGGESTIONS FOR DE LUXE *CHIRASHI ZUSHI*

Fishcake "*kamaboko*" slices or strips
Boiled prawns
Raw fish *sashimi*, tuna, halibut, porgy, squid, sea bass, yellowtail, etc.
Add a dab of *wasabi* paste with the fish.

MIXED *SUSHI* WITH CRAB CALIFORNIA STYLE

For 6–8 servings:
1 *recipe* sushi *rice for* Chirashi
1 *recipe cooked vegetable (carrots and celery)*
¼–½ *lb. (115–225 g) cooked crab meat*

Seasoned Vinegar:
2 *tablespoons vinegar*
½ *teaspoon soy sauce*
½ *teaspoon sugar*

1 *dill pickled cucumber, chopped*
¼ *cup chopped parsley*

1. Mix the rice with the cooked vegetables, ¼ cup of the crab, and a little pickle.
2. Mix the rest of crab meat with the seasoned vinegar and let stand 10 minutes.
3. Arrange on dishes and sprinkle the crab, pickles and parsley on the top of the rice mixture.

PRESSED SUSHI (*Oshi Zushi*) ★ *page 177*

This garnish-decorated and pressed *sushi* looks like a cake and makes a beautiful party dish. You can prepare it in the morning and keep it pressed until serving time.

Equipment and Materials:
— A cake pan 8–9″ (20–23 cm) square and about 2″ (5 cm) deep
— A slightly smaller tray or board which will fit inside the pan
— Plastic wraps 20″ (50 cm) long and 12″ (30 cm) long
— A weight of 4–5 lb. (1.8–2 kg)—this could be 4 or 5 cans of 1 lb. (450 g) canned food, or 1 brick which has been washed well and dried.

1. Egg Crepes: Make 2–3 crepes from one recipe, but bake

at 300°F. (150°C.) oven for 5 minutes in 2 or 3 greased, non-stick pans. Baked at low temperature, crepes have smoother surface and better color.

2. Stack 2 crepes together and cut a 4″ (10 cm) square through both layers. Cut the square diagonally to make 4 triangles. Cut the scraps into strips.

3. Devein the prawns and cook in salted, boiling water for 1 minute. Cool in the liquid and shell.

Molding the Pressed *Sushi*:

1. Place the 20″ plastic sheet over the pan. Fit it into the corners. Make the decoration on the bottom of the pan by placing 4 egg crepe triangles and peas in the four corners.

2. Spoon on fluffy shrimp over the prawns to fill in the inside square which has been framed by the egg crepe triangles.

3. Carefully spread half the rice onto the decoration. Sprinkle on the cooked vegetables, egg strips, *shiitake* and fluffy shrimp if there is any left.

4. Spread on the rest of the rice. Lay the second sheet of plastic wrap over this. Put the board on the rice and fold the corners of the plastic sheets over it.

5. Weigh the board down with weights. Let this stand 1 hour to 5–6 hours in a cool place, but not in a refrigerator.

6. Remove weights, plastic sheet and the board. Open up the plastic sheets. Place a platter upside down over the mold. Turn it over and remove the plastic wrap. Put shredded ginger in the center and add the remaining ginger at the side. To serve, cut with a sharp knife wiping the knife often with a well-wrung cloth.

For 8–10 servings:
1 recipe sweet egg crepe (page 110)
¼ lb. (115 g) small prawns
1 recipe sushi rice for Pressed Sushi (page 240)
1 recipe Fluffy Shrimp (page 243)
½ recipe cooked vegetables (page 244)
½ recipe shiitake (page 244)
12 small snow peas (page 245 green garnish)
¼ cup sweet, pickled ginger (page 241) or red pickled ginger

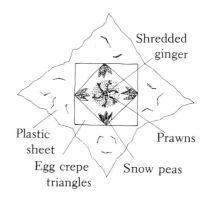

Shredded ginger

Plastic sheet

Prawns

Egg crepe triangles

Snow peas

STRIPED *SUSHI* (*Tazuna Zushi*)   ★ *page 179*

This is a rolled *sushi* with a beautiful striped design.

1. Boil prawns following directions on page 244. Shell and cut into two fillets.

2. Soak cucumber strips in salted water (1 teaspoon salt per 1 cup water) to soften, then drain.

3. Place a plastic sheet on a bamboo mat and arrange the prawn fillets and cucumber strips alternately to make diagonal stripes.

4. Smear *wasabi* paste on the garnish. Then put *sushi* rice on the center in a rod shape.

5. Roll, holding the plastic and the mat.

6. Pull the far end of the mat and the plastic with your left hand while holding the roll with your right hand to firm up the roll. Pull the mat. Roll back and forth.

7. Unroll the mat. Twist the ends of the plastic sheets.

8. Place the rolls on a tray. Top with a board and a 1–2 lb. (450–900 g) weight such as a book. Let it stand one hour.

9. Cut through the plastic into slices. Peel off before serving.

For 3 Rolls:
1½–2 cups sushi rice for pressed sushi

Garnish:
About 20 medium prawns
24–30 cucumber strips (½″ × 3½″ × ⅛″ thick) (1.3 × 9 × 3 mm)
1 teaspoon wasabi paste
Diluted vinegar for hands (half vinegar and half water)
Equipment and materials:
—Plastic sheet
—Bamboo matchstick mat (Makisu, page 39) or a dish towel

THREE-COLOR STRIPED *SUSHI* ★ *page 179*

Add skinned, lightly salted raw smelt fillets to prawns and cucumber strips to make three-color stripe *sushi*.

SMOKED SALMON ROLL (Smoked Salmon *Zushi*)
★ *page 179*

Follow the direction for Striped *Sushi*, but replace cucumbers and prawns with thin slices of lox-type smoked salmon. First place lemon slices in the center of a plastic sheet, arrange salmon slices over them, smear on *wasabi* paste, then pile *sushi* rice on salmon slices in a rod shape and roll. Lemon slices make a lovely pattern on the roll.

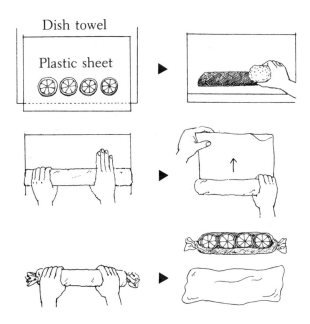

STUFFED *TOFU* PUFF *SUSHI* (Inari Zushi)
★ *page 177*

For 15 Sushi:
1 *can* Inari Zushi no Moto (contains 15 bags, cooked) (Fried tofu puffs are cut into two and cooked in seasoned liquid, but the puffs sold here are too narrow so buy the canned ones.)
About 4½ cups sweet sushi rice for Chirashi Zushi (1½ cups raw rice)
2 tablespoons black or white sesame seeds, toasted
2 tablespoons red pickled ginger, shredded

1. Warm (but do not boil) the unopened can in hot water for 10 minutes. This will make it easier to separate the puffs. Open the can and press out the liquid into the rice. *Inari Zushi* is eaten without soy sauce, so the rice should be well-seasoned.
2. Mix in the toasted sesame seeds with the rice.
3. Carefully open the cut end of the puff and fill it with rice. Shape it nicely and serve with red pickled ginger.

NORI ROLL (*Futo Maki Zushi*) ★ *page 179*

Equipment:
A bamboo mat *"makisu"* (page 39) or use a dish towel and plastic sheet as shown on pages for Striped *Sushi*.
Diluted vinegar (half water) for wetting hands.

1. Place the *nori* right side down on the *makisu*. Use the narrower side as the width and the 8½″ (21.5 cm) side as the length which will be rolled. Spread *sushi* rice onto the *nori*, leaving about 2″ (5 cm) as margin at the farther end and ⅓″ (1 cm) at the end nearest you. Fillings for *Nori* Roll are called *"gu"* and can be made ahead except for egg, which is better if baked on the same day. On top of the *sushi* rice, place the fillings (*gu*):
   Fluffy shrimp
   Kampyō
   Golden egg strip
   Shiitake
   Green vegetable
   Red pickled ginger
2. Make a roll with the *makisu,* holding firmly to keep *gu* from falling down. Hold and press the fillings in as you roll so they will be in the center.

For 1 Roll:
1 large sheet nori 6½″ × 8½″
   (16.5 × 21.5 cm)
1½ cups sushi *rice for*
   Chirashi
1 golden egg strip (page 242)
2 tablespoons fluffy shrimp
   (page 243)
14″ (35 cm) long kampyō
   (page 243)
1 or 2 shiitake (page 244)
7″ (18 cm) long cucumber
   stick or 2 boiled spinach
   leaves
½ tablespoon red pickled
   ginger

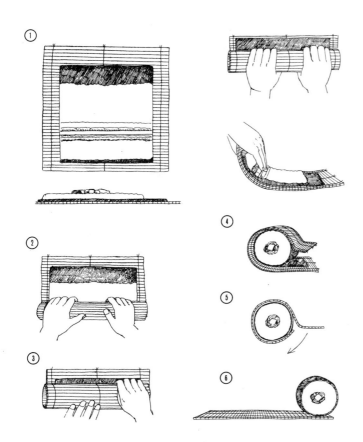

3. Keep rolling further. At this point press in both ends to push any rice back into the roll.
4. Lift the end of the mat and keep rolling.
5. Roll up and down.
6. When turned over, the roll is now finished. Repeat the rolling motion to firm up the roll. *Nori* Roll will keep one day in a cool place, but do not put into the refrigerator. It is better to cut the roll just before serving. Wrap the roll with plastic wrap. Slice with a sharp knife, wiping the knife often with a well-wrung cloth.

THIN *NORI* ROLLS (*Hoso Maki Zushi*)   ★ *page 178*

Equipment:
A makisu *or a dish towel and plastic wrap*
Diluted vinegar (half water) for wetting hands

For 1 Roll:
Half a sheet of *nori 4" × 7" (10 × 18 cm)*
About ¾ cup sushi *rice for* nigiri *(page 240)*
One of the fillings suggested on the next page
Wasabi *paste for seafood*

Thin rolls made from half a *nori* sheet make neat, one-bite *sushi* which are marvelous as appetizers or finger food at a buffet party.

1. Spread the rice on the *nori* sheet, leaving a margin of ⅓" (1 cm) at the end nearest you and 1" (2.5 cm) at the farther end.
2. Place the fillings a little closer to you than the center.
3. Follow the same directions for rolling as given for regular *norimaki* page 249.

DEW DROP THIN ROLLS
Place the filling at the far end of the rice and roll. Press down on the *nori* where the filling is. When sliced, this makes a dew drop shape.

Nori sheet

Thin *Nori* Rolls

Dew Drop Thin Rolls

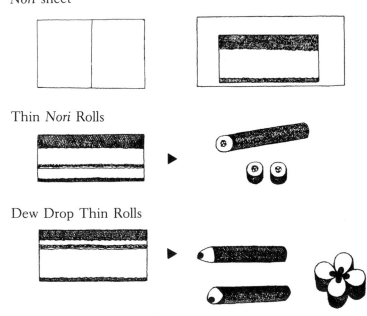

Sample Fillings
Tuna rod with *wasabi* (*Tekka Maki*)
Cucumber rod, slightly salted (*Kappa Maki*)
Kampyō and *shiitake* (page 243 and 244)
Smoked salmon and capers
Cocktail sausage and pickles
Fluffy shrimp and *kampyō* (page 243)
Crab meat, red caviar, sweet pickled ginger threads and chopped parsley
Golden egg threads and boiled spinach stems
Pickled *daikon* (*takuan*, page 27) or pickles in *sake* lees (*narazuke*, page 29)

MAKE-YOUR-OWN-SUSHI (*Okonomi Zushi*)

★ *page 180*

Here is the ideal *sushi* party! Just prepare and put all the ingredients for making *Nigiri Zushi* on the table and let everybody make his own *sushi*. Each person can choose the amount of rice he likes and pick his favorite garnishes. "*Okonomi*" means "favorite."

Method:
Place a sheet of *nori* on your left palm. Put about 1 tablespoon rice on it, add a dab of *wasabi*, then put on a topping. You may dip the topping in soy sauce if you wish. Roll it up and eat!

For 6–8 servings:
1 recipe sushi *rice for* nigiri *(page 240)*
About 30 large sheets of toasted nori, *each cut into 6 small pieces provide 20–30 small sheets per person.*
Wasabi *paste and soy sauce*
½ cup sweet pickled ginger (page 241) for nibbling between sushi *and to cleanse the palate.*

Toppings:
Choose whatever is available from this list:

Raw Seafood
Sliced like sashimi *or sticks: tuna, halibut, sea bass, snapper, yellowtail, abalone, scallops, horseneck clams, squid, sea urchin roe*

Cooked
Prawns (page 244), octopus, smoked salmon, thick baked egg (page 242), kampyō (page 243), shiitake (page 244), canned, water-packed tuna, crab meat

Pickles
Pickled daikon (takuan, *page 27),
Rice wine lee pickles (narazuke, page 29), kosher dill
pickles*

Salted
*Caviar, red caviar, "tobiko"
(flying fish roe)*

Raw Vegetables
*Japanese or English cucum-
ber cut into strips, salted
lightly with sesame seeds
sprinkled on if you wish
Celery cut into strips
Shiso leaves (perilla), sometimes available at Japanese
stores. These add flavor
and can be used instead
of or with nori as sushi
wrappers.*

NIGIRI ZUSHI   ★ *page 181*

Ingredients:
Sushi *rice for* nigiri *(page
240)*
    1 cup sushi *rice makes about*
    8 nigiri
Wasabi *paste to add to fish*
Nori *cut into strips*
    *½" × 4" (1.2 × 10 cm) to
    use as a band on squid
    and baked egg sushi*
    *1" × 8" (2.5 × 20 cm) for
    boat-shaped sushi (see
    tobiko, red caviar and sea
    urchin roe below)*
    *Sweet pickled ginger to pass
    around*
    *Soy sauce in small dishes for
    dipping*

"*Nigiri,*" the hand-formed *sushi* with various raw and cooked topping, is the ultimate of *sushi* served at professional *sushi* bars.
But you too can make it with some practice. Just follow these
directions on page 254.

Various *sushi* served at *Nigiri Sushi* Bars:

Prawns (page 244)   Tuna

Smoked salmon   Squid

Baked egg (page 242)   Thin egg (page 244)

            Thin egg

                                     Scallop
                                     Horseneck clam

    Abalone

Tobiko (flying
fish roe)

Red caviar

Sea urchin roe

Kappa (page 251)
Cucumber roll

Tekka (page 251)
Tuna roll

Shiso maki
Shiso (perilla leaves)
and salt pickled
plum paste (page
26) are added to
cucumber roll

Halibut, sea bass, red
snapper or porgy,
yellowtail

Broiled eel or
Conger eel
Boiled octopus
(sold cooked)
Brush on
Nitsume glaze
(page 241)

Boat-shaped
sushi

HAND-ROLLED SUSHI (*Temaki Zushi*)   ★ *page 178*

Rice and toppings are rolled in quartered sheets of *nori*. Popular
garnishes are pickled *daikon* (*takuan*) and vegetables which have
been pickled in *sake* lees (*narazuke*) blanched *daikon* sprouts
(*kaiware*) with bonito flakes mixed with soy sauce. In the San
Francisco area, crab meat and avocado are popular and are called "California *Sushi*."

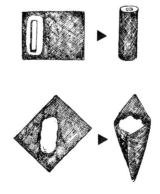

MAKING *NIGIRI ZUSHI*

1. Wet your hands well—the top of your hands as well as your palms—with *tezu* (diluted vinegar). Pick up "*tane*" (fish slice) with your left hand.
2. Turn your left hand over. The "*tane*" is now on the palm. Take a small handful of rice with your right hand.
3. With the forefinger of your right hand, still holding the rice, put some *wasabi* on the fish.
4. Place rice on the fish slice and press hard with the thumb on the rice.
5. As you press with your left thumb on the end, press the top and side of the rice with the first and second fingers of your right hand.
6. Open your left hand, rolling the *sushi* to your fingertips with the fish coming up on top. Holding the sides of the *sushi*, move it back onto your palm.
7. With the thumb and middle finger of your right hand, press hard on both sides.
8. As the first and middle fingers of your right hand press on the "*tane*," clench your left hand with your left thumb pressing the end of the *sushi*. Repeat this several times, turning end over end. "*Nigiri*" means clenching.

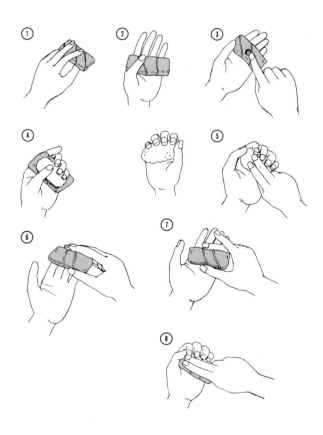

Pickles

PICKLED VEGETABLES "TSUKEMONO"

At the end of a meal, the Japanese like to have one or more kinds of "*tsukemono*" with green tea to finish up their rice. So keeping a supply of these pickles is a must in Japanese households. Many kinds of pickles are sold in stores, but here are some simple ones that you can make easily.

Salt Pickling
Salt is now regarded as an enemy of health, but it does play a vital role in the pickling process. It breaks through the cells of the materials, draws the juice out, works as a preservative and also provides seasoning.

Salt Pickling with Weights
Pressing the materials down with a weight helps the salt to break down the cells and to reduce the natural water content. Use a weight equal to the weight of the vegetables to be pickled. Press with the weight until the liquid comes up. Then reduce the weight to half. After the pickles are ready to eat, continue to keep them in the liquid.

Pickling Equipment
An improvised pickling container:

Glass or ceramic container with a drop-lid, using canned foods as the weight.

Screw-top pickle maker, sold in Japanese stores

Proportions of salt
To keep pickles
 for one day...........................Use 2% of the weight of
  the materials.
  for 3–4 days...........................Use 3%
  for one week........................Use 4%
  for 2–3 weeks.....................Use 5%

For example, to pickle 4 cups shredded cabbage (9 oz. or 250 g)
 to keep for one day...............Use 1 t.   (5 g) salt (2%)
 to keep for 3–4 days ....Use ½T. (7.5 g) salt (3%)
 to keep for one week...........Use 2 t. (10 g) salt (4%)
 to keep for 2–3 weeks...........Use 1 T. (15 g) salt (5%)

SALT PICKLING WITHOUT WEIGHT

This is a simple and quick method. You use more salt, but much
of it is washed away.

1. Mix the vegetables with twice the amount of salt, explained
   above. For example, for 4 cups shredded cabbage, use 2 teaspoons to 1 tablespoon salt.
2. Let stand two hours to overnight until the vegetables are
   limp and the bulk is reduced to nearly half.
3. Rinse with water, drain and squeeze out the water.
4. Pack into a jar with additional seasonings.

INSTANT RUBBED CABBAGE PICKLE
(*Sokuseki-zuke*)

Hand rubbing makes this the quickest pickle to prepare—it takes
about 10 minutes. It will keep in the refrigerator for one day.

4 cups cabbage or Chinese cab-
bage, shredded
1 teaspoon salt

Optional spices to choose:
1 teaspoon ginger, grated
2 teaspoons toasted sesame
seeds
1 red cayenne pepper, seeded
and chopped, or a dash of
cayenne pepper
1 teaspoon lemon peel, cut
needle thin
A dash of MSG
1–2 shiso *leaves, shredded*
fine

Mix cabbage leaves with salt and rub vigorously with both hands
until the leaves are tender and the quantity is less than half.
Squeeze out some juice and add one or two spices. The pickle
is ready to serve.

Note: You can use the same method with sliced cucumbers or
eggplants. With the eggplants, since they exude a dark juice, let
them stand 15 minutes after mixing with salt, then rub and
squeeze out the juice. Rinse with water, squeeze the water out
again and add some salt.

REFRIGERATOR CHINESE CABBAGE PICKLES
(Hakusai Reizoko-zuke) ★ *page 182*

In early winter, everywhere in Japan, Chinese cabbages are salt-pickled in big barrels or crocks with heavy rocks pressing down and weighting the lids. These are kept for several weeks or longer. They develop a delicious sour taste. You can create a similar taste by adding raisins or a little sugar to cabbage.

1. Wash the leaves well and cut into 1″ (2.5 cm) lengths. Place in a big bowl.
2. Sprinkle on 2 tablespoons salt and mix well. Cover and let stand about 2 hours. May be left overnight in the refrigerator.
3. By handfuls, squeeze out the liquid from the cabbage leaves.
4. Place 2 handfuls of cabbage into the jar and press into the bottom. Sprinkle on a little bit of each of the seasonings in layers. Repeat in layers until all the leaves are added and packed down and the remaining seasonings have been added. When sugar is used instead of the raisins, place it only on the top layer.
5. Fill the jar with water to cover cabbage. Cover tightly and let stand at room temperature for 24 hours—to let the sugar turn sour. After a while, open the jar and taste the liquid. Add more salt and water if needed.
6. Place the jar in the refrigerator after one day. It is ready to eat on the third day.

Variation: Add 1 or 2 cloves of garlic, peeled and chopped; 1 red cayenne pepper, seeded and chopped (or ¼ teaspoon cayenne pepper) to make a more robust pickle.

A *1-quart jar with a wide mouth, sterilized*
8 *cups Chinese cabbage (1.1 lb. or 500 g)*
2 *tablespoons salt*
1–2 *teaspoons salt*
1 *tablespoon ginger, cut needle thin*
1 *teaspoon lemon rind, cut needle thin*
1 *tablespoon kombu, cut into strips (or ½ teaspoon* MSG*)*
1 *teaspoon raisins (or ¼ teaspoon sugar)*
1 *dried cayenne pepper*

Note: Regular round cabbage alone or mixed with chinese cabbage makes a very nice pickle.

CELERY PICKLE (Celery *Sokuseki-zuke*) ★ *page 182*

1. Boil the celery stalks in boiling water with 1 teaspoon salt for 2–3 minutes to the half-tender stage. Drain and plunge into cold water to make them green. Drain.
2. Peel off the outside fibers and cut the stalks into 1½–2″ (4–5 cm) lengths.
3. Pack the stalks into a screw top pickling jar, or any container which will accomodate a drop-in lid. Pour in the pickling liquid and screw on the top or place a one-pound can on as a weight and pickle for one day.

4–5 *stalks of celery (10–11 oz. or 300 g)*
1 *teaspoon salt*

Pickling Liquid:
Mix to dissolve:
2 *teaspoons salt*
2 *tablespoons sake, sherry or white wine*
1 *tablespoon mirin (or 1 teaspoon sugar)*
¼ *teaspoon* MSG

THOUSAND SLICE TURNIP PICKLE (*Kabu Senmai-zuke*)

★ *page 182*

Make this pickle when you have fresh turnips with smooth white skins. The addition of vinegar makes it possible to use less salt.

A 1-quart jar
2 lb. (900 g) turnips (about 5 medium size)
2 tablespoons salt
½ tablespoon ginger, shredded
1 small red pepper, seeded and chopped (or cayenne pepper)
3″ (8 cm) square kombu, cut into strips. (Kombu adds so much to this pickle, but if unavailable, just use ¼ teaspoon MSG).

Pickling Liquid
Mix well to dissolve:
¼ cup rice vinegar
½ teaspoon salt
1 teaspoon sugar
½ cup water

1. Wash turnips. Peel the skin if they are blemished. Cut in half lengthwise, and slice crosswise as thin as possible (like ¹⁄₁₆″ or 1.5 mm).
2. Place in a big bowl and sprinkle on 2 tablespoons salt. Mix and let stand half an hour. Or mix with your hands until the turnips are soft and juicy.
3. Squeeze the juice out of the turnips. Pack in layers into a clean jar by the handfuls, sprinkling with ginger, pepper, and *kombu*. Repeat until all the turnip slices are packed tightly.
4. Pour in the pickling liquid. If it is well-packed, this amount will cover to the top. If it does not, add more water.
5. Cover tightly and refrigerate. After 3 days, it is ready to eat but it is better after 5 or 6 days. It will keep about 3 weeks in the refrigerator.

Note: *Daikon* may be prepared in the same way.

GREEN PICKLE (*Midori-zuke*)

★ *page 182*

When *daikon* comes with fresh green tops (which are usually thrown away), this is an excellent way to use them. Mustard greens, spinach or watercress also may be used. It is a refreshing, instant pickle.

4 cups leaves and stems of daikon *or other greens,* chopped
2 teaspoons salt
½ teaspoon salt
¼ MSG
½ teaspoon ginger, grated
1 teaspoon toasted sesame seeds

1. Wash and chop the leaves and stems fine.
2. Sprinkle on 2 teaspoons salt. Mix and let stand 15–20 minutes until moist.
3. Squeeze the dark juice out of the leaves and place them in a colander.
4. Pour over boiling water. Cool under running water.
5. Squeeze out the water and mix with salt, ginger, MSG, and toasted sesame seeds. It is ready to eat. Keeps in the refrigerator for several days.

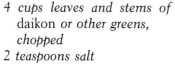

SWEET-SOUR PICKLED DRIED *DAIKON* (*Hari Hari-zuke*) ★ *page 182*

If you can get dried *daikon* (*kiri boshi daikon*) in Japanese stores, it is very simple to make this. Dried *daikon* has a natural, concentrated sweetness that adds to the taste. Dried *daikon* comes in two shapes: Small disks or long noodle-like strings which need to be cut into 1″ (2.5 cm) lengths.

1. Place the *daikon* in a colander and rinse quickly to wash.
2. Squeeze out the moisture and put it into the jar.
3. Mix the rest of the ingredients and pour over the *daikon*.
4. Cover and let stand several hours until the *daikon* soaks up the liquid and expands. It will keep indefinitely in the refrigerator. If you like things hot, chopped red cayenne pepper may be added.

A *one pint jar (2 cups)*
¼ package dried daikon *(1.5 oz–40 g) (page 27)*
2 tablespoons needle-thin ginger
⅓–½ cup sugar
½ cup soy sauce
⅓ cup vinegar
1 cup water

Desserts and Japanese Sweets

In a Western dinner, the dessert course is very important. It might even be the climax of a dinner. But in Japanese meals, desserts have always been something additional or extra.

The dainty tea cakes that are served with powdered green tea are like confections, and Japanese sweets are usually too heavy to eat following a dinner. Very often fresh fruits are served. If something more is wanted, we must borrow Western dessert ideas, modify Japanese sweets or concoct something new. So here are some light desserts which are suitable to serve after a Japanese dinner.

DESSERTS

BASIC FRUIT ICES

STRAWBERRY ICE

Since this is made of pure fruit purée, it is very refreshing. The same method works with other fruits.

For 8 servings:
1 quart (4 cups) ripe strawberries, hulled and sliced
½–¾ cups sugar
2 tablespoons lemon juice

1. Mix the sugar with the strawberries and let stand for one hour to draw the juice from the berries.
2. Add the lemon juice. Whirl in a blender, a food processor or put through a sieve. Strain to remove seeds.
3. Put into a bowl and freeze.
4. When it has frozen to about 1″ (2.5 cm) from the side of the bowl (2 hours at the coldest), take it out and beat the purée to break it up. Return it to the freezer.
5. Repeat beating two or three times. Whirling the purée in a food processor can make it very smooth. Freeze for several hours before serving.

Note: By adding one very stiffly beaten egg white, this becomes a sherbet. By adding ½–1 cup of whipped cream, this becomes good ice cream. Either addition should be mixed in after the ice has been frozen and beaten.

CANTALOUPE MELON ICE WITH GREEN GRAPES AND LEMON CREAM SAUCE

★ *page 183*

Fresh green grapes add sparkle to this light, orange-colored ice, and the sabayon-like, creamy sauce makes this dessert very satisfying.

1. In the top of a double boiler, beat the yolks and sugar until they are pale and creamy.
2. Heat water in bottom of double boiler to simmer. Set the yolks and sugar over the simmering water and continue to beat. Add the lemon juice and keep beating until thick enough to form ribbons.
3. Remove from the hot pot, set it in a bowl filled with water and ice. Beat until it is cold.
4. Whip the heavy cream to soft-peak stage and add to the yolk mixture. Keep the sauce in the refrigerator until serving. If this sauce is frozen it makes a delicious ice cream.
5. To assemble dessert, pile the cantaloupe ice into serving bowls, scatter on some grapes, pour over some lemon cream sauce and serve.

For 8–10 servings:
Cantaloupe Ice:
4 cups ripe cantaloupe melon, cut up
½ cup sugar
⅓–½ cup lemon juice
Whirl in a food processor and make ice as for strawberry ice

1 cup green seedless grapes, washed

Lemon Cream Sauce:
4 egg yolks
¼–½ cup sugar
¼ cup lemon juice
⅔ cup heavy cream

PERSIMMON ICE CUPS   ★ *page 183*

If you are able to get the flat, *"fuyū"* type persimmons which are sweet while still firm, you can make this festive dessert. Use one persimmon per person unless they are large—then one would serve two people.

1. Cut off the stem ends of the persimmons and save them. Scoop out pulp, leaving a cup with walls ¼″ (6 mm) thick. With large persimmons, cut in half crosswise to make two cups, then scoop cut.
2. Whirl the pulp in a food processor. Add the lemon juice, orange juice and sugar to taste.
3. Freeze the purée and proceed as for basic fruit ice.
4. Fill the chilled persimmon cups with the ice, add the saved tops and serve.

Note: Instead of using fresh orange juice, you may substitute orange sherbert, using about ¼–⅓ the amount of the persimmon ice. Decrease amount of sugar you add to the persimmon purée when using orange sherbet.

For 8 servings:
8 medium size fuyū *persimmons (or 4 large)*
¼–⅓ cup lemon juice
½ cup sugar
1 cup orange juice

261

GREEN TEA ICE CREAM

Powdered green tea used for the tea ceremony is available in small cans at Japanese grocery stores, and it can be stored in the freezer.

For 8 servings:
½ cup sugar
1½ cups water
1 tablespoon green tea powder
Few drops of green food coloring
1 cup whipping cream, whipped
2 egg whites
2 tablespoons sugar

1. Boil the sugar and water to make a syrup.
2. In a bowl, mix the green tea powder with the syrup, beating well to dissolve. Cool the mixture.
3. Cover the bowl with aluminum foil and freeze.
4. After about 3 hours, when it is beginning to freeze, take the bowl out of the freezer and beat the mixture, proceeding as for a basic fruit ice (page 260).
5. When the ice is the consistency of a sherbet, add the whipped cream and mix well. Color with green food color. Freeze for one hour.
6. Beat the egg whites until stiff, sprinkle in 2 tablespoons sugar, and beat well. Combine with the tea mixture. Freeze until serving time.
7. *Variations*: Add ½ cup mini marshmallows or chocolate chips. Japanese guests would enjoy the addition of 1 small can of *yude azuki* (sweet red beans) or ½ cup *ama natto* (candied red beans).

Note: A quick and easy green tea ice cream is made by just mixing green tea powder and green food coloring into vanilla ice cream.

CHESTNUT PARFAIT

For 8 servings:
1 cup chestnut purée (if sweet, decrease the amount of sugar)
2 tablespoons vermouth or brandy
6 egg yolks
¼ cup water
½–¾ cup sugar
2 cups whipping cream, whipped

1. Beat the yolks with water until frothy.
2. Continue beating over a double boiler, adding sugar gradually. Cook until mixture is thick enough to form a ribbon when drizzled from a spoon.
3. Place the pan in cold water and beat until cooled.
4. Mix in the chestnut purée, vermouth or brandy, and the whipped cream. Freeze until firm.

WINE SHERBET ★ *page 183*

Sorbet is served between the main courses in French dinners, and it also makes a delightful, light dessert. Scatter well-washed cherry blossom petals (in spring when they are available), or one or two rose petals on pink sherbet made with rosé wine. Decorate champagne or white wine sherbet with jasmine or violet flowers.

1. Boil the water with sugar and simmer for 5 minutes.
2. Remove from the heat and cool. Add the lemon juice and wine.
3. Pour into a bowl, cover and freeze.
4. Proceed as for basic fruit ice (page 260).
5. Beat the egg whites stiff and mix into the ice. The two must be of similar textures to blend well, Freeze several hours before serving.
6. Serve in chilled glasses or bowls.

For 8–10 servings:
2 cups water
2/3 cup sugar
3–4 tablespoons lemon juice
2 cups wine (rosé, white or champagne)
2 egg whites

GINGER SHERBET

Use ginger ale instead of wine in the wine sherbet recipe, or half ginger ale and half white wine. Add 2–3 tablespoons chopped, candied ginger before freezing.

FLOATING ICE
★ *page 183*

This is a very cool and low calorie dessert. The jelly is made with water and is completely unflavored an served with syrup.

1. Make clear, unseasoned jelly from softened gelatin and water. Pour into a bowl and chill.
2. Boil the sugar and water. Remove from the heat and add the other ingredients. Cool and chill well in the refrigerator.
3. Chill the serving glasses or bowls.
4. Break up the jelly with a fork or a spoon and pile into glasses.
5. Pour over the green syrup and serve. Vodka may be added to the syrup before serving.

For 8 servings:
2 envelopes (2 tablespoons or 16 g) unflavored gelatin soaked in 1/2 cup water
2 1/2 cups water

Syrup:
1 3/4 cups water
1/3–1/2 cup sugar
2–4 tablespoons lemon juice
2 tablespoons creme de menthe

Optional:
1/4 cup vodka

SPARKLING JELLY

Here is another light jelly that is good served in wine glasses.

1. Add 1/4 cup hot water and sugar to the softened gelatin and bring to a boil.
2. Remove from the heat and add wine and lemon juice. When it is completely cool, add the ginger ale.
3. Pour into glasses, add the garnish of your choice and chill.

For 6 servings:
1 envelope (2 2/3 teaspoons or 8 g) unflavored gelatin soaked in 1/4 cup water
1/4–1/3 cup sugar
1/4 cup hot water
1/2 cup white wine
2 tablespoons lemon juice
1 cup ginger ale

Garnish:
2 slices of lemon, cut into six pieces, or 1/4 cup sliced strawberries

263

SNOW JELLY WITH STRAWBERRY SAUCE
(*Awayuki-kan*) ★ *page 183*

There is a Japanese sweet called Snow Jelly (*Awayuki-kan*) made with agar-agar. This jelly using gelatin is lighter and fluffier. It is beautiful served with fresh strawberry sauce.

For 8–10 servings:
1 envelope (2⅔ teaspoons or 8
  g) unflavored gelatin soaked
  in ¼ cup water
1¼ cups water
⅓ cup sugar
2 tablespoons lemon juice
2 egg whites
2 tablespoons sugar
8–10 strawberries, sliced

Fresh Strawberry Sauce:
1 basket (2 cups) strawberries
  minus 8–10 berries, sliced
⅓ cup sugar
2 tablespoons kirsch

1. Add ½ cup water and ⅓ cup sugar to the softened gelatin and bring to a boil.
2. Remove from the heat and add the rest of the water and the lemon juice.
3. Chill the pan in ice and water.
4. Meanwhile, beat the egg whites until they reach the soft peak stage. Sprinkle on 2 tablespoons sugar and beat until stiff peaks are formed.
5. When the jelly begins to set and is the consistency of egg white, beat until more than doubled and frothy like meringue.
6. Combine the meringue and the meringue-like jelly. Mix in the sliced strawberries.
7. Divide into wet glasses or molds, and chill.
8. Make Strawberry Sauce by whirling the rest of the strawberries in a food processor or in a blender. Add sugar to taste and flavor with kirsch. Keep in the refrigerator.
9. Unmold and pour the sauce over the jelly or spoon into glasses. Top with the sauce and serve.

PLUM WINE JELLY ★ *page 184*

Plum wine is a sweet liqueur made with green plums and sold in Japanese groceries. It is good served as an after-dinner drink, and it is said to aid digestion.

For 6 servings:
1 envelope (2⅔ teaspoons or 8
  g) unflavored gelatin soaked
  in ¼ cup water
¼ cup hot water
1–2 tablespoons lemon juice
3 tablespoons sugar
¾ cup plum wine
12 green seedless grapes,
  washed
Plastic wrap

1. Add hot water and sugar to the softened gelatin and cook until completely dissolved.
2. Remove from the heat and add lemon juice and the plum wine. Cool.
3. Cut plastic wrap into squares and place on small tea cups or bowls. Spoon in some of the jelly mixture, and one grape, and twist the ends of the plastic wrap. Secure ends with a wire tie.
4. Chill in the cups.
5. The jelly may be served with the wrap by changing the wire tie with ribon or gold cord. Or unwrap jelly by dipping into hot water, and serve on a dish lined with a washed, green maple leaf.

RIPE PERSIMMONS WITH LEMON CREAM SAUCE

The most common persimmons sold in markets in the U.S. are the "*hachiya*" variety—the pointed, tall kind with a brilliant orange-red color. These persimmons are bitter until very soft and ripe, but when fully ripe, they are so sweet and soft they melt in your mouth.

Peel the ripe, tender persimmons by dipping them in boiling water for 5 seconds like peeling tomatoes. Keep them whole and chill them. Prepare Lemon Cream Sauce (page 261) and chill it. Pour the sauce over the persimmons and serve with spoons. This is a "natural" pudding.

ORANGE COMPOTE

Served well-chilled, this is a very refreshing dessert.

1. Peel the oranges. Remove the white membrane and slice about ⅛"–¼" (3–5 mm) thick. Arrange slices in glass bowl.
2. Place all the ingredients for the syrup in a pot and bring to a boil. Simmer for 15 minutes.
3. Pour the hot syrup onto the orange slices. Cool and cover with plastic wrap and chill for several hours. This can be made one day in advance and refrigerated until serving time.
4. Remove the spices and serve in compote dishes. Cookies complement this dessert nicely.

Note: Any leftover syrup can be frozen like basic fruit ice.

For 4–6 servings:
4 medium oranges

Syrup:
½ cup sugar
¾ cup water
¾ cup red or rosé wine
2 cloves
2" (5 cm) stick of cinnamon
1" (2.5 cm) of vanilla bean or
  ¼ teaspoon vanilla extract
2 thin slices of ginger

SESAME CRISPS   ★ *page 183*

These paper thin cookeis do not contain flour and are so light they make perfect accompaniments for sherbets, ice cream or compotes.

1. Mix all the ingredients in a bowl.
2. Grease 3 large cookie sheets and line them with the aluminum foil. Grease the foil.
3. Drop the mixture by teaspoonfuls about 3" (7.5 cm) apart. Flatten with the back of a wet teaspoon to make a disk about 1" (2.5 cm) in diameter.
4. Bake at preheated 350°F. (180°C.) oven about 8 minutes until golden.
5. Remove from the oven and let cool a few minutes until the cookies harden slightly. Peel off the foil. Move cookies to a rack and let them cool.
6. Store in a tightly covered can.

For 70–100 Cookies:
1¼ cups white sesame seeds
1 cup sugar
1 egg
½ tablespoon butter
½ teaspoon baking powder
½ teaspoon vanilla extract
A pinch of salt
Aluminum foil

CHESTNUTS WITH CHOCOLATE SAUCE

For 8 servings:
1 lb. (450 g) chestnuts in shells
 (or ³⁄₄ lb. chestnut purée).
 See page 21 for preparing
 chestnuts.
¹⁄₄–¹⁄₃ cup sugar
2 tablespoons brandy
¹⁄₄ teaspoon vanilla extract

Chocolate Sauce:
2 oz. (2 squares 56 g) semi-
 sweet chocolate
¹⁄₄ cup milk or cream
2 tablespoons corn syrup

1. Boil chestnuts in shells until they are tender. ★ *page 183*
2. Cut the nuts in half and scoop out the meat with a spoon.
3. Process in a food processor until smooth. Mix in sugar, brandy and vanilla.
4. Cut a square of plastic wrap. Place about 3 tablespoonfuls on it and twist the ends of the sheet to make a chestnut shape.
5. Cut the chocolate into small pieces and cook in a double boiler with milk and the syrup, stirring to make a velvety sauce.
6. Peel off the plastic sheet from the chestnuts, place them on small individual serving dishes, pour over the chocolate sauce and serve.

JAPANESE SWEETS

Here are some traditional Japanese sweets you can make using local products.

"*An*" (sweet bean paste) made from "*azuki*" (small red beans) is the base for many sweets. It is sold in 1 lb. 2 oz. (about 500 g) cans and is labeled Sweetened Red Bean Paste. "*Koshian*" or "*nerian*" are smooth pastes. "*Tsubushian*" is a crushed bean paste.

You can make the bean paste yourself also. If "*azuki*" beans are not available, use red beans or kidney beans. Split peas are quick cooking and easiest to make. Green split peas make a nice green "*an*." Lima beans make a delicate white "*an*," but they must be rinsed well in water or they will become sticky and elastic.

SWEET BEAN PASTE (An)
SMOOTH BEAN PASTE (Koshi-An)

Makes 5–6 cups:
1 lb. (450 g) beans (about
 2¹⁄₄–2¹⁄₂ cups) azuki, red
 beans, kidney beans or
 split peas
1³⁄₄–2 cups sugar
¹⁄₈ teaspoon salt

1. Cover the beans with plenty of water and bring to a boil.
2. Lower the heat to medium and continue to cook.
3. When the beans have absorbed water and the wrinkles of the bean skins have disappeared, drain the beans in a colander. Changing the water will remove the dark juice from beans. It is not necessary for split peas.
4. Cover the beans with plenty of water again using three times as much water as beans. Bring to a boil. Lower the heat to medium low and cook, removing any scum and adding water as needed to keep the beans covered until they have cooked very tender.
5. Drain the beans in a colander with a dish towel lining it. Gather up the ends of the towel and squeeze out the water.

6. Whirl the beans in a food processor or blender until they become a smooth paste.
7. Place the bean purée in a large pot, add sugar and salt, and cook over medium heat, stirring with a wooden spoon. First the melted sugar will make the purée softer, but continue stirring over heat until the *"an"* is thick enough so you can see the bottom of the pot for about 10 seconds as you stir.
8. Remove from the heat and let cool, stirring from time to time. This can be stored in the refrigerator up to one week, or can be frozen.

CRUSHED BEAN PASTE (*Tsubushi-An*)

1. Follow the directions 1 to 4 given above for Smooth Bean Paste.
2. Add sugar and salt to the tender beans in the pot. Lower the heat and continue to cook until the beans begin to crumble and the liquid has evaporated.
3. Stir the beans to crush some of the beans.

WHITE BEAN PASTE (*Shiro-An*)

1. Follow the directions 1 to 3 given above for Smooth Bean Paste.
2. Rinse with water. If you are using lima beans, rub the beans to loosen the skins. Cover with water and stir around, then pour out the water with the skins. If using small white beans or baby lima beans, there is no need to remove the skins.
3. Cover beans with plenty of water and cook until they are crumbly.
4. Spread a dish towel in a colander, pour the beans in and drain.
5. Whirl the drained beans in a food processor, blender, or put through a sieve. Add 2–3 cups water and stir to dilute the purée.
6. Pour the liquid purée into a large bowl, add more water and stir. Let stand for 30 minutes.
7. Pour out the clear water. Using a dish towel, make a cloth bag and pour the bean mixture from the bottom of the bowl into this bag.
8. Place the bag into a bowl. Cover with water and knead the bag in the water. Squeeze the water out of the bag and change the water. Repeat this process several times. The lima bean purée will exude a sticky, starch substance which must be thoroughly washed away in this manner or the *"an"* will be sticky.
9. After pressing out any remaining water, return the *"an"* to a cooking pot, add sugar and salt, and cook according to the directions (7) for Smooth Bean Paste.

Makes 3½–4 cups:
1 lb. (450 g) lima beans, baby lima beans, or small white beans
1¾ cups sugar
⅛ teaspoon salt

SUMMER BEAN PASTE JELLY (*Mizu Yōkan*)

"Kanten" (agar agar) is made of seaweed and is used for traditional Japanese sweets. It jells at a higher temperature than gelatin—jelling in cold tap water even in summer. The standard proportions are 1 stick of *kanten* to 2 cups water. But in this recipe, 3 cups of water are used to make a soft jelly to be eaten with a spoon.

1 stick agar-agar (kanten, *page 17*) *(about 5–6 g)*
or substitute 2 envelopes (about 5 teaspoons or 16 g) unflavored gelatin
3 cups water
A can of koshi-an *or* neri-an *(smooth bean paste)—1 lb. 2 oz. (500 g) can or 2 cups homemade smooth "an"*
¼ teaspoon salt
Optional sugar to taste

1. Soak *kanten* stick in water for 1 hour.
2. Squeeze out the water and tear into small pieces. Add 2 cups water and bring to a boil. Lower the heat and simmer about 5 minutes, stirring until it is completely dissolved.
3. Place the *"an"* in a mixing bowl and gradually add the *kanten* liquid to dissolve. Return to the pot and cook over low heat. Taste and add more sugar and salt to your taste.
4. Remove from the heat and add 1 cup water. Place the pot in cold water in a larger bowl and stir until the mixture is lukewarm. (The jelly will have a clear top if not treated this way.)
5. Pour the mixture into wet individual molds or a square cake pan.
6. Cool in cold water and then refrigerate.
7. When set, loosen around the edge with a knife and turn out onto serving dishes. If you have made a large square, cut into small, thick slices.

Note: Attractive dish liners for this dessert are well washed green leaves of Japanese maple, cherry or bamboo which suggest coolness.

STEAMED CHESTNUT-BEAN SQUARES
(*Kuri Mushi Yōkan*) ★ *page 184*

A can of koshi-an *or* neri-an *(smooth bean paste) 1 lb. 2 oz. (500 g) can or 2 cups homemade smooth sweet bean paste*
½ cup all-purpose flour
2 tablespoons cornstarch
⅓ cup sugar
⅓ cup water
About 12 chestnuts in syrup, drained (sold in a can or jar)
Plastic wrap
An 8″ × 8″ (20 × 20 cm) square pan, 1½″–2″ (4–5 cm) deep. Or use a bread pan 4″ × 8″ × 2½″ (10 × 20 × 6.5 cm)

1. Sift the flour, cornstarch and sugar together into a large bowl.
2. Gradually add ⅓ cup water to make a smooth paste.
3. Add the bean paste to the mixture and blend in well. Stir with a paddle. When you are able to see the bottom of the bowl for a few seconds while stirring, the consistency is right. If mixture is too thin, add a little sifted flour; if it is too thick, add a little more water. (Canned *"an"* varies in thickness according to the brand).
4. Cut a sheet of plastic wrap large enough for the ends to extend over the sides of the pan. Place in the pan.
5. Pour in the mixture and smooth out the surface. If using a bread pan, make a slight indentation in the center since this area will rise while cooking. Cover with a sheet of aluminum foil.
6. Place the pan in a steamer with plenty of boiling water and steam for 30 minutes over high heat.

268

7. Remove from the steamer and push the chestnuts into the half-cooked pudding. Cover again and return to the steamer. Steam for 30 minutes more if using a square pan or for one hour more if using a bread pan. (The bread pan produces a thicker loaf and takes much longer to cook).
8. Test for doneness by poking a bamboo skewer into the center. If soft bean paste comes out of the hole, it is not yet done. If it is fully cooked, the hole will stay clean.
9. When cooked, let it cool completely in the pan. When cold, lift it out of the pan with the plastic liner. Cut into thick slices to serve. To keep, wrap in a plastic sheet, then in aluminum foil, and refrigerate.

JAPANESE WAFFLES (*Dora Yaki*) ★ *page 184*

These spongy sweet waffles are put together with *"tsubushi-an,"* a crushed bean paste, or with a split pea paste. They are also good with jams, thick custard cream fillings, or sweetened cream cheese.

1. Break eggs into a bowl. Add sugar and beat over warm water.
2. Add corn syrup, *mirin* and soy sauce (added to make the waffle brown nicely). Beat until light and fluffy.
3. Add the soda mixed with water. Fold in flour alternately with water, mixing lightly with a wire whisk. The batter will be the consistency of a thick custard sauce.
4. Cover and let stand 10 minutes.
5. Heat a heavy iron griddle. Pour on 1 tablespoon salad oil and tilt and rotate the griddle to coat it well. Wipe the griddle with a cotton ball or a paper towel.
6. Pour about 3 tablespoons of batter from a ladle onto the griddle, holding it still to let the batter spread gradually.
7. Cook over medium-low heat. When bubbles appear, turn it over with a spatula and cook the other side. The batter browns quickly. Transfer to a cake rack to cool.
8. When completely cold, put 2 waffles together with bean paste filling which has been softened with 2 tablespoons corn syrup.

Note: Kept in a plastic bag, these will remain soft and moist for several days in the refrigerator. They may also be frozen. For a cream cheese filling, cream softened cream cheese with sugar to your taste.

For about 20 waffles, each 3½" (9 cm) diameter, yielding 10 cakes:
3 eggs
½–¾ cup sugar
1 tablespoon light corn syrup or honey
1 tablespoon mirin or 1 tablespoon sake or sherry with 1 teaspoon sugar
1 teaspoon soy sauce
½ teaspoon baking soda mixed with 1 tablespoon water
2 cups cake flour, sifted three times
⅓–½ cup water
A heavy-gauge iron griddle or frying pan

Filling:
Mixture of ½–1 can (1 lb. 2 oz) "tsubushi-an" (crushed bean paste), or 1–2 cups homemade crushed bean paste, or split pea paste mixed with 2 tablespoons light corn syrup.

This is called chestnut pastry even though the filling does not contain chestnuts. The glossy brown top of the pastry resembles the chestnut color, hence the name. This is a slightly modified version of a recipe created by Japanese people living in California yearning for the sweets of home.

Yields about 30
Filling:
1 recipe white bean paste
(page 267)

Pastry:
¼ lb. (110 g) butter or
*   margarine*
½ cup sugar
1 whole egg plus 2 egg whites
2 tablespoons light corn syrup

3 cups all-purpose flour ⎫
1 teaspoon baking soda ⎬
Sift together. ⎭

Glaze:
2 eggs yolks ⎫
1 teaspoon mirin ⎬
½ teaspoon soy sauce ⎭
Mix all together.

1. Make the white bean paste one day before. Cool completely and roll into 30 small balls.
2. Melt butter and add sugar while the butter is still hot.
3. Beat with a wooden spoon and gradually add one whole egg, the two egg whites and the corn syrup.
4. Blend in the flour which has been sifted with the baking soda. If the dough is too soft, let it rest in the refrigerator for 15–20 minutes.
5. On a floured board, roll the dough into slender rolls of 1¼″ (3 cm) diameter. Cut into 30 pieces.
6. Roll out each piece of dough into a circle about 3″ (9 cm) in diameter. Place the bean paste ball in the center and wrap the dough around it.
7. Turn the gathered side down onto the floured board and rotate it between your hands to form a smooth ball. Then flatten the top and shape it into an oval. Or you could shape it like a chestnut. Keep the finished ones covered with a dry cloth while you work.
8. Place on greased cookie sheets 1″ (3 cm) apart. Brush the tops and sides with the glaze.
9. Preheat the oven to 375°F. (200°C.). Bake for 15 minutes until the pastries are nicely browned.

Note: For a more deluxe pastry, mix cut-up, drained chestnuts (canned or in jars) into the lima bean paste. These will keep several days in the refrigerator. They also freeze very well.

PART-IV
Menu Planning
Sample Menus
with Preparation Schedules

A festive table setting for a New Year dinner.

The fan motif is repeated on the lacquer tray and on the chopstick holders, signifying a prosperous future, while the looped willow branches symbolize the fulfillment of one's wishes.

A summer dinner table features a water scene with an arrangement of iris and a sand-painted stream.

Menu Planning

Making one or two Japanese dishes and serving them as part of a Western menu will provide you with some interesting combinations!

Planning a Japanese menu is not different from planning a Western meal. Let us start from simple menus—family suppers that we serve for everyday. For a family meal, everything is placed on the table at the beginning so the cook can eat at the same time as everyone else. Rice and pickles are always served—like bread and butter—and are not listed on the following menus unless they are a special kind.

To simplify any of the following menus, you may delete items shown in parentheses.

Pork *Miso* Soup
Sashimi
Marinated Spinach

(Clear Soup with *Tofu*)
Tempura
Rice Bowl
Cucumber Salad

Miso Soup with *Tofu* Puffs and Onions
(Baked Eggplant)
Poached Beef & Potato

(Chilled *Tofu*)
(Stirred Egg Soup)
Pan-Fried *Teriyaki* Fish
"*Namasu*" *Daikon* Salad
Green Pea Rice

(Peanut *Tofu*)
Vegetable Medley Soup
Pork *Sashimi* with Several Vegetable Garnishes
(Stir-Fried Eggplant with *Miso*)

When drinks such as *sake*, beer or white wine are served, rice is not served until last. By adding some appetizers or salad, these will be nice company dinners.

The most common approach in planning menus is to start from a main dish.

WITH *TEMPURA* AS THE MAIN COURSE:

For Non-Drinkers

Clear Soup
Tempura
Enoki Mushroom (Marinated Salad)
Floating Ice

For Drinkers

Enoki Mushroom Salad
Tempura
Miso Soup
Fresh Fruits

Sashimi Tidbits
Enoki Mushroom Salad
Tempura
Soup
Ginger Sherbet

WITH *NABEMONO* TABLE COOKING AS THE MAIN COURSE:
Nabemono using varied materials can be a meal in itself. For a dry type of casserole, soup and salad with fruit as the dessert are good additions. For soupy type casseroles, no soup or simmered dish is necessary.

Oyster Mushroom Salad with Snow Dressing
Sukiyaki
Fresh Fruit

(Mini *Zushi*)
Shabu Shabu
Oyster Mushroom Salad
Noodles Cooked in Broth
Cantaloup Ice with Lemon Sauce

Japanese Salad Platter
"Teppan Yaki" (Iron Griddle Cooking)
Miso Soup
Wine Sherbet
Sesame Crisps

THE FORMAL JAPANESE DINNER

Formal dinners at restaurants are called *"kaiseki"* dinners. But there are two kinds of *kaiseki*. One is also called *"cha kaiseki,"* a tea ceremony dinner. The word *"kaiseki"* 懐石 (bosom stone) comes from an alleged practice of *zen* priests who would ward off hunger by putting a warm stone in the bosom of their robes. It is a metaphor for a simple repast which is served before the powdered green tea.

The other *kaiseki*, 会席 more frequently served, means a party banquet. It was developed in the 18th century, influenced by the tea ceremony *"kaiseki"* and by *"honzen ryori,"* a highly ceremonious dinner served at the court circle and in the prestigious warrior class. This *kaiseki* does not have such rigid rules of formality, and the emphasis is on good eating with *sake* to drink in a leisurely fashion. Each course is brought in separately, carefully arranged on dishes that change from course to course—for a change of scenery! This is the reason that no uniform set of dishes is used.

Here are some key points for menu planning:
1. Variety and Contrast
    Variety in materials, tastes, colors, textures and cooking methods are very important. Courses are named for the cooking method used, for example, Grilled Foods, or Fried Foods, rather than by the name of the materials used in the various dishes.
2. Dramatic Rhythm
    Each menu should have its high peaks and low points. One or two climaxes in a meal are fine, but too many impressive courses are tiring.
3. Workability
    To be able to deliver a dinner at a given time, all the work should be carefully scheduled. Following the timetables for the sample menus will be helpful.
4. A Feeling for the Seasons
    A successful Japanese dinner is like a poem—one is reminded of the season by the materials, the choice of dishes on which the food is served or by the manner in which food is arranged—with a leaf or two. Heightening the diner's awareness of nature makes one feel like celebrating the season with *sake*!

THE ORDER OF COURSES

Here is a sample menu for a party banquet *kaiseki* dinner—not the tea ceremony *kaiseki*. The dishes can be prepared with locally available foods. Of course, you need not be bound by this sequence, but it is nice to know.

The numbers explain the order in which the courses can be served.

Menu for:	9 courses	7 courses	5 courses	4 courses	3 courses
Appetizer*	1 Red Caviar in Snow	1 1	1 1 1	1	1
Soup**	2 Clear Soup Crab Stick	2 2 2	2 3 2	1 2	1 1 2
*Sashimi***	3 Halibut or Tuna	3 3 1	3 2 2 1	2 1 2	2 3 1
Grilled Food	4 Beef Pickle Rolls	4 4 3	4 3	3 3	3 2
Fried Food	5 Deep Fried *Tofu*	5 4	4 3	3	2
Salad****	6 Spinach with Sesame Dress.	5	4		3
Steamed Food	7 Steamed Turnip	5	5		
Simmered Food	8 Bamboo Shoots & Celery	6 6 6	5 4 5	4 4	
Finishing Soup	9 *Miso* Soup, Chicken meatballs, Small Onions Rice & Pickles Green Tea	7 7 7	5	4	3
Dessert	Plum Wine Jelly				

   *   Appetizer may be served in more than one course or as an assortment on a tray which could appear in the middle of the courses.

  **   There is no definite rule, but when two soups are served, usually the first soup is clear soup and the last one is *miso* soup.

 *** *Sashimi* may precede soup, this being treated like an appetizer.

**** Often served in small portions as a side dish. It may be served as an appetizer, and does not have a set position in the order of the courses.

SMALL IS BEAUTIFUL

For informal family dinners, hearty meals in generous portions are always good. However for more sophisticated dinners, overly generous servings have a negative effect—at least in the Japanese psyche. It is always quality, rather than quantity, that counts in a Japanese dinner!

Sample Menus with Preparation Schedules

In Japan the season of the year is supremely important in planning nearly every event. This seasonal consciousness carries into meal planning, where the particular season is foremost in the mind of the host when planning entertainment for guests. In this chapter I have provided a party menu for each of the seasons, focusing on and including the choice foods of each and suggesting table settings which will emphasize the beauties of each season.

Also in this chapter you will find timetables to guide you through the organization and production of each menu. This will help to insure that everything is ready at the appropriate time. These timetables are based on the assumption that the cook is working alone. Underlined procedures in the timetables indicate the length of time needed to complete it. "PR" means to process in a food processor.

For each menu section, you will find a complete shopping list for items needed for that menu. Please adjust menus to your working speed, eliminating dishes if necessary.

SPRING: A LUNCHEON FOR THE DOLL FESTIVAL

Fresh Materials

16 small, live clams
1/2 lb. cooked shrimp
5 eggs (sushi *and* dessert)
1/2 cup regular tofu
3 carrots (sushi *and* salad)
1 bunch thin green asparagus

1/2 cup snow peas or string
   beans
1 small piece of ginger
1 lemon

1 basket of strawberries

Staples

Salt
Sugar
Soy Sauce
Sake
Mirin
Rice Vinegar
Instant Dashi

Dry or Canned Food

3 cups rice, Japanese type or
   short grain
1 small can bamboo shoots
1/2 oz. (15 g) kampyō (dried
   gourd rind)
1/2 oz. dried shiitake
   mushrooms
1/4 cup red pickled ginger
1 sheet nori (dried seaweed)
1 envelope unflavored gelatin
1 tablespoon white sesame
   seeds

Green Tea
1 bottle rosé wine
2 tablespoons kirsch

Clam Soup (page 205)
Mixed *Sushi* (*Chirashi Zushi* page 245)
Green Asparagus & Carrot with *Tofu* Dressing (page 220)
Rosé Wine for adults
   Soft Drinks for children
Snow Jelly with Strawberry Sauce (page 264)
Green Tea

March 3 is the day Japanese families celebrate the Doll Festival for Girls. They display a set of dolls representing the royal court, arrange peach blossom branches and offer diamond-shaped, three-layered rice cake. Why not have a children's party or invite your friends to celebrate the arrival of Spring?

TABLE SETTING

The color scheme comes from the layered rice cake. Pink (representing flowers), white (snow), green (the green grass of spring), and red (the covering used on the display shelves for the dolls).

Centerpiece:
   A pair of "*hina*" dolls made with folded napkins and flowers placed on a rectangular piece of red felt. Add a branch of peach blossom.
Emperor:
   1 large napkin in a dark color such as black, navy, brown or dark green
   1 white tulip, narcissus or daisy
Empress:
   1 large napkin—coral, orange or pink colored
   1 pink, single camellia or rose
How to fold the napkins for Emperor and Empress:
   Tuck in the end.
   Press down the lower ends so it will stand up.
   Tuck in a flower.
Place Mats:
   Put the small pink paper on the large green paper.
   Large: 18″ × 12″ (45 × 30 cm), light green paper
   Small: 13″ × 7″ (33 × 18 cm), pink paper
Napkins:
   A white napkin is folded into a knot, after the ancient custom of delivering a letter or poem tied onto a branch.
Chopstick Holder:
   A short twig of peach branch, with blossoms

CLAM SOUP (page 205)

This is very simple to make, however, the clams must be absolutely fresh, preferably alive. Substitutes: A Clear Soup (page 202) with a garnish of either *Kamaboko* Flowers (page 205) or Hard-boiled Egg Plum Flower (page 204).

MIXED SUSHI (*Chirashi Zushi*, page 245)

Chirashi Zushi is a popular choice for the Doll Festival because it is pretty, doesn't require much technique and everybody likes it. Follow the directions on page 245. Mold the mixed *sushi* in a rice bowl or a tea cup, turn out on serving dishes and decorate with the toppings.

SPRING LUNCHEON

PREPARATION TIMETABLES

Underlines indicate approximate time needed for process.

ON THE DAY BEFORE THE LUNCHEON

	1:00 p.m.	2:00 p.m.	3:00 p.m.	4:00 p.m.	5:00 p.m.
Clams	Let the clams excrete sand			Wash, refrigerate	
Sushi Garnishes					
Fluffy Shrimp	PR. Cook				
Kampyō	Parboil	Cut. Cook			
Shiitake	Soften				
Vegetable		Cut. Cook		Refrigerate all.	
Green Vegetable			Cut. Cook		
Egg Threads			Cook. Cut		

Green Aspragus & Carrot with *Tofu* Dressing					
Carrots			Cut. Cook Cool. Chill		Refrigerate
Green Asparagus			Cut. Parboil		
Tofu Dressing		Press *tofu*.	PR. Chill.	Refrigerate	
Snow Jelly			Soak. Cook. Chill. gelatin. Beat whites.	Beat. Mold. Chill	

Cut papers for place mats.
Centerpieces and napkins folded.

281

	9:00 a.m.	10:00 a.m.	11:00 a.m.	12:00 a.m.	1:00 p.m.
Clam Soup				Cook.	Serve
Mixed *Sushi*					
Sushi Rice	Wash. Soak. Cook.	Mix.	Dish		Serve
		Add garnishes			
Green Asparagus&					
Carrot with *Tofu* Dressing			Mix. Dish up		Serve
Drink	Chill				Serve
Snow Jelly	Unmold. Chill				
Strawberry Sauce	PR. Chill				Serve
Green Tea				Boil water.	Serve
Table Setting	Set the table.				

Note: Fluffy Shrimp and other cooked garnishes can be made ahead and kept frozen. There are also canned *sushi* garnishes (vegetables) and colored fluffy fish *"soboro"* sold at Japanese groceries.

SUMMER: A BARBECUE PATIO DINNER

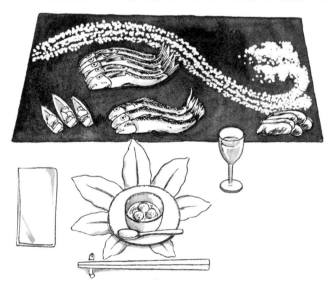

SHOPPING LIST FOR
 BARBECUE PATIO
 DINNER
(for 8 servings)

Fresh Materials

8 trout
*5 eggs (Custard Soup and
 Dessert)*
2 cups seedless green grapes
2 large cucumbers
½ cake kamaboko *(fishcake)*

Cocktails
  Rice crackers
  Roasted pecans
Green Jade Cup (page 217)
White Wine
Chilled Custard Soup (page 114)
Salt Grilled Trout (page 92)
Sweet Pickled Ginger (page 241)
Baked Eggplant (page 138)
Japanese Salad Platter (page 223)
Parsley Rice (page 236)
Instant Cabbage Pickle (page 256)
Green Tea
Green Tea Ice Cream (page 262)

Summer is the time for a barbecue so I planned this menu around a barbecue in which trout and eggplant are grilled over charcoal. For a heartier dinner, add skewered chicken (see *Yakitori* on page 105). The initial cocktail hour was added because it is so popular in the USA.

TABLE SETTING
Cover your patio table with a tablecloth in a quiet color such as beige, moss green or navy blue. For place mats, use large aralia leaves.

Centerpiece:
  You may omit the centerpiece, merely placing the grilled fish on a tray which is decorated with salt which has been brushed into a wave design. In traditional Japanese dinners, no centerpiece is used on the table since each plate is the focus of attention. However, if your table looks bare, make a water arrangement by filling a shallow container, tray or glass casserole with water. In this, make a design with pebbles and float some flowers or leaves. There are also leaf-shaped candles which float and which can be lit as it gets dark.

Chopstick Holders:
  Use well-washed pebbles. (Or the dinner may be served with regular knife, fork and spoon)

ROASTED PECANS

2 cups pecans with skins
1 tablespoon soy sauce

1. Line a pan with aluminum foil. Spread the pecans out on the foil and roast at 300°F. (150°C.) for 15 minutes.
2. Put the nuts into a bowl, sprinkle on the soy sauce and mix them so the nuts are coated. Spread out again on the foil.
3. Return to the oven and dry the nuts at 250°F. (120°C.) for another 15 minutes. When cool, put into a jar.

Note: This recipe is also good with walnuts or blanched almonds.

GREEN JADE CUP (page 217, Green Jade Salad)

Prepare the double amount at least 2–3 hours before serving. Divide into individual glass bowls and refrigerate.

8 *Japanese eggplants (or 2 small American ones)*
6 *okra*
5 *lemons*
1/4 *lb. ginger (pickles and baked eggs)*
1 *butter lettuce*
1–2 *carrots*
2–3 *stalks celery*
1 *large tomato*
1 *cup string beans*
8 *fresh* shiitake *mushrooms if available*
4 *cups cabbage (for pickles)*
1 *bunch parsley*
1 *cup whipping cream*

Staples

Salt
Sugar
Soy Sauce
Sake
Vinegar
Mustard
White Miso
Charcoal
Mirin
Salad Oil
Green Food Color

Dry or Canned Food

1–2 *bags rice crackers*
2 *cups pecans*
2–3 *cups Japanese type rice*
1/4 *cup white sesame seeds*
Bonito flakes
Kombu (dried kelp) or Instant dashi
Handful "wakame" (dried strips of seaweed)
2 *bottles dry white wine*
Green tea
1 *tablespoon powdered green tea*
1 *dried cayenne red pepper*

CHILLED CUSTARD SOUP (page 114)

For 8 servings:
Medium Firm Custard:

3 eggs
1½ cups dashi
½ teaspoon salt
⅓ teaspoon each soy sauce
and mirin

Garnishes for Custard:

½ cup cubed kamaboko
(fishcake)
4 tablespoons sliced okra

Clear Soup:

4 cups dashi
2½ teaspoons soy sauce
1 teaspoon salt
3 tablespoons sake
A dash of MSG

Prepare in the morning or the day before. Refrigerate the custard in bowls and the soup in a jar. Just before serving, gently pour the soup over the custard.

SALT GRILLED TROUT (*Masu Shio Yaki*)

See Salt Broiling on page 92.
Skewer the fish so it looks as if it is swimming in a stream. See "*Odori Gushi*" on page 95.

For the garnish, Sweet Pickled Ginger (page 241) on bamboo leaf boats adds a nice touch. You may use pickled baby ginger (*hajikami*) which is sold in jars.

Bamboo Leaf Boat
1. 2. 3. Put one bent loop into the other loop.
4. 5. Bend the tip of the leaf up.

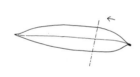
1

2

4

3

5

BAKED EGGPLANT (page 139)

Allow one slender Japanese or Chinese eggplant per person. If using large eggplants, cut into two, lengthwise, and soak in salted water to remove bitterness. Wipe dry and brush the cut surface with oil. Follow the recipe and barbecue over charcoal until tender. Drop into water to cool. Then peel.

ASSEMBLING THE TRAY

Japanese chefs get inspiration from traditional Japanese arts which produce esthetic effects in their presentation of food. This presentation is inspired by Japanese *bonseki* (sand painting) in a design of mountains and seascapes of white sand on a black lacquer tray.

1. Make a wave with salt. Repeat three or four times. To define the edge of the wave, sweep the brush left to right, dipping downward, then sweeping upward.
2. At the right side, make a pile of eggplant to look like a rock. Sprinkle with grated ginger.
3. Group the fish together, as if they are swimming.
4. Add the bamboo leaf boats at the lower left and put pickled ginger on them. Serve soy sauce with either lemon wedges or Celery Vinegar Sauce (page 93).

1 good-sized rectangular black lacquer board, or a black plastic board, cut to suit your table
Table salt in a shaker with a V-shaped spout
Pastry brush or a wide paint brush

JAPANESE SALAD PLATTER (page 223)

With vegetables in four colors, this salad is very healthful and refreshing. Various vegetables may be prepared ahead of time and chilled in separate containers. Arrange each item in a separate pile on a bed of lettuce. Here is a sample combination:

White

1 cup celery cut into fine julienne, salted to soften, washed and drained.

Green

1 cup string beans boiled in boiling water, plunged into cold water and cut into strips.

Yellow-Red

1 cup carrot cut into fine julienne. Treated the same way with celery
1 large tomato, sliced.

Dark

A handful of dried seaweed "wakame" softened in water and cut into strips removing hard veins.
8 fresh shiitake mushroom caps grilled on charcoal and cut into strips.

Sesame Miso Dressing on page 223.

PARSLEY RICE

See Green Leaf Rice on page 236. Serve in rice bowls accompanied with pickles served in small dishes. If Western flatware is used, serve the rice on a bread plate, with pickles at the side.

GREEN TEA ICE CREAM

Make it several days ahead. Or a quick way is to add green tea powder and green food coloring to vanilla ice cream.

SUMMER BARBECUE DINNER

PREPARATION TIMETABLE

This is based on one worker. Guests arrive at 6:00 p.m.; dinner is served at 7:00 p.m.

One day before:
Make the Ice Cream and freeze.
Prepare custard and soup and chill.
Make Sweet Pickled Ginger.
Roast pecans.

In the morning:
Buy trout. Clean and chill.
Make Celery Vinegar Sauce in the food processor.
Make Instant Cabbage Pickle.
Set the table.

Afternoon Timetable:

	2:00	3:00	4:00	5:00	6:00	7:00	8:00	9:00
Pecans					Serve Cocktails			
Jade Green Cup	Prepare.	Chill				Serve		
White Wine	Chill					Serve		
Custard Soup	Chill					Serve		
Grilled Trout	Chill		Skewer & Chill			Grill.		
Celery Vinegar					Start Charcoal.		Serve	
Grilled Eggplant						Grill. Peel		
Salad			Prepare vegetables. Arrange & Chill				Serve	
Salad Dressing				Prepare. Chill				
Parsley Rice				Wash. Soak. Chop parsley		Cook.	Serve	
Tea							Boil water Serve.	
Ice Cream							Serve	

286

AUTUMN: MOON VIEWING DINNER

Persimmon Cup with Fall Leaves (page 288)
Warmed *Sake*
Hazy Full Moon *Tofu* Soup (page 204)
Sashimi (page 85)
   Halibut and Tuna
Salt Baked Casserole "*Hōroku Yaki*" (page 96)
Marinated Spinach (page 146)
Mushroon Rice (page 237)
Green Pickles (page 258)
Green Tea
Chestnuts with Chocolate Sauce (page 266)

It is an ancient Japanese custom to observe a Moon Viewing Party in September and October when the moon is full. People enjoy a pleasant evening, basking in the moonlight on the balcony. Newly harvested "*satoimo*" (Japanese taro page 32), fresh soy beans (page 19), chestnuts, persimmons and other fall fruits are offered to the moon, arranged on a table with Japanese pampas grass and wild flowers. The round white dumplings made of rice flour which symbolize the full moon are piled on a ceremonial wooden stand.

Here is a menu suitable for fall evenings to celebrate the season and to enjoy the new harvest of fruits and vegetables.

SHOPPING LIST FOR MOON VIEWING DINNER (for 8 servings)

Fresh Materials
¼ *lb. crab meat*
1 *lb. tuna for* sashimi
1 *lb. halibut for* sashimi (2 lb. if whole and not filleted)
16 *prawns*
1 *chicken breast*
8 *"fuyū" persimmons*
3 *limes*
1 *cucumber (or cabbage) for* sashimi *garnish*
1 *bunch parsley*
8 *cherry tomatoes*
½ *lb. oyster, shiitake or pine mushrooms*
½ *lb. mushrooms for rice (pick a different kind from the ones used in the casserole.)*
1 *sweet potato (casserole)*
1 *potato (appetizer)*
1 *large carrot (appetizer)*
24–40 *snow peas*
1 daikon *with green top (If there is no green top, add a bunch of mustard greens for pickles)*
1–2 *bunches spinach*
1 *lemon*
Small ginger root
8 *string beans (soup)*
1 *lb. chestnuts (plus 16 if used for appetizer)*
2 *boxes soft tofu*
Handfuls of pine needles.

Staples
Salt
Sugar
Soy Sauce
Sake
Instant Dashi
MSG
Milk
Vanilla
Cayenne Peppers
Frying Oil

Cornstarch
Corn Syrup

Dry or Canned Food
Rock Salt
Wasabi *Powder*
2–3 cups Japanese type rice
1 teaspoon white sesame
seeds
4" × 5" (10 × 13 cm) kombu
for frying

For Soup Stock:
Bonito flakes ⎫
Kombu *or Instant* ⎬
Dashi ⎭

1 bottle of sake
Green tea
2 squares (60 g) semi-sweet
chocolate
2 tablespoons brandy
20 green tea vermicelli
1 small jar gingko nuts

1 small "fuyū"* persimmon
per person
1 lime per 2–3 persimmons
*"Fuyū" is a type of persim-
mon that is sweet while
still firm. It is flat-topped
and is now available in
markets on the West
Coast.

TABLE SETTING

Table:
A bare table, or cover with a quiet-colored tablecloth in earthy toned tan, beige, brown, mustard, gray or navy blue with matching napkins.
Place Mats:
Matchstick bamboo mats, or a bamboo stick window shade cut into long runners. Or combination of double sheets of paper in harmonious fall colors.
Centerpiece:
Fall fruits and nuts can be placed on a base of natural wood or a bamboo stick base, with an arrangement of wild flowers and grasses.
Dishes:
Use rustic, earthy, pottery dishes, wood tray and baskets. But adding one or two porcelain or Imari type dish or bowl is effective.
Chopstick Holders:
Fall leaf-shaped ceramic holders.

PERSIMMON CUPS

1. Cut off the stem end of the fruit and save it to use as the lid. Wipe the cut surface with a slice of lime to prevent the persimmon from becoming dark.
2. Scoop out the pulp with a small spoon, leaving a shell about ¼" (6 mm) thick.
3. Cut the pulp into bite sized pieces, mix with lime juice, and return the pulp to the cups.
4. Cover with the top and refrigerate until serving time.
5. Place the persimmon cups on individual baskets, trays or folded papers and surround with edible fall leaves or nuts.

FALL LEAVES
Choose from the following list.
Fried Kelp Leaves (page 199)
Gingko Leaf Potato Chips (page 199)
Carrot Maple Leaves (page 199)
Noodle Pine Needles (page 199)
Roasted Chestnuts (page 200)
Gingko Nuts (canned) strung on real pine needles.

WARMING *SAKE*

Warm the *sake* to make it fragrant and mellow tasting. See page 299.

HAZY FULL MOON SOUP (page 204)

This is a thickened soup with crab meat. An alternate choice is Full Moon *Tofu* in Basic Clear Soup (page 203).

SASHIMI

If you have a Japanese market, you can buy fish trimmed just to slice for *sashimi*. Allow ¼ to ½ lb. (110 to 150 g) per person. If you are serving tuna and halibut, about 1 pound of each would serve up to eight people. See directions on page 87 for slicing. If you must bone and cut, read page 86. Tuna is tender, so cut it about ⅜″ (1 cm) thick. Halibut is firm-fleshed, so cut it thinner than ¼″ (6 mm).

Make thinly shredded cabbage or cucumber to lay on individual plates, arrange *sashimi* slices—5 tuna slices in the rear (away form you) and 6 halibut slices, slightly overlapping, in front (closer to you). Add a sprig of parsley or a chrysanthemum leaf for a green touch. *Wasabi* paste may be served in a cherry tomato cut like a flower. Arrange them before the guests arrive. Cover with plastic wrap and refrigerate. Serve with soy sauce in a small dish.

SALT BAKED CASSEROLE (page 96)

Baked in the oven, this is a wonderful way to cook fall vegetables with seafood and chicken. Double the amount for eight servings, and omit chestnuts as they are used as dessert. If your casserole is not large enough, use two.

MARINATED SPINACH SALAD (page 146)

This is a kind of stand-by vegetable dish for Japanese family meals. If you have chrysanthemums in your garden, wash the plucked petals well and blanch them in boiling water with a little vinegar. Drain and rinse with water and add to the spinach to make this dish more elegant. Chrysanthemums from florists are not recommended to eat because chemicals may have been used.

MUSHROOM RICE (page 237)

Fall is the season for mushrooms. The expensive pine mushrooms "*matsutake*" have a great deal of aroma, but other fresh mushrooms such as oyster mushrooms, *shiitake*, or regular mushrooms are also nice.

If you have individual-sized pottery cauldrons or small

casseroles, cook the rice in them in the oven to serve individually. This will also keep the rice warm.

CHESTNUTS WITH CHOCOLATE SAUCE
(page 266)

Chestnut purée is shaped like a chestnut here and chocolate sauce is poured over it. Serve with good green tea.

PREPARATION TIMETABLE

One day to a few days before:
Make the fall leaves in your spare time. Cool and store in tightly covered cans or jars.
In the morning:
Boil the chestnuts. Scoop out and make purée. Shape the purée into chestnut shapes.
Set the table.
Prepare the Persimmon Cups.

Afternon Timetable:

	1:00	2:00	3:00	4:00	5:00	6:00	7:00	8:00	9:00
Persimon cups	Chill					Dish up.	Serve		
Fall Leaves	(Made ahead.)								
Sake							Warm. Serve		
Soup					Make *Dashi*		Heat		
Crab Meat				PR.				Serve	
Tofu					Cut out		Warm		
String Beans					Cut. Parboil				
Sashimi, Garnishes		Slice. arrange. Cover with plastic sheet & refrigerate					Serve		
Casserole		Prepare					Heat		
Chicken			Slice. Refrigerate						
Prawns			Devein. Refrigerate						
Mushrooms							Cut Arrange		
Sweet Potato				Cut. Soak				Bake Serve	
Snow Peas				Trim					
Pine needles				Wash. Drain					
Dipping Sauce				Prepare. Set aside					
Marinated Spinach					Boil		Marinate. dish up	Serve	
Mushroom Rice						Wash rice		Cook. Serve	
						Cut mushrooms			
Pickles	(Made in the morning.)							Serve	
Tea								Boil water Serve.	
Chestnuts with Chocolate Sauce	(Made in the morning.) Make sauce							Heat	Serve

290

WINTER: A CASSEROLE DINNER

Nandina Caviar (page 189)
Warmed *Sake* (page 299) or Beer
Crab Salad (page 215)
Boiled Chicken Casserole (*Mizu-taki*, page 228)
Stir-Fried Celery (*Kimpira*, page 136)
Rice Porridge (*Zōsui*, page 228)
Thousand Slice Turnip Pickles (page 258)
Toasted Tea (page 297)
Wine Sherbet (page 262)
Sesame Crisps (page 265)

Here is a hearty dinner for chilly winter evenings. The soupy casserole is warming and serves as the soup, main dish and the vegetable course because you use so many kinds of things in it. Start with the picturesque red caviar appetizer. The salad fills the time until the casserole starts cooking.

Since the casserole is so light, stir-fried *kimpira* is added for a contrast.

After being thoroughly warmed by the delicious casserole, cold Wine Sherbet is a refreshing ending with delicious, delicate sesame cookies.

TABLE SETTING
Folk art "*mingei*" theme would be most appropriate for the simple table setting.

Table:
Bare, with a cotton runner or mats.

SHOPPING LIST FOR A CASSEROLE DINNER
(for 8 servings)

Fresh Materials
1/2–1 cup red caviar
1 lb. crab meat, cooked
1 large chicken 4½–5 lb.
1 box regular tofu
3 eggs (sherbet and cookies)
1 daikon
1 cucumber
1 Chinese cabbage
1 bunch spinach
2 bunches green onions
2 cups (½ lb.) fresh mush-
    rooms (oyster, shiitake, *pine*
    or regular mushrooms)
¼ lb. snow peas
1 bunch chives
6–8 stalks celery
2 lb. turnips
3 lemons
1 small ginger
Twigs of nandina shrub
Optional: 4 eggs for rice
    porridge

Staples
Salt
Sugar
Soy Sauce
Sake
Vinegar
Vanilla
Butter
Baking Powder
Instant Dashi
Aluminum Foil

Dry or Canned Food
1½ cups Japanese type rice
1¼ cups white sesame seeds
1 dry red cayenne pepper
2″ × 3″ (5 × 8 cm) kombu
2 cups white or rosé wine
1 bottle sake
Bancha (*cheapest kind of*
    green tea)
3 cans chicken broth

Centerpiece:
No flower-centerpiece. The materials for the casserole are arranged beautifully on a platter and placed in the center of the table. Electric skillets (one for every 3–4 persons) should be set out.

Dishes and Chopstick Holders:
Use rustic potteries.

NANDINA CAVIAR (page 189)

This is very easy to prepare. Choose a plain dish to set off the design.

CRAB SALAD (Crab meat with Vinegar Dressing page 215)

This is another easy dish to prepare. One pound of crab meat will serve 8. Cucumber fans (page 49) add a nice touch.

BOILED CHICKEN CASSEROLE
(*Mizu-daki*, page 228)

Originally only chicken was boiled and eaten with lemon soy sauce. But adding vegetables is good, especially for family dinners. The freshness of the chicken is important. Boiling the chicken may be done one day ahead. Chill it and remove the fat that has congealed. In Japan an earthenware pot with an unglazed bottom, called "*donabe*," is used on the tabletop gas burner. A deep electric skillet is also very handy to use. One recipe with enough vegetables will serve eight. Use Chinese cabbage, spinach, green onions, some kind of mushrooms and snow peas.

STIR-FRIED CELERY (Celery *Kimpira* page 136)

This is one of those dishes the Japanese like to have on hand for an extra item. For the Japanese, *kimpira* means stir-fried burdock, but I like the one made with celery. Serve this with the casserole to nibble in between.

RICE PORRIDGE (*Zōsui*, page 228)

A wonderful ending to the casserole! Rice porridge made with the delicious casserole broth cannot be beaten! Use 3–4 cups leftover cooked rice or cook 1½ cup raw rice for 8 servings.

THOUSAND SLICE TURNIP PICKLE (page 258)

Make the pickles 5 or 6 days in advance so the flavor mellows.

TOASTED TEA (*Hōji Cha*, page 297)

Freshly toasted tea has delightful fragrance. It may be served to non-drinkers throughout the dinner if you like.

WINE SHERBET (page 262)

2 cups white or rosé wine, or champagne and 2 egg whites makes 8 to 10 servings. Can be made several days in advance.

WINTER CASSEROLE DINNER

PREPARATION TIMETABLE

Five days before:
Make Thousand Slice Turnip Pickles. Refrigerate.
Several days before:
Make Wine Sherbet
Bake Sesame Crisps.
One day before:
Boil the chicken. Cool and chill the whole pot.
Collect Nandina twigs.
In the morning:
Set the table
Make Stir-Fried Celery *"Kimpira"*

Afternoon Timetable:

	2:00	3:00	4:00	5:00	6:00	7:00	8:00	9:00
Nandina Caviar	....			} Dish up		Serve		
Daikon	.... Grate			}				
Sake	....				Warm. Serve			
Crab Salad								
Crab Meat	....		Dish up. Chill			} Serve		
Cucumber fans	........Make fans. }		Make Dressing					
Casserole								
Boiled Chicken			Arrange					
Vegetables	Prepare }		on platter			Cook. Serve		
Tofu						Add rice & serve		
Rice Porridge	....			Wash. Soak. Cook.				
Sauce	....		Make sauce.					
Tea	....						Boil water. }Serve ....Toast Tea. }	
Sherbet	} ....(Made ahead)							Serve
Sesame Crisps								

293

PART-V
Making Tea
Serving Sake

Making Tea

Offering a cup of tea to guests at home and in a business office is customary Japanese hospitality. Green tea is drunk without the addition of sugar or milk and is a very refreshing and healthful drink. Get acquainted with the many varieties of tea and their individual preparation methods.

SENCHA
This is the most commonly used green tea in Japan. It is made from young tender leaves. There is a wide price range depending on the quality of the tea. *Sencha* has a refreshing taste and aroma. It can be served with meals, with sweets or just by itself.

BANCHA
Bancha is the tea for every day use. Made from mature leaves and stems, it is the least expensive tea.

HŌJICHA (Toasted Tea)
When *bancha* is toasted (or roasted), it becomes very fragrant and makes delightful tea. Even though *hōjicha* is sold already roasted, the aroma keeps for only 1 or 2 weeks, at most. So it is best to toast it yourself just before you make tea.

    Bancha can be toasted in a dry frying pan by shaking the pan over heat until the tea becomes fragrant. There is a small roasting pan sold at Japanese markets. (page 39)

    Hōjicha is good with meals. Some *sushi* restaurants serve a big cup of *hōjicha* as soon as the customer sits down.

GYOKURO (Jade Dew Tea)
Gyokuro is the most expensive tea and is made from the young, new leaves grown sheltered under reed screens. It is tea to be prepared carefully and appreciated in small sips from a small, thin cup. Infused in warm water, this tea has a delightful aroma and a rather strong taste with a mellow sweetness. It is a tea for the connoisseur, to be served with sweets.

MATCHA (Powdered Green Tea)
Made from the best young tea leaves, as for *gyokuro*, *matcha* is used exclusively in the tea ceremony. Prepared according to a ritual, *matcha* is served with sweets. *Matcha* is not brewed, but a teaspoonful is beaten with hot water in a tea bowl with a whisk. The whisk is made of finely split bamboo and is called *"chasen."*

COMMON RULES FOR BREWING TEA

1. Warm the pot and cups by rinsing them with boiling water.
2. When the tea is brewed, the pot should be drained to the last drop.
3. For the second brewing, use hot water with a higher temperature than the first and pour it immediately. After the second brewing, discard the leaves.

TO BREW 4 SERVINGS OF TEA:

	Water Temperature	Water Quantity	Tea	Steeping	Utensils
Sencha	175°F. (80°C.)	1½ cups	2 T.	1–2 minutes	
Bancha	210°F. (100°C.)	2 cups	3 T.	Immediately	
Hōjicha	210°F. (100°C.)	2 cups	3 T.	Immediately	
Gyokuro	140–150°F. (60–65°C.)	1 cup	2 T.	2–3 minutes	

COLD WATER INFUSION

Sencha or *gyokuro* can be infused in cold water. It is good served chilled or on the rocks in warm weather.

For each cup of tap water, add 2 tablespoons tea. Let stand for 30 minutes at temperatures above 75°F. (25°C.). Let stand longer at lower temperatures. Strain and chill. You may use the tea leaves 3 or 4 times.

Serving Sake

SERVING *SAKE*

Sake has an alcohol content of 16%. "*Genshu*," a variety of *sake* made for serving chilled or on the rocks, contains 19% alcohol. *Sake* is usually served warm, but it may also be served at room temperature or chilled.

WARMING *SAKE*

Warming *sake* seems to make it lighter and releases its aroma. Pottery bottles for warming and serving *sake* are called "*tokkuri*," and hold about 1 cup. Fill the bottle with *sake* to just below the neck and place it in boiling water in a small pot over low heat.

To serve:	Temperature	Approximate Heating Time
Tepid	110°F. (43°C.)	2–3 minutes
Medium Hot	122°F. (50°C.)	3–4 minutes
Hot	135°F. (55°C.)	4–5 minutes

Select the degree of warmth which you prefer. The climate also will influence how hot one warms *sake*. When the weather is hot, warm only to tepid; when the weather is cold, perhaps you will enjoy hot *sake*. Although we say "hot" (*atsu kan*), *sake* should never be too hot. When the *sake* cup touches one's lips, it should be just comfortably warm.

Do not overheat *sake*. Once it has been warmed, any unused *sake* is no longer good for serving as a drink. However, it can be used in cooking.

Index

Italicized numbers designate illustrations.

302

V

W